Studies on the Vignettes from Chapter 17 of the Book of the Dead

I

The Image of *mś.w Bdšt* in Ancient Egyptian Mythology

Mykola Tarasenko

Archaeopress Egyptology 16

Archaeopress Publishing Ltd
Gordon House
276 Banbury Road
Oxford OX2 7ED

www.archaeopress.com

ISBN 978 1 78491 450 9
ISBN 978 1 78491 451 6 (e-Pdf)

Printed in England by Oxuniprint, Oxford

This book is available direct from Archaeopress or from our website www.archaeopress.com

Contents

Preface .... **v**

Chapter 1: The scene with the cat, serpent and sacred tree, 19th–21st Dynasties **1**

§ 1.1. The *Book of the Dead* Vignette with the cat, serpent and sacred tree... 1

18th Dynasty 1

§ 1.2. The vignette with the cat, serpent and sacred tree in Theban tomb decorations and coffins (19th–21st Dynasties) 13

§ 1.3. The iconography of the scene 19

Chapter 2: Correlation between text and visual image **23**

§ 2.1. The textual source for the vignette 23

§ 2.2. Participants of the scene: the problem of identification 25

Chapter 3: *Mś.w Bdšt* – the sources and the plot **36**

Chapter 4: *Mś.w Bdšt* in the context of BD 175A, BD 123, CT Sp. 409, pBrooklyn 47.218.84 and the *Book of Heavenly Cow* – the Cosmogonic myth dénouement **48**

Chapter 5: *Mś.w Bdšt* in the *Book of Gates* **72**

Chapter 6: *Mś.w Bdšt* – the name and the image **88**

Chapter 7: Essence of *mś.w Bdšt* in the Egyptian world view **98**

Conclusion **105**

Appendix 1: Catalogue of sources **111**

Appendix 2: Selected texts **115**

Abbreviations **125**

Bibliography **128**

List of Figures

Figure 1 The BD 17 vignette in p*Nḫt* pLondon BM EA 10471, 18th Dynasty (© Trustees of the British Museum)........ 1
Figure 2 The BD 17 vignette in p*Nḫt-ʿ-Ỉmn* pBerlin P. 3002, 19th Dynasty (after Munro 1997: Photo-Taf. 5).
Figure 2a The BD 17 vignette in p*Nḫt-ʿ-Ỉmn* pBerlin P. 3002 (drawing after Naville 1886 I: Taf. XXX (Ba); Lüscher 2014: Taf. 13)........ 2
Figure 3 The BD 17 vignette in p*Ḳnn3* pLeiden T 2, 19th Dynasty (after Leemans 1882: pl. XI, 1)
Figure 3a The BD 17 vignette in p*Ḳnn3* pLeiden T 2 (drawing after Naville 1886 I: Taf. XXX (La))........ 3
Figure 4 The BD 17 vignette in p*Hw-nfr* pLondon BM EA 9901, 19th Dynasty (after Malek 2000: 85, pl. 52).
Figure 4a–4b The BD 17 vignette in p*Hw-nfr* pLondon BM EA 9901 (drawing after Naville 1886 I: Taf. XXX (Ag))........ 3
Figure 5 The BD 17 vignette in p*3nj* pLondon BM EA 10470, 19th Dynasty (after Malek 2000, p. 85, pl. 51).
Figure 5a The BD 17 vignette in p*3nj* pLondon BM EA 10470 (after Faulkner 1998: pl. 10)... 4
Figure 6 The BD 17 vignette in pDublin 4 (TCLM 1661), 19th Dynasty (drawing after Naville 1886 I: Taf. XXX (Da))........ 5
Figure 7 The BD 17 vignette in p*P3-ḳrr* pLeiden T 4 (AMS 14), 20th Dynasty (photo by © Leiden, Rijksmuseum van Oudheden)........ 6
Figure 8 The BD 17 vignette in p*Mw.t-m-wj3* pBerlin P. 3157, 21st Dynasty (drawing after Naville, 1886 I: Taf. XXX (Bb).)........ 7
Figure 9,10,11 The BD 17 vignettes in p*Nsj-t3-nb.t-išrw* pLondon BM EA 10554 (= pGreenfield), 21st – 22nd Dynasties (© Trustees of the British Museum)........ 8
Figure 12 The scene in p*T3-wḏ3.t-Rʿ* pCairo S.R. VII. 11496, 21st Dynasty (after Piankoff 1957, II: pl. 15.)........ 9
Figure 13 The BD 17 vignette in p*Ỉni-pḥ=f-nḫt* pCologny-Geneva C (Bibliotheca Bodmeriana), 21st Dynasty (after Bissing 1928: Taf. I)........ 10
Figure 14 The BD 17 vignette in p*Diw-sw-n-Mw.t* pLondon BM 9948, 21st Dynasty (after Shorter 1938: pl. X)........ 11
Figure 15–15a The *Amduat* papyrus of *P3-n-pj* pCologny-Geneva CVII (Bibliotheca Bodmeriana), 21st Dynasty (after Valloggia 1989: 131–144: pl. 5; 144, fig. 44)........ 12
Figure 16 The BD 17 vignette in the tomb of *Sn-nḏm*, TT 1 (after Wilkinson, Hill 1983: 138, fig. 30.4.1; Pinch 2002: 107, fig. 22)........ 13
Figure 17 The BD 17 vignette in the tomb of *Sn-nḏm*, TT 1, Deir el-Medina, 19th Dynasty (after Bruyère 1959: pl. XVIII, no. 1)........ 13
Figure 18 The BD 17 vignette in the tomb of *Pn-bwi* and *K3-s3*, TT 10, Deir el-Medina, 19th Dynasty (Ramses II) (photos by *Archives Scientifiques de l'IFAO*; © Institut Français d'Archéologie Orientale, Revault)........ 14
Figure 19 The BD 17 vignette in the tomb of *Ḏḥwtj-mśw*, TT 32, El-Khokha, 19th Dynasty (drawing after Kákosy, Bács, Bartos, Fábián, Gaál 2004 I: p. 199)........ 14
Figure 20–20a The BD 17 vignette in the tomb of *Nfr-ḥtp*, TT 216, Deir el-Medina, 19th Dynasty (Ramses II) (photos by *Archives Scientifiques de l'IFAO*; © Institut Français d'Archéologie Orientale, Ihab Mhd Ibrahim)........ 15
Figure 21 The BD 17 vignette in the tomb of *P3-šdw*, Deir el-Medina, TT 292, 19th Dynasty (Ramses II) (photos by *Archives Scientifiques de l'IFAO*; © Institut Français d'Archéologie Orientale, Revault)........ 15

Figure 22–22a The BD 17 vignette in the tomb of *Nḫt.w-Ỉmn*, TT 335, Deir el-Medina, 19th Dynasty (after Bruyère 1926: 163, fig. 109; 171, fig. 113) 16
Figure 23–23a The BD 17 vignette in the tomb of *Ỉnj-ḥr-ḫˁw*, TT 359, Deir el-Medina, 20th Dynasty (after Cherpion, Corteggiani 2010, II: 65, fig. 98; Bruyère 1933: pl. XXI)................ 17
Figure 24 The BD 17 vignette in the tomb of *Ỉni-ḥr.t-ms* at El-Mashayikh (Lepidotonpolis), 19th Dynasty (drawing after Ockinga, al-Masri 1988: 7–8 (Scene 5); pl. 11)....... 18
Figure 25 The scene on the coffin of *Ḫ3-ˁs.t*, J.E. 29665; CG 6076, 21st Dynasty (drawing after Niwiński 1996: 105, fig. 82).. 18
Figure 26 The scene on the coffin of *Ḫnśw-mś*, Turin 2238; CGT 10106b, 21st Dynasty (drawing after Lanzone 1884, Tav. CLII) 19
Figure 27–27a The scenes on the inner coffin of *P3-di-Ḫnśw*,Lyon Musée des Beaux-Arts H 2320–2321, © photo F. Jamen 19
Figure 28 The BD 17 vignette in the p*Ns-Mnw* pNew Jersey University, Ptolemaic Period (after Clère 1987, pl. V)
Figure 29 The BD 17 vignette in the p*Nḥm-s-Rˁt-t3wi* pLouvre N. 3149, Ptolemaic Period (after Broze 1991: 111, fig. 55) 21
Figure 30 The BD 17 vignette in the p*Ỉw=f-ˁnḫ* pTurin 1791, Ptolemaic Period (after Lepsius 1842: Taf. IX)
Figure 31 The BD 17 vignette in the p*Nḥm-s-Rˁt-t3wi* pLouvre N. 3087, Ptolemaic Period (after Broze 1991: 111, fig. 56) 22
Figure 32 The BD 17 vignette in the p*Ỉrti-w-r-w* pChicago OIM 10486 (= pMilbank), Ptolemaic Period (after Allen 1960, pl. LXI)
Figure 33 The BD 17 vignette in the p*Nfrt-ii* (*Nfr-ii-n-i*) pBerlin P. 10477, Ptolemaic Period (after Lüscher 2000, Photo-Taf. 6) 22
Figure 34–34a Photos of serval (*Felix serval* or *Leptailurus serval*); from the open Internet resources (http://www.naturephoto-cz.com/serval-photo-12476.html; http://hq-oboi.ru/wall/koshka_serval).. 26
Figure 35 The scene from the "Great Litany of Re" in the tomb of Thutmose III (KV 34), 18th Dynasty (after Piankoff 1964: 14, fig. B, reg. 5 (67); Hornung 1999: 147, fig. 90... 27
Figure 36 Stele Oxford Ashmolean Museum 1961. 232, Deir el-Medina, 19th Dynasty (after Malek 2000: 88, fig. 56).. 27
Figure 37 The scene of the 7th Hour of *Amduat* in the tomb of Thutmose III (KV 34), 18th Dynasty (after Hornung 1963 I: Taf. 7; Karlshausen 1991: 103, fig. 51; Hornung, Abt 2007: 214)
Figure 38 The scene on the on the "magical knife" New York MMA 15.3.197, Middle Kingdom (after Altenmüller 1965, II, S. 119, Abb. 13).. 28
Figure 39–39a Photos of the *Balanites aegyptiaca* (L.; Del.) from open Internet resources (http://bg-aqaba.ju.edu.jo/pages-tree/Balanites%20aegyptiaca.aspx; http://agroforesttrees.cisat.jmu.edu/tree_detail. asp?id=20)....................................... 29
Figure 40 The vignette of BD 108 in the p*Ḳnn3* pLeiden T 2, 19th Dynasty (drawing after Naville 1886 I: Taf. CXIX; Quirke 2013: 238)... 30
Figure 41 The scene on the "magical knife" Moscow Pushkin State Museum of Fine Arts No. 6736, Middle Kingdom (after Ходжаш 1960: 247)... 32
Figure 42 The scene on the "magical knife" Moscow Pushkin State Museum of Fine Arts No. 6736, Middle Kingdom (after Ходжаш 1960: 247)
Figure 43 The scene on the "magical knife" London College UC 35309, Middle Kingdom (© Petrie Museum, London College) 33
Figure 44 The scene of the 12th Hour of the *Book of Gates* (lower register) (drawing after Hornung 1979–1980, II, S. 285, 286 (Szene 100): Taf. 12 (Zwölfte Stunde); Karlshausen 1991: 103, fig. 52) 33

Figure 45 The vignette of BD 146 in the p*Ỉw=f-ʿnḫ* pTurin 1791, Ptolemaic Period (after Lepsius 1842: Taf. LXVI) 34
Figure 46 The vignette of BD 146 on the mummy shrouds Vleeshuis Fr. 5 No. 4946 2/2 (Antwerp), Ptolemaic Period (after Caluwé 1993: 205: pl. XIX) 34
Figure 47 pRamesseum XV verso I, late Middle Kingdom (after Gardiner 1955: pl. XLVII)... 41
Figure 48 BD 175A in p*Ḥʿ* pTurin A, Suppl. 8438, 18th Dynasty (after Schiaparelli 1937: 59–60).
Figure 49 BD 175A in p*ꜣnj* pLondon BM EA 10470, 19th Dynasty (after Faulkner 1998: pl. XX IX).
Figure 50 BD 175A in p*Rʿ* pLeiden T 5, 19th Dynasty (after Naville, 1886 I: Taf. CXCVIII)..... 49
Figure 51 BD 175A in p*Ptḥ-mś* pKrakow MNK IX–752, 19th Dynasty (after Luft 1977: Taf. III)... 49
Figure 52 Scene No. 69 of the 11th hour of the *Book of Gates* in the tomb of Ramses VI (KV 9) (after Piankoff 1954, II: pl. 58–59) 72
Figure 53 Scene No. 69 of the 11th hour of the *Book of Gates* (drawing after Hornung 1979–1980, II, S. 247) 72
Figure 54 Scene on the on the coffin of *Mn-ḫprw-Rʿ*, Cairo J.E. 29628; CG 6271, 21st Dynasty (drawing after Niwiński 1989a , p, 56, fig. 3) 75
Figure 55 Sheet of the p*Ḫnmw-m-ḥb* pLondon UC 32365 (Frag. 10), 19th Dynasty (after Shorter 1937, pl. X) 77
Figure 56 Scene of the ritual protection of the graves of Osiris, Taharqa's cenotaph at Kom Jem, east wall of the chamber 'E', 25th Dynasty (drawing after Parker, Leclant, Goyon 1979: pl. XXV) 80
Figure 57 Scene in the p*Ḏd-Ḫnśw-iw=f-ʿnḫ* II, pCairo S.R. VII. 10266, 21st Dynasty (drawing after Piankoff 1957, p. 174, fig. 67) 82
Figure 58 The Judgment scene in the p*Hw-nfr* pLondon BM EA 9901, 19th Dynasty (© Trustees of the British Museum).
Figure 59 The Judgment scene in the p*ꜣnj* pLondon BM EA 10470, 19th Dynasty (© Trustees of the British Museum) 83
Figure 60 The Judgment scene in the p*Ns-Mnw* pHermitage No. 3531, Ptolemaic Period (Landa, Lapis 1974, pl. 135) 84
Figure 61 The Judgment scene in the p*ꜣnj* pLondon BM EA 10470, 19th Dynasty (© Trustees of the British Museum) 84
Figure 62 The BD 100 vignette in the p*Nb-snj* pLondon BM EA 9900, 18th Dynasty (© Trustees of the British Museum) 85
Figure 63 The scene from BD 110 in the p*Nb-snj* pLondon BM EA 9900 (© Trustees of the British Museum) 85
Figure 64 The scene from BD 110 in the p*Jwjꜣ* pCairo CG 51189, 18th Dynasty (after Davies 1908: pl. XVIII). 85
Figure 65 Scene of CT Sp. 465, V, 361 (B_1C) (after Piankoff 1972, fig. 1). 86
Figure 66 Scene No. 8 of the 2nd hour of the *Book of Gates*, tomb of Seti I (KV 17), 19th Dynasty, (photo after Hornung 1999: 60, fig. 27; drawing after Hornung 1999 p. 67, fig. 31 103
Figure 67 Scene No. 8 of the 2nd hour of the *Book of Gates*, tomb of Seti I (KV 17), 19th Dynasty, (photo after Hornung 1999: 60, fig. 27; drawing after Hornung 1999 p. 67, fig. 31 104

Preface

The present monograph investigates on the problem of how ancient Egyptian mythological concepts were reflected in the semantics of pictures accompanying the funerary collection '*Book of going forth by day*' (Egyptian title transliterated as *r.w nw prt m hrw*), named in the science as the *Book of the Dead* (further: BD).

Both BD texts and pictures (so-called *vignettes*) express how the Egyptians viewed the Afterworld and Afterlife. Vignettes did not just illustrate the spells, but often carried their meaning, substantially supplementing and broadening the texts in the pictorial and symbolic form (in particular in the case of chapters, accompanied by friezes or registers of scenes, such as 1, 17, 110, 125, 151 etc.). The sense and the meaning of the vignettes could be revealed not only through the written content of spells, but also through the decryption of their internal symbolism. In other words, these scenes could be read as an isographic text carrying an independent sense in the corresponding (semiotic) system of signs.

Noteworthy is the fact that BD documents compose the most numerous group of Egyptian illustrated papyri. Textual and pictorial content of this funerary collection also suffered from the practically continuing thousand year's evolution.[1] Consequently, from the variety of Egyptian papyrological sources, only found in the BD, we are able to follow such a particular historical and cultural phenomenon as the *pictorial tradition* of book miniature,[2] which has no analogues in the world history and represents the unique opportunity for the study of the number of categories forming the religious and mythological worldview of the ancient Egyptians.[3]

Compared to the vast majority of publications dedicated to the textual study of the ancient Egyptian *Book of the Dead*, studies on the research of its pictorial component are not so numerous. Reproductions and short descriptions of the vignettes are found in the summarizing works on the BD and different publications of its translations, in particular of P. Barguet, R. O. Faulkner, E. Hornung, and St. Quirke.[4] As for the specialized studies and typologization of the vignettes, four basic approaches have been selected.[5]

The first approach focuses on analytic study of the vignettes in concrete document (often used for publication of documents).[6] The model study for this type of

[1] In general see the essay by I. Munro in: Taylor 2010: 54–78; for canonical formation of BD cf. also: Gee 2010: 23–33.
[2] See: Чегодаев 2004.
[3] Cf. Milde 2011: 43–56.
[4] Barguet 1967; Hornung 1979; Faulkner 1998: 2001; Quirke 2013.
[5] See in details: Тарасенко 2010: 100–126.
[6] Verhoven 1993: I–III; Lapp 2004; Mosher 2001.

research is that of H. Milde on vignettes p*Nfr-rnpt* pBrusseles E 5043 of the 19th Dynasty.[7] Similar are those, for example, of M. Jr. Mosher (publication of p*Ḥr* pLondon BM 10479: Ptolemaic Period),[8] and R. Lucarelli (excursus on the vignettes in p*Gꜣt-sšn* pCairo J.E. 95838; S.R. IV 936, 21st Dynasty).[9]

The *second approach* focuses on iconography, typology, semantics and evolution of vignettes of separate BD chapters on different media. This approach has gained an excellent reputation in a number of specialized publications, including monographs and dissertations: Chr. Seeber on the Judgment scene / *Totengerichtszene* (BD 30A and 125 vignettes),[10] J. S. Gesellensetter on the pictures of BD 110,[11] B. Lüscher on the vignettes of the BD 151,[12] N. Billing on the iconographic images of the goddess of the Tree of Life (BD 109/149),[13] T. S. Tawfik on the vignettes of the BD 1, and G. Lapp on BD 15/16.[14]

Sporadically, scholars have studied vignettes of different BD spells in separate articles: K. Sethe, H. Schäfer, E. Hornung, J. Budek (BD 15/16);[15] G. Lenzo Marchese (introductory vignettes of the 21st Dynasty papyri);[16] H. Refai (the final pictures of the 21st Dynasty papyri); S.-A. Naguib, M. Gabolde, H. Gaber (BD 30/125 vignettes);[17] N. Guilhou (BD 36, 40, 144–147, and 182 vignettes);[18] N. Billing (BD 59 vignettes);[19] W. R. Dawson (BD 85 vignette in the pParis Louvre N 3074);[20] O. E. Kaper (BD 94 vignettes);[21] R. Lucarelli (BD 40, and 182 vignettes);[22] S. Demichelis (unique BD 100 vignettes);[23] M. Hummel, M. Heerma van Voss, J. Masquelier-Loorius (BD 110 vignette);[24] M.-A. Calmettes (BD 151 vignettes).[25] The illustrative frieze of BD 17 and its unique scenes has been the subject of a number of specialized articles: M. Broze, P. Koemoth, H. Goedicke, O. Keel, S. Schroer, D. Budde, and H. Kockelmann.[26] The remarquable article of

[7] Milde 1991.
[8] Mosher 2001.
[9] Lucarelli 2006: 198ff.
[10] Seeber 1976.
[11] Gesellensetter 1997.
[12] Lüscher 1998.
[13] Billing 2003; 2004: 35–50.
[14] Tawfik 2008. Cf. also: Barthelmess 1992: 157–166, Lapp 2015.
[15] Sethe 1928: 259–284; Schäfer 1928; 1935: 15–38; Hornung 1981: 183–237; 1992: 317–323; Budek 2008: 19–48.
[16] Lenzo Marchese 2004: 43–62.
[17] Naguib 1998: 68–88; Gabolde 2006: 11–22; Gaber 2009: 1–15.
[18] Guilhou 2006: 31–38; 2014: 63–76; 2014a: 23–32; 2015: 184–187.
[19] Billing 2004: 35–50.
[20] Dawson 1924: 40.
[21] Kaper 2002: 109–126.
[22] Lucarelli 2007: 1181–1186; 2012: 79–91.
[23] Demichelis 2000: 267–273.
[24] Hummel 1983: 43–45; Heerma van Voss 2006: 115–120; Masquelier-Loorius 2006: 95–107.
[25] Calmettes 2006: 23–30.
[26] Broze 1991: 109–115; Koemoth 1993: 19–31; Goedicke 1998: 38–45; 1999: 87–106; Keel, Schroer 1998: 13–29; Budde 2000: 116–135; Kockelmann 2006: 77–94.

L. E. Diaz-Iglesias Llanos, dedicated to the image with the deities Heh and Uadj-ur and the sacred lake of Herishef in Heracleopolis in BD 17,[27] is noteworthy for the careful study of the iconography of the image that included both source database (papyri, paintings on the tombs, temples and coffins, mummy linen) and chronological frames of scene. To my mind it can be acknowledged as a model analysis of the BD 17 pictorial component.

The third approach focuses on BD vignettes on separate groups of monuments. Among these, the monograph of M. Saleh reviews BD text and vignettes, from New Kingdom mural paintings of private Theban tombs.[28] One of the most interesting and least studied group of monuments that have scenes from BD are the so-called 'Mythological papyri' and '*Amduat* papyri' the production of which falls within the Third Intermediate Period. The works of A. Piankoff, N. Rambova, F. Sadek Abd al-Aziz and N. V. Lavrentyeva are dedicated to these sources.[29] But the most significant contribution in that field was made by A. Niwiński, specially with a fundamental publication[30] and a number of papers dedicated to the issue of general and special problems of painting iconography and semantics on funerary papyri and coffins of the 21st Dynasty.[31] A general summary was published in 2000: in which A. Niwiński singled out five stages in the development of the 21st Dynasty religious iconography and underlined the connection of its evolution with the political and social changes in the state.[32]

The fourth approach focuses on the typology / classification of BD vignettes in the context of the whole collection and all kinds of sources. However, a 'general' typology of vignettes, which all the Egyptologists would accept, does not yet exist. Three studies can be singled out: that of I. Munro on the early manners of BD illustrating (18th Dynasty),[33] the unpublished dissertation of M. Jr. Mosher on vignettes of late tradition[34] and generalizing 'art studies' typology and study of vignettes by M. A. Chegodaev.[35]

In sum, this short historiographical review of the subject has evidenced four approaches to study BD illustrations. Among these, to my mind, the most useful one for understanding New Kingdom BD pictorial tradition is *the second approach* as the most methodologically reasonable and effective. It studies the vignettes for each separate spell. Taking into account the unstable structure of the BD 'Theban

[27] Díaz-Iglesias Llanos 2005: 31–106. Her analyzes of a number of BD vignettes see now: Idem 2014.
[28] Saleh 1984.
[29] Piankoff 1957; Sadek Abd al-Aziz 1985.
[30] Niwiński 1989.
[31] Niwiński 1988a: 315–325; 2006: 245–264; 2008: 11–12; 2009: 133–162.
[32] Niwiński 2000: 21–43.
[33] Munro 1988.
[34] Mosher 1990.
[35] Чегодаев 2004.

Recension', and considering concrete scenes enables to consider chronologically and evolutionally close groups of images. It thus gives the possibility to determine their typology and the connection between vignette, text and context of spells on the same semantic level.

Thus, this monograph concentrates on the second of the admitted methodological approaches to study the BD illustration heritage. This study was initiated in 2007: when I began investigating the vignettes of BD 17. The graphic frieze of BD 17 vignettes, which developed during the 19th Dynasty, is a collection of two dozens of independent scenes related to a plot from the mythological text of the spell. In the course of the study, the need to examine these scenes as the separate visual motives which had spread outside the context of BD 17 became evident. Among these motives my attention was drawn by the scene with the cat, serpent and *i̓šd*-tree and a so-called 'double-lion' scene. In 2012: the analysis of these motives became part of my doctoral dissertation defended at the A. Yu. Krymskyi Institute of Oriental Studies of the National Academy of Sciences of Ukraine (Kyiv). Sources for this research are underlined in this book with additions and extensions due to the emergence of new literature and sources.

The mythological character of 'Children of Weakness' (*mś.w Bdst*) here considered is directly related to the above mentioned scene of BD 17 and has not yet been the object of an independent study / monograph and remains largely mysterious. This last is explained by the fact that the 'Children of Weakness' could be defined as a negative image of the mythical enemy of the creator-god and the king. However, as this study will show, at the same time they were also an important component of the Cosmogonic myth, and disclosure of the value of their name allows us to investigate some fundamental features of the ancient Egyptian's worldview.

Publishing this research would have been impossible without the essential help and advices from my numerous colleagues. In this regard, I would like to express my gratitude to Dr. Irmtraut Munro (Bonn), Dr. Prof. Andrzej Niwiński (Warsaw), Dr. Prof. John Baines (Oxford), Dr. Prof. Steven Quirke (London), Dr. Nadine Guilhou (Montpellier), Dr. Alain Dautant (Bordeaux), and Dr. Éva Liptay (Budapest).

I'm deeply thankful to Dr. Daniele Michaux-Colombot (Orleans) for reading my English and helpful commentaries on the content of the book.

Preparation of this monograph was supported by the Fellowship of 'Stiftungsfonds für Postgraduates der Ägyptologie' (Institute of Egyptology, University of Vienna) for year 2014.

Chapter 1

The scene with the cat, serpent and sacred tree, 19th–21st Dynasties

§ 1.1. The *Book of the Dead* Vignette with the cat, serpent and sacred tree

The subject of this chapter is iconographic and semantic analysis of the scene, attributed to vignettes from the *Book of the Dead* (BD) chapter 17, in which three main participants are usually represented: a cat, a sacred tree and a serpent, and where the cat cuts off the snake's head.[36]

A number of vignettes from BD 17 were edited in the post-Amarna period – early 19th Dynasty. Of the twenty-seven sources found seventeen scenes are displayed on funerary papyri – in fifteen cases among BD 17 vignettes, and twice as independent scenes in related papyri of the 21st Dynasty. Chronologically *one* scroll is dated back to the late 18th Dynasty, *five* – to the 19th Dynasty, *one* – to the 20th Dynasty and *ten* – to the 21st Dynasty. The scene also appears on the painting of the *eight* tombs (*six* – from the 19th Dynasty, and *one* – from the 20th Dynasty) and on *two* coffins of the 21st Dynasty (see Appendix 1).

18th Dynasty

1) The earliest example of this BD 17 vignette[37] is represented in p*Nḫt* pLondon BM EA 10471 (***Figure 1***).[38] One should note the absence of the tree in this picture.

FIGURE 1

[36] Naville 1886 I: Taf. XXX; Milde 1991: 38, Scene XV.
[37] See in details: Тарасенко 2013: 3–17; Tarasenko 2014: 241–254.
[38] © Trustees of the British Museum; Тарасенко 2013: 10 (Сц. 11), табл. 1, *4*; Tarasenko 2014: 248 (Sc. 11) (drawing).

The colored scene is located in the middle of sheet 5 of the scroll (underneath is the text of BD 18), between the image of Horus-falcon on the pedestal on the left and the 'resurrection' composition of the deceased out of the canopic box surrounded by the Sons of Horus on the right. Here, as well as on other colored pictures, the cat's body is orange-yellow, and the serpent is painted in the blue.

19th Dynasty

2) In p*Nḫt-ˁ-Ỉmn* pBerlin P. 3002 (***Figure 2***,[39] ***2a***[40]) there are colored BD 17 vignettes. Similar to the previous scroll, the tree is not present. The cat strikes the snake with two knives, one of which is held by his hind paw; another two knives are thrust directly into the back of the reptile, thus recomposing the hieroglyph-determinative for Apophis. In addition, the shape of the serpent resembles the hieroglyph / *ḏw*, clearly noting the term 'evil': *ḏw*[41] / *ḏw.t.*[42]

FIGURE 2

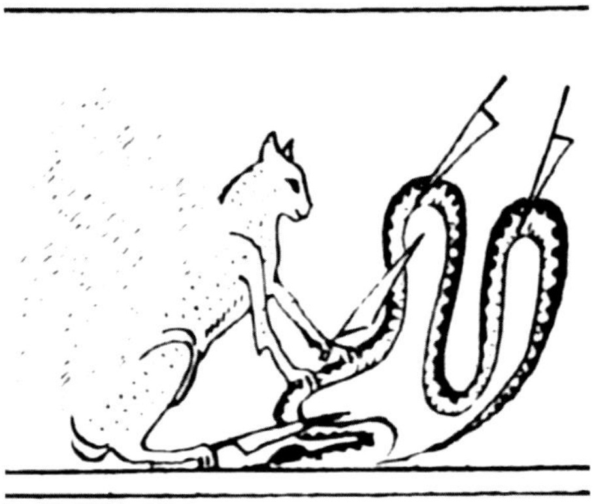

FIGURE 2A

L. Kákosy describes a number of later monuments with similar semantics,43 depicting deities sitting on pedestals, inside of which the figure of Ouroboros is placed as sign / *ḏw*.[44] The left side of the cat's body and a part of space behind him in в p*Nḫt-ˁ-Ỉmn* is destroyed, but according to the surviving fragments one can conclude that there was a scene of 'resurrection' of the deceased surrounded by Sons of Horus (it is on the right in the p*Nḫt*). The following image is the owner of the scroll in the worshiping posture in front of the 'horizon' sign.

---

[39] Munro 1997: Photo-Taf. 5.

[40] Naville 1886 I: Taf. XXX (Ba); Lüscher 2014: Taf. 12, 13.

[41] Wb., V, 545.3; Faulkner 1962: 320; Hannig 1995: 1000.

[42] Wb., V, 547.2; Faulkner 1962: 320; Hannig 1995: 1000.

[43] Kákosy 1995: 124.

[44] Kákosy 1995: 128, Figure 1–3; 129, Figure 4.

FIGURE 3

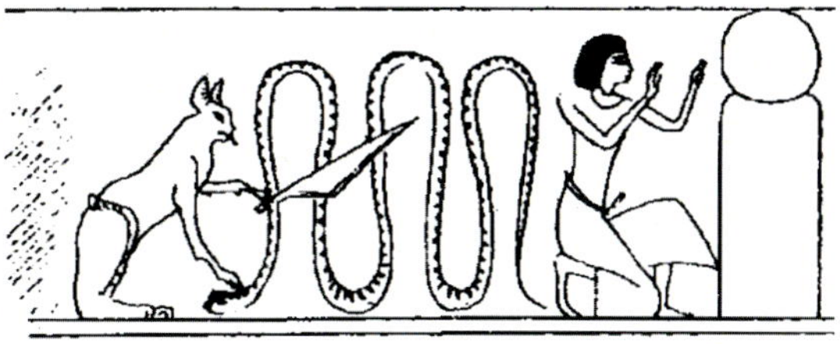

FIGURE 3A

3) In p*Ḳnn3* pLeiden T 2 the image of the cat and the snake (without the tree) completes the series of BD 17 vignettes (***Figure 3***).[45] The scene is displayed from left to right instead of right to left on the drawing by E. Naville (***Figure 3a***).[46] The striped serpent's body (on the left) has three symmetrical bends. With his left paw the cat presses the serpent's head to the ground, and cuts his body with his right paw. To the right of the scene with the cat and snake, similar to the previous document, the scroll's owner is shown in front of the *3ḫ.t*-symbol.

FIGURE 4

FIGURE 4A

4) In p*Hw-nfr* pLondon BM EA 9901 the scene is the last illustration of the BD 17 vignettes group (***Figure 4;***[47] ***4a).***[48] The dark blue spotted snake's body is depicted beneath the branches of the sacred tree and has two bends (a probable 'reference' to the *ḏw*-sign). With his left paw the cat cuts off the serpent's head with a knife, and presses it with his right paw. In front of this composition figures a scene of worship of the deceased to five ram-headed deities (their *b3*-souls) on the pedestal (***Figure 4b***).[49]

---

[45] Leemans 1882: pl. XI, 1.

[46] Naville 1886 I: Taf. XXX (La).

[47] Faulkner 2001: 48; Malek 2000: 85: pl.52.

[48] Naville 1886 I: Taf. XXX (Ag).

[49] Naville, 1886 I: Taf. XXX (Ag). Cf. ***Figure 6*** (pDublin TCLM 1661), ***Figure 7*** (p*Mw.t-m-wj3* pBerlin P. 3157). See: Milde 1991: 38 (Sc. XIV).

FIGURE 4B

FIGURE 5

FIGURE 5A

5) The p*ꜣnj* pLondon BM EA 10470 also provides a colorful vignette (***Figure 5,***[50] ***5a***).[51] Compared to the previous examples, the scene is contracted: the snake's body (on the right) has only one bend. The cat is shown under the sacred tree; he cuts off the serpent's head. The number of characters in p*ꜣnj* is expanded: there are three deities with knives in their hands behind the snake (apparently they are assistants of cat-Re?). O. Goelets' comments of this picture are uncommitting: 'the essence of the three gods, armed with knives, sitting in front of the serpent Apophis is incomprehensible'.[52] On the left of the scene there is a unique image of *bꜣ*-souls of Re and Osiris sitting on *ḏd*-columns (***Figure 5a***). The right side displays the scroll owner and his wife, worshiping the boat of Khepri.

6) The anonymous pDublin 4 (TCLM 1661) displays a polychrome vignette with the cat, serpent, and tree (***Figure 6***).[53] The cat is placed in the middle of the serpent ring, thus suggesting the image of *Ouroboros*, which is a unique case for the iconography of this vignette. With one paw the cat pulls the serpent's head, and with the other paw he cuts off its head. The tree is behind the cat. Shown to the left of the scene is the papyrus owner, worshiping five Ram-headed deities, similar to picture in the p*Hw-nfr*. The Khepri's bark is drawn on the right.

[50] Malek 2000: 85: pl. 51.
[51] Faulkner 1998: pl. 10.
[52] Faulkner 1998: 160.
[53] Naville 1886 I: Taf. XXX (Da).

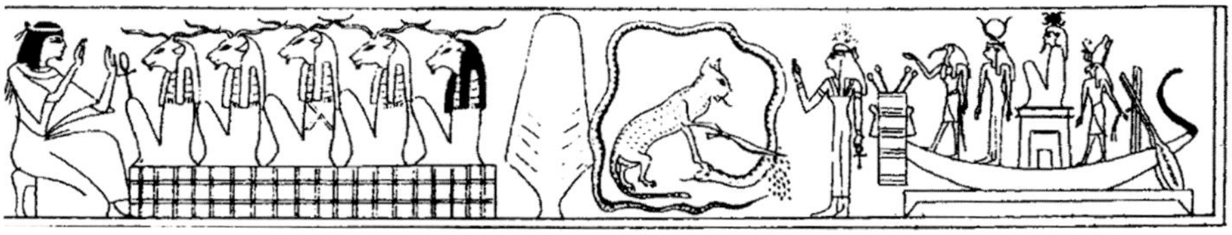

Figure 6

The posture of the serpent on this vignette is, seemingly, not accidental, since in addition to the temporal and chthonic qualities of the *Ouroboros*-serpent,[54] his essence as Apophis (and wider – *Evil*) becomes visible.[55] Moreover, the annular shape had to neutralize the power of Evil serpent, as indicated already in the *Pyramid Texts*, informing about the protective formula directed against *Šnṯ*-serpent in the Spell 393 (Pyr. § 689a-d): *śd=k tp r=k*[56] *Šnṯ pẖr pẖr=k kꜣ-wr* – 'Thy tail shall be in thy mouth, *Šnṯ*-serpent. Turn yourself around,[57] turn around, the Great Bull'[58] (PT 393, Pyr. § 689b (T)).[59]

In the magical papyrus of *Ns-Mnw* pBremner-Rhind = pLondon BM EA 10188 (30th Dynasty – early Ptolemaic Period), there is an indication that for annihilation of Apophis it is necessary to create the drawing of *Ouroboros*-serpent on a blank (lit.: 'new' – *mꜣw*) sheet of papyrus (which shall be punctured and burned during the ritual (32, 43–44)), signed above the back as *ꜥꜣpp ḫr bṯw* – 'Apophis, the fallen, *bṯw*-serpent' (32, 45–46).[60] It is reported in the other place how Re is to gain victory over Apophis: *wnn śd=k rdit rn r(ꜣ)=k wšꜥ=k mskw=k ḏś=k* – 'Your tail shall be placed in your mouth, (and) you shall chew your own skin' (30, 16).[61]

Although direct images of Apophis in the form of *Ouroboros* are unknown, there are numerous examples of pictures where Apophis is shown biting his own body.[62] Researchers, who have dealt with the figure of the Egyptian *Ouroboros*, as, in particular, L. Kákosy, believed that connection between Apophis and this figure is strange,[63] considering that basically *Ouroboros* had quite a positive function in Egyptian mythology.

---

[54] Тарасенко 2005: 14–37.
[55] Kákosy 1995: 123; 1986: Kol. 888–889.
[56] In the edition of K. Sethe here, apparently, the sign is given mistakenly, all translators understand it as =*k* – 2nd person pronoun, masculine, singular (but compare: Pyr. Komm. II: 223 (Pyr. § 443c)).
[57] Literally: 'Turn your appeal'.
[58] Cf. translation by S. A. B. Mercer: 'Thy tail shall be in thy mouth, combat-serpent. Turn thyself around thy turning, great bull' (Mercer 1952 I: 136). J. P. Allen translates: 'Your tail is in your mouth, shunned snake, your surrounding has been surrounded, great bull' (Allen 2015: 94 (Teti 393)).
[59] Allen 2013 III: 238; Cf. Kákosy 1986: Kol. 888.
[60] Faulkner 1933: 91; 1938: 52.
[61] Faulkner 1933: 79; 1938: 44.
[62] See: ***Figure 55*** (p*Ḫnmw-m-ḥb* pLondon UC 32365) and ***Figure 12*** (p*Tꜣ-wḏꜣ.t-Rꜥ* pCairo SR VII. 11496).
[63] Kákosy 1986: Kol. 888.

We assume that identification of Apophis with *Ouroboros* is explicable, firstly, by the fact that both images were directly related to the primitive state of the Universe: it was the first to embody the phenomenon of Evil (*iśf.t*), as antagonist to Order and Justice (*mꜣꜥ.t*), and the second is a serpent-like amorphous and latent state of the Universe before the Creation self-unfolding act. Secondly, the purpose of this identification was to bring Apophis to the state, safe for the Creator-god. Since the total destruction of the Evil serpent was impossible in the Egyptian notion, he had to be defeated in a state of impotence, passivity and inertia, and *Ouroboros* was the most appropriate visual form of the serpent for representation of these conditions.[64] It may be assumed that the shape of a serpent biting himself advocated special visual marker for his 'weakness'.

20th Dynasty

7) Iconography of this Dynasty is represented by the polychrome BD 17 vignette in p*Pꜣ-ḳrr* pLeiden T 4 (AMS 14)[65] (***Figure*** *7*).[66] The body of the snake here has three bends. The cat, represented in the sole picture, pulls the serpent's head with one paw, while cutting off the snake's head with the other paw. Unfortunately, the damaged state of the papyrus does not allow clarifying whether there was a tree, but the photo confirms the picture of a branch (?) testifying the presence of this component.

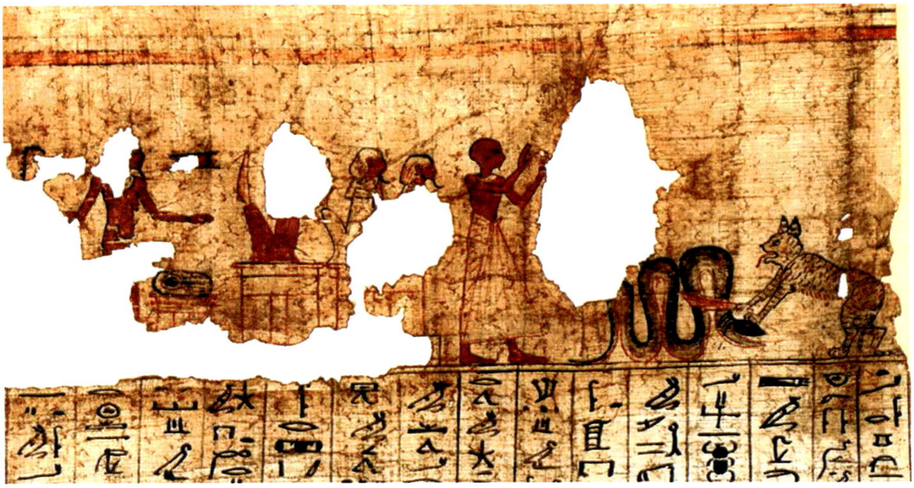

FIGURE 7

[64] Тарасенко 2005: 15–17.
[65] Unpublished. Totenbuchprojekt Bonn, TM 134347: <totenbuch.awk.nrw.de/objekt/tm134347>.
[66] © Photo by Leiden, Rijksmuseum van Oudheden.

21st – 22nd Dynasties

Characteristic for the Third Intermediate Period, well attested with many funerary papyri, is a reduced number of BD scrolls with the *complete visual series* of BD 17 vignettes. There are only three scrolls of this type (p*Mw.t-m-wjꜣ* pBerlin P. 3157; p*Nḏm(w).t* pLondon BM EA 10541 + pLouvre E. 6258 (Fr. 1); and p*Nsj-tꜣ-nb.t-išrw* pLondon BM EA 10554), but the scene in question is found only in two documents.

8) In p*Mw.t-m-wjꜣ* pBerlin P. 3157 the polychrome vignette with the cat and snake completes the illustrated series of BD 17 (***Figure 8***).[67] The cat, represented in in a rare manor, pulls serpent's head with one paw, while cutting off the serpent's head with the other paw. The tree stands behind the cat. In front of the vignette the scroll owner worships the seven deities on the pedestal (three of them have ram heads).

FIGURE 8

9) The p*Nsj-tꜣ-nb.t-išrw* pLondon BM EA 10554 (= pGreenfield) is the latest document of the BD with spell 17 vignettes for the Third Intermediate Period, considering that *Nsj-tꜣ-nb.t-išrw* probably previously died in the 22nd Dynasty.[68] Her impressive scroll (40.53 m) is written in Hieratic, a common practice for the BD of late 21st Dynasty, whence the only Hieroglyphic chapter is BD 125B. This document, copiously illustrated with monochrome drawings, follows New Kingdom tradition in terms of vignette design (upper frieze). It is characteristic that the order of the spells are similar in the manuscripts of *Nsj-tꜣ-nb.t-išrw* and her father *Pꜣ-nḏm* II pLondon BM EA 10793 (= pCampbell).[69] The Hieratic papyrus of the latter is completely deprived of illustrations (except for the introductory 'étiquette' vignette).[70] This fact makes pGreenfield unique for its time.[71] Nothing explains what made them provide Hieratic scroll with pictures in the period when BD copies were not illustrated. I can assume that one of the reasons is that *Nsj-tꜣ-nb.t-išrw*, taking into account one of her rare titles

---

[67] Naville, 1886 I: Taf. XXX (Bb). In the Naville's edition the vignettes are incorrectly oriented from the left to right, however the original 'reads' them from the right to left.

[68] Kees 1964: 74–76; Niwiński 1984: 80; 1992: 457–458 (1); Kitchen 1986: 65–66 (§ 53B); Naguib 1994: 171ff.

[69] Munro 1996; Zaluskowski 1996: 15–16.

[70] Munro 1996: 52–53, Photo-Taf. 1; Taylor 2010: 268, Figure 79, 307; See also: Maspero 1889: pl. I (here is given the photo of the introductory vignette without its later damages).

[71] The type BD.III.2 by A. Niwiński (Niwiński 1989: 155, 157).

(),[72] could have been a servant in the temple archive (*ipw*) at Thebes, and had access to its bookstores, took advantage of this chance when ordering the design for her own scroll.[73]

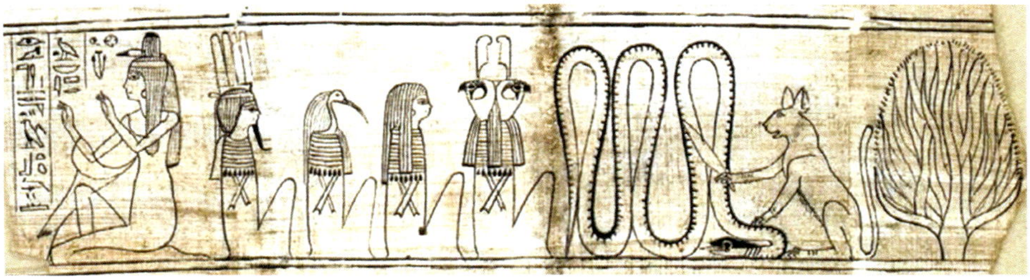

FIGURE 9

FIGURE 10

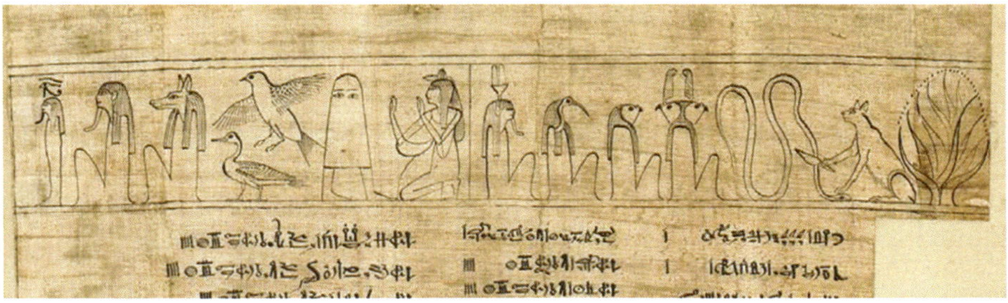

FIGURE 11

However, the vignettes in pGreenfield show evident confusion and repetition, that also applies to BD 17 scenes that are duplicated and 'illustrated' in various spells and hymns. The scene with the cat and snake in pGreenfield is repeated three times on sheets 11, 37 and 76 over the text of different utterances (BD 17, 124/125 and

[72] *bꜣk.t* (*n.t*) *pꜣ ipw n Ỉmn-Rꜥ nsw nṯr.w* – 'Servant in the archive (?) of Amun-Re, king of the gods' (Niwiński 1992: 458; Quirke 1993: 50 (No. 145)).
[73] See in details: Тарасенко 2015: 234–258.

Hymns to Re and Osiris)[74] (***Figure 9,***[75] ***10,***[76] ***11***[77]). In all cases, the body of the snake has different iconographical features. On sheet 11 it is shown with three bends, on sheet 76 – with two, and on sheet 37 – with one. In all three scenes the cat pulls serpent's head with one paw, while cutting off the serpent's head with his other paw. The sacred tree is shown behind the cat on sheets 11 and 76. These two scenes are oriented from right to left and before them there are four deities with two-headed Horus in front of them. Contrariwise, on sheet 37 the scene is oriented from left to right and there is no image of sacred tree. Here the god Heh is shown behind the cat. Probably, these types of scenes were drawn from different master-copies.

10) The p*T3-wḏ3.t-Rꜥ* pCairo S.R. VII. 11496 is a combination of the 'Mythological papyrus' and BD.[78] It contains a series of polychrome pictures, partly dating back to the BD (vignettes of chapters 77, 85, 17, 86, 110 and 126) and the text of a single spell – BD 125ᴮ. BD 17 is represented solely the cat scene, serpent and the sacred tree (***Figure 12***).[79] The body of serpent has three bends and it is shown snapping its own neck. The tree is drawn behind the reptile. Noteworthy is that the cat depicted here is a female one. J. Malek explains this by the fact that the scroll was designed for a woman,[80] an acceptable proposition. The text over the animal informs on the killing (*šm3*) of Apophis by the *miw.t ꜥnḫ* – 'living (female) cat'.

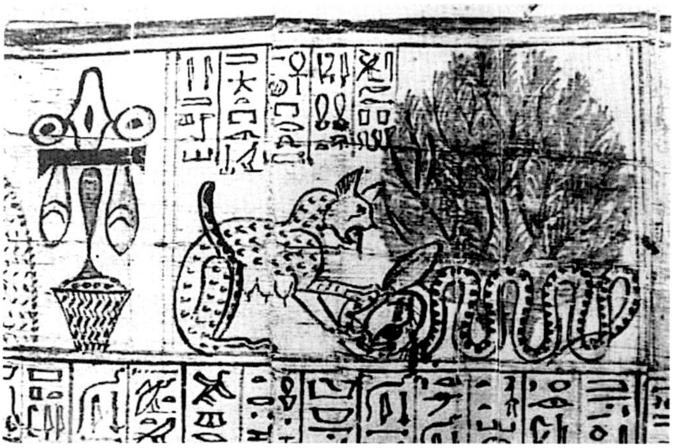

FIGURE 12

11) The relatively small (3.78 m) p*Ini-pḥ=f-nḫt* pCologny-Geneva C (Bibliotheca Bodmeriana) consists of ten BD chapters, two of which are accompanied by

[74] Zaluskowski 1996: 145–150, Taf, XVII.
[75] pGreenfield, Sh. 11 – © Trustees of the British Museum = Budge 1912: pl. XIV.
[76] pGreenfield, Sh. 37 – © Trustees of the British Museum = Budge 1912: pl. XLIII.
[77] pGreenfield, Sh. 76 – © Trustees of the British Museum = Budge 1912: pl. LXXXVII.
[78] Piankoff 1957 I: 133–142 (Pap. No. 15).
[79] Piankoff 1957 II: pl. 15.
[80] Malek 2000: 84.

polychrome vignettes, – spells 17 and 125B. The papyrus ends with the picture of BD 110 (in full height of the scroll sheet). In sum, the BD 17 scenes in the p*Ỉni-pḥ=f-nḫt* are divided into four independent 'blocks' (only two of them are published)[81] separated by columns of the text. The vignette with the cat, cutting off the serpent's head and the goddesses Isis and Nephthys is represented in the first 'block'. Behind them is pictured a Khepri's bark with a divine crew (***Figure 13***).[82]

Figure 13

Identical, but monochrome, a scene with the cat and snake (also containing the image of Isis and Nephthys) are represented in an interesting series of five 'replicated' or 'unified' scrolls with illustrated BD 17 dated back to the second half of the 21st Dynasty. Only one of these documents is partially published (pLondon BM EA 9948). These scrolls form a compact typological and chronological group. They may date to a period immediately preceding the beginning of the dominance of the Hieratic version of the BD, devoid of accompanying vignettes (type BD.I.2 by A. Niwiński).[83] They clearly represent the last stage in development of pictorial Hieroglyphic BD 'Theban redaction'.[84]

12) pʿ*nḫ=f(-n)-Ḫnśw* pCologny-Geneva CI (Bibliotheca Bodmeriana);[85]
13) p*Ṯnt-imnt.t-hr-ib* pCologny-Geneva CII (Bibliotheca Bodmeriana);[86]
14) p*Ns(j)-Ḫnśw* pTurin 1818;[87]
15) p*Ḏd-Ḫnśw*, Saint-Petersburg, Hermitage Museum No. 18587;
16) p*Diw-sw-n-Mw.t* pLondon BM 9948 (***Figure 14***).[88] Exactly the same order of chapters and a number of illustrations of BD 17 as in the previous four documents appear, but at the end there is a picture, perhaps related to BD 18 illustrations, which, however, is based only on A. Shorter's identification.[89]

[81] Bissing 1928: 37–39, Taf. I; Bickel 2001: 117–134, Figure 32, 39; Tarasenko 2012: 383, Figure 4a–b.
[82] Bissing 1928: Taf. I; Bickel 2001: 128–129, Figure 39; Tarasenko 2012: 383, Figure 4a.
[83] Niwiński 1989: 113–118.
[84] Tarasenko 2012: 379–394.
[85] Unpublished, Totenbuchprojekt Bonn, TM 134678: <totenbuch.awk.nrw.de/objekt/tm134678>.
[86] Unpublished, Totenbuchprojekt Bonn, TM 134677: <totenbuch.awk.nrw.de/objekt/tm134677>.
[87] Unpublished, Totenbuchprojekt Bonn, TM 134600: <totenbuch.awk.nrw.de/objekt/tm134600>.
[88] Shorter 1938: pl. X.
[89] Shorter 1938: 2.

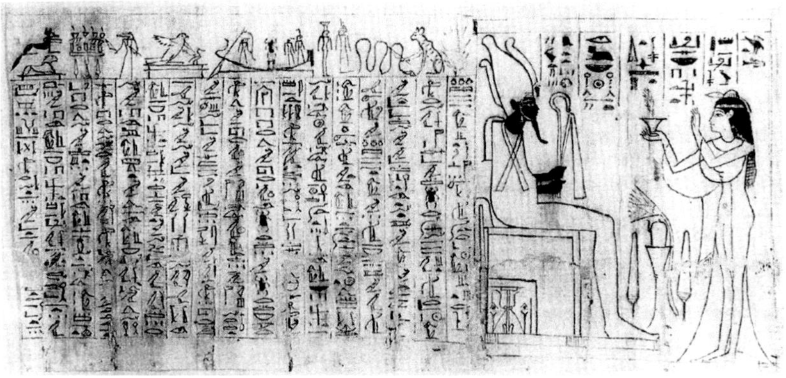

FIGURE 14

Noteworthy is the fact that these papyri duplicate not only the text, but also the iconic series, created perhaps by the same artist. The documents consist of (*a*) the introductory vignette (individual for each scroll, moreover in two papyri from Geneva the vignettes are polychrome, whereas in three other they are monochrome), (*b*) the BD 17 text and BD 1, which is accompanied by (*c*) selected and randomly arranged vignettes of BD 17 placed in the upper frieze. Given below is the sequence of visual scenes, presented in the documents.

1. The scene with the cat, serpent and tree, with Isis and Nephthys behind the composition (scene XV).[90] One should note placement of this scene at the beginning of the graphic line while the scrolls of the New Kingdom always depict it at the end of the illustration.
2. The Khepri bark with the divine crew (scene XXI).
3. Image of the goose and the falcon on the pedestal (scene XVIII).
4. The dog-headed (or crocodile-headed) 'demon' with knives in his hands in front of the altar and two lamps (scene XX).
5. The jackal (Anubis) and lion (scenes XXI and XXIII).
6. The *wḏ3.t*-eye on the pedestal (scene X / XXI).
7. The deceased in adoration posture in front of the Heavenly cow on the pedestal (scene XI).
8. Image of three 'demons' (scene XVII (– XVIII?)).[91]
9. Deity in front of the offerings table.
10. Four deities in front of the offerings table.
11. The scroll owner in worshiping posture in front of four deity figures. The final scene has several variants.

[90] Given here and below are the numbers of scenes corresponding to the BD 'Theban redaction' by H. Milde (Milde 1991: 31–42).
[91] This scene has no direct analogies with New Kingdom BD 17 vignettes and probably was created during the 21st Dynasty (see in details: Milde 1991: 44–45, Figure 15; Тарасенко 2009a: 82–88).

12. The pʿnḫ=f-(n-)Ḫnśw and pṮnt-imnt.t-hr-ib (pCologny-Geneva CI and CII) display the deceased in adoration posture in front of three deities.
12a. In pNs(j)-Ḫnśw pTurin 1818 the deceased is depicted in front of the only god. Obviously, there was not enough space on the sheet to place the figures of two more deities, and the scene had to be shortened.[92]
12b. The pDiw-sw-n-Mw.t pLondon BM 9948: the longest document, on the contrary, has surplus space left and after the scene of the deceased worshiping three gods (12), identical to those in pʿnḫ=f-n-Ḫnśw and pT3-nt-imnt.t-hrt-ib, there is another composition, originating perhaps from BD 18 vignettes, where the scroll owner is shown in front of deities (perhaps created by another artist, as indicated by minor stylistic differences and larger figures).

17) Another example of a single BD 17 vignette is represented in the combined '*Amduat* papyrus' – p*P3-n-pj* pCologny-Geneva CVII (Bibliotheca Bodmeriana) (***Figure 15***).[93] The scroll has a hymn to Re-Atum-Horakhty, the variant of a solar hymn of BD 15 and the monochrome picture from the 12th Hour of *Amduat*. The upper register (the left side) of this *Amduat* composition contains the scene of the cat and serpent (***Figure 15a***).[94] A distinctive feature of this image is that both characters are turned to the right (the cat is shown sitting on the serpent's neck) while usually they are pictured opposite to each other.

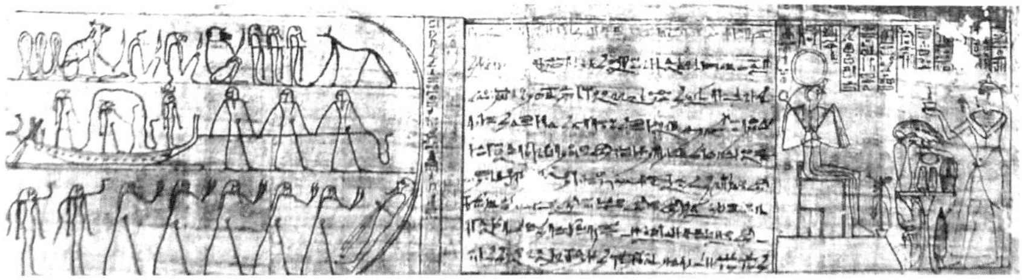

FIGURE 15

FIGURE 15A

[92] Unfortunately, the length of p*Nsj-Ḫnśw* is not exactly known to us. The length of pʿ*nḫ=f-(n-)Ḫnśw* is 1.18 m, p*Ṯnt-imnt.t-hr-ib* – 1.2 m, p*Diw-sw-n-Mw.t* – 1.21 m. Due to poor condition it is impossible to identify the original length of p*Ḏd-Ḫnśw*. The height of the sheets of the examined scrolls ranges from 21.6 cm to 25 cm (data from *Bonn Totenbuchprojekt*).
[93] Valloggia 1989: 131–144: pl. 5.
[94] Valloggia 1989: 144, Figure 44.

§ 1.2. The vignette with the cat, serpent and sacred tree in Theban tomb decorations and coffins (19th–21st Dynasties)

From the second half of the New Kingdom the text and vignettes of BD 17 are incorporated to the plot of Theban tombs painting. Although the number of scenes from BD 17 in the Theban tombs does not exceed five.[95] The scene with the cat and serpent, as noted by M. Abdul-Qader Muhammed and H. Milde, is one of the most popular scenes from BD 17 (along with the images of playing *snt*-game and so-called *Rw.tj*-scene)[96].[97] It appears in seven tombs.

1) TT 1, *Sn-nḏm*, Deir el-Medina, 19th Dynasty (Ramses II).[98] The picture is located on the eastern wall of the corridor to the Innermost Chamber[99] (***Figure 16,***[100] ***17***).[101] Noteworthy is the strange correlation between the vignettes and the text in this tomb, when under the image of the scene in question there is the text, associated with *Rw.tj*-scene, portrayed on the opposite western wall. The picture shows the body of the serpent with two bends; the cat cuts off the serpent's head; the tree is placed behind the cat's back.

FIGURE 16

FIGURE 17

[95] Saleh 1984: 19, Tab. IV.
[96] For this scene see: Tarasenko 2013: 77–122.
[97] Abdul-Qader Muhammed 1966: 253–255; Milde 1991: 49. Cf. Saleh 1984: 19, Tab. IV.
[98] PM ²I. 1: 1–5.
[99] PM ²I. 1: 1 (5).
[100] Wilkinson, Hill 1983: 138, Figure 30.4.1; Pinch 2002: 107, Figure 22.
[101] Bruyère 1959: pl. XVIII, no. 1; cf. Saura i Senjaume 2006: 61, Figure 5.2; 64, Figure 5.5.

2) TT 10, *Pn-bwi* and *Kꜣ-sꜣ*, Deir el-Medina, 19th Dynasty (Ramses II).[102] The scene is placed in the Chapel wall painting and is not published.[103] The image is in very bad state of preservation (***Figure 18***).[104]

FIGURE 18

3) TT 32, *Ḏḥwtj-mśw*, El-Khokha, 19th Dynasty (Ramses II)[105] (***Figure 19***).[106] The scene is located on the ceiling painting of the cross Pillared Hall and is badly damaged. The body of the serpent (blue) is shown with three bends; the cat presses the serpent's head with one paw and cuts off his head with the other; the tree is placed behind the back of the serpent.

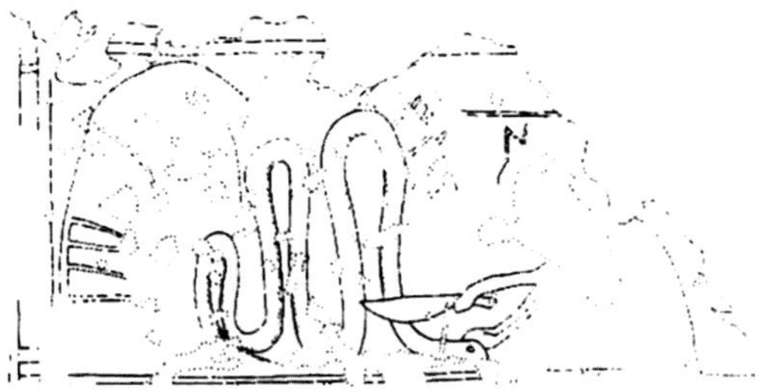

FIGURE 19

4) TT 216, *Nfr-ḥtp*, Deir el-Medina, 19th Dynasty (Ramses II).[107] The scene is placed on the Western Wall painting of the Innermost Chamber 'D'[108] (***Figure 20, 20a***).[109]

[102] PM ²I. 1: 20–21.
[103] Saleh 1984: 18–19; PM ²I. 1: 21 (5).
[104] © Institut Français d'Archéologie Orientale, Revault. Photos by *Archives Scientifiques de l'IFAO.*
[105] PM ²I. 1: 49–50.
[106] Kákosy, Bács, Bartos, Fábián, Gaál 2004 I: 199.
[107] PM ²I. 1: 312–315.
[108] PM ²I. 1: 314; Saleh 1984: 18–19; Bruyère 1925: Tab. 2.
[109] © Institut Français d'Archéologie Orientale, Ihab Mhd Ibrahim. Photos by *Archives Scientifiques de l'IFAO.*

FIGURE 20

FIGURE 20A

5) TT 292, *P3-šdw*, Deir el-Medina, 19th Dynasty (Ramses II).[110] The scene is placed on the ceiling painting of the Chapel and is not published[111] (***Figure 21***).[112]

FIGURE 21

6) TT 335, *Nḫt.w-Ỉmn*, Deir el-Medina, 19th Dynasty[113] (***Figure 22, 22a*** (detail)).[114] The scene is placed on the ceiling of the burial Chamber 'C'. The serpent has three bends; the cat cuts off its head with a knife (two more knives are shown already thrust into the serpent's body). The tree is not represented.

[110] PM ^{2}I. 1: 374–376.
[111] PM ^{2}I. 1: 375; Saleh 1984: 18, Anm. 88.
[112] © Institut Français d'Archéologie Orientale, Revault. Photos by *Archives Scientifiques de l'IFAO*.
[113] PM ^{2}I. 1: 401–404.
[114] Bruyère 1926: 163, Figure 109, 171, Figure 113.

FIGURE 22

FIGURE 22A

7) TT 359, *Ỉnj-ḥr-ḫˁw*, Deir el-Medina, 20th Dynasty (Ramses III / IV)[115] (***Figure 23;***[116] ***23a).***[117] The scene is on the West wall of the inner Chamber 'G'.[118] The blue body of the serpent has two bends. The cat presses the snake's head with one paw and holds a knife, cutting it roughly in half with his other paw. The emphasis is placed on the disproportionately long ears of the animal.[119] The sacred tree is shown between the curves of the serpent's body.

8) Tomb of *Ỉnỉ-ḥr.t-ms* at El-Mashayikh (Lepidotonpolis, VIII (Thinite) nome of Upper Egypt), 19th Dynasty (Merneptah)[120] (***Figure 24***).[121] The image is in a bad state of preservation. The scene is located on the Eastern wall of the burial chamber.

[115] PM ²I. 1: 421–424; Saleh 1984: 18–19.

[116] Cherpion, Corteggiani 2010 II: 65, Figure 98. See also: Saleh 1984: 19, Abb. 22; Corteggiani 1995: 146, Figure 2; Malek 2000: 87: pl. 55; Hodel-Hoenes 2000: 285, Figure 212; Keller 2001: colour pl. 26,3; Dodson, Ikram 2008: 267, Figure 289; Angenot 2011: pl. 2b.

[117] Bruyère 1933: pl. XXI.

[118] PM ²I. 1: 423 (11). This scene is unique not only in its special iconography (cf. Mekhitarian 1991: 30; Sweeney 2009: 535–536), but in the fact that it is the only one, whose artist is known for sure – it is the draughtsman in the 'Places of Truth' (*ś.t mꜣˁ.t*) *Ḥr-Mnw* (I) (see: Bruyère 1933: 67; Keller 2001: 80; for this person see: Davies 1999: 23–54). His 'signature occupies the final (left) column of the text' near the vignette: *iri in ... sš ḳd.wt m ꜣḫ.t nḥḥ Ḥr-Mnw mꜣˁ-ḫrw* – 'made by ... the Draughtsman in the Horizon of Eternity Hormin, true of voice ' (Keller 2001: 80; colour pl. 26,3; Cherpion, Corteggiani 2010 I: 226–227).

[119] Cherpion, Corteggiani 2010 II: 65, Figure 99. Most remarkable in this scene is the image of the cat's ears shown disproportionately long. Some scholars believe that they are the ears of a hare (Bruyère 1933: 6; Corteggiani 1995: 147; Sweeney 2009: 536; Cherpion, Corteggiani 2010 I: 113, n. 641). According to S. Aufrère, the assimilation is due to the lunar associations of these animals (Aufrère 2004: 55, 59). Other researchers suggest that the cat donkey ears. V. Angenot offered to 'decode' the scene as a *rebus* for the name *miw ˁꜣ*, based on homonyms *ˁꜣ* – 'great' and *ˁꜣ* – 'donkey' (Angenot 2016 *in press*; Cannuyer 2014: 48; cf. also: Guilhou 2015: 188–189). The whole scene is conceived by researcher as a 'cultural metaphor' (Angenot 2011: 260). Chr. Cannuyer agrees with V. Angenot, but assumes this image not only as *rebus*, but also as an image of a dual cat-donkey (*miw-ˁꜣ*) (Cannuyer 2014: 49 ('conjonction de deux animaux alliés dans l'extermination de l'ennemi matinal du soleil')). Thereupon, it is reasonable to surmise that the fragment of BD 125 mentions a conversation of cat and donkey (Cannuyer 2014: 55–56; *sḏm.n=i twy ḏd ṯn ˁꜣ ḥnꜣ miw* – Lapp 2008: 182 (pꞽwiꜣ)) in the context of the reference to 'split of the *išd*-tree in *Re-Setau*' (*iw mꜣꜣ.n=i pšn išd m-ḫnw Rꜣ-śṯꜣw* – Lapp 2008: 184, 186 (pꞽwiꜣ)) – Lapp 2008: 184, 186 (pꞽwiꜣ)). Unfortunately, this mythem is too obscure to connect its plot with the scene in TT 359. Besides, we should not forget that the scene shows a serval (judging by the hair color, see below), the animal, which itself has long and large ears (Figure 34, 34a).

[120] PM V: 28–29; Ockinga, al-Masri 1988.

[121] Ockinga, al-Masri 1988: 7–8 (Scene 5); pl. 11.

FIGURE 23

FIGURE 23A

FIGURE 24

The BD 17 vignette with the cat and serpent appears three times on 21st Dynasty's **coffins**.

1) The bottom of *Ḫꜣ-ʿs.t*'s outer coffin Cairo J.E. 29665; CG 6076[122] has four registers of pictures. The scene in question is given in the fourth one. The serpent is shown wriggling on the branches of the sacred tree, its body has three bends and is curved round to form a ring. The cat presses the serpent's head with one paw, and cuts off its head with the other (***Figure 25***).[123]

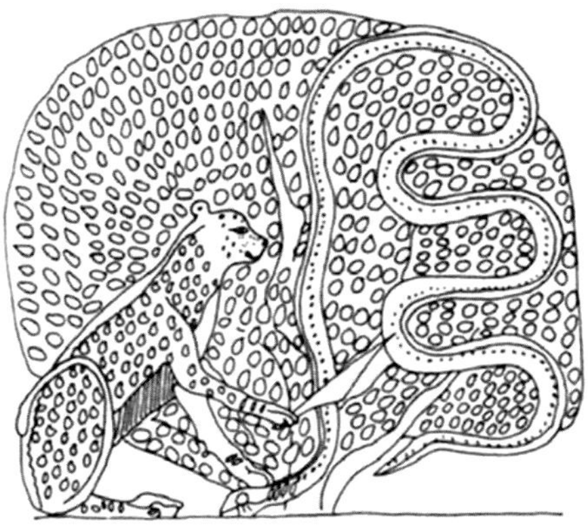

FIGURE 25

2) At the bottom of the *Ḫnśw-mś* inner coffin Turin 2238; CGT 10106b,[124] the scene with the cat and serpent is placed below the feet of the goddess Nut (***Figure 26***).[125] The cat and serpent are shown in the background of the sacred tree; the body of the reptile has one bend; the cat presses its head with one paw, and holds a knife in the other.

3) On the inner walls of the lid of *Pꜣ-dỉ-Ḫnśw* inner coffin Lyon Musée des Beaux-Arts H 2320–2321[126] the scene with the cat, serpent and sacred tree is placed among other BD 17 vignettes (***Figure 27***).[127] These pictures are monochrome and belong to the same iconographic tradition with the group of five papyri discussed

[122] Niwiński 1988: 124 (108); 1996: 102–110.
[123] Niwiński 1996: 105, Figure 82.
[124] el-Sayed 1981: 163–173; Niwiński 1988: 173 (Nr. 386); 2004: 62–80.
[125] Lanzone 1884: Tav. CLII (drawing); see also: Niwiński 2004: Tav. XI. 2 (photo).
[126] See: Jamen 2015.
[127] © Photo by F. Jamen; see also: Jamen 2015: 100, Figure 36.

FIGURE 26

above (Nos. 12–16). For instance, here is shown the image of a *Mḏd*-demon (***Figure 27a***),[128] which represents the idea of invisibility and known only in the mentioned group of documents and several other scrolls of the 21st Dynasty.[129]

FIGURE 27

FIGURE 27A

§ 1.3. The iconography of the scene

The **iconography** of the scene has no significant variants in the 'Theban BD recension'. Its three components are: 1) the ***cat*** with a ***knife***; 2) the ***serpent***, and

[128] © Photo by F. Jamen; see also: Jamen 2015: 100, Figure 39.

[129] See: Тарасенко 2005a: 104–125; 2009a: 82–88; Tarasenko 2012: 385.

3) the ***sacred tree***). Only in p*ꜣnj* pLondon BM EA 10470 this scheme has been added with the image of three deities with knives (***Figure 5, 5a***).

The third component may be excluded: there are no pictures of the sacred tree in p*Nḫt* pLondon BM EA 10471; p*Nḫt-ꜥ-Ỉmn* pBerlin P. 3002; p*Ḳnnꜣ* pLeiden T2; p*Pꜣ-ḳrr* pLeiden T 4; p*Ỉni-pḥ=f-nḫt* pCologny-Geneva C; p*Pꜣ-n-pj* pCologny-Geneva CVII and in the tomb of *Nḫt.w-Ỉmn* TT 335.

There are several ways to display the body of the serpent:

a. – the body of the serpent has *one* bend (p*ꜣnj* pLondon BM EA 10470; p*Nsj-tꜣ-nb.t-išrw* pLondon BM EA 10554 (Sh. 37); tomb of *Ỉni-ḥr.t-ms* at El-Mashayikh; coffin of *Ḫnśw-mś* Turin 2238; CGT 10106b);

b. – the body of the serpent has *two* bends (p*Nḫt-ꜥ-Ỉmn* pBerlin P. 3002; p*Hw-nfr* pLondon BM EA 9901; p*Mw.t-m-wjꜣ* pBerlin P. 3157; p*Nsj-tꜣ-nb.t-išrw* pLondon BM EA 10554 (Sh. 76); tombs of *Sn-nḏm* TT 1, *Nfr-ḥtp* TT 216, *Ỉnj-ḥr-ḫꜥw* TT 359);

c. – the body of the serpent has *three* bends (p*Ḳnnꜣ* pLeiden T 2; p*Pꜣ-ḳrr* pLeiden T 4; p*Nsj-tꜣ-nb.t-išrw* pLondon BM EA 10554 (Sh. 11); p*Ỉni-pḥ=f-nḫt* pCologny-Geneva C; p*ꜥnḫ=f-(n-)Ḫnśw* pCologny-Geneva CI; p*Ṯnt-imnt.t-hr-ib* pCologny-Geneva CII; p*Ns(j)-Ḫnśw* pTurin 1818; p*Ḏd-Ḫnśw* Hermitage 18587; p*Diw-sw-n-Mw.t* pLondon BM EA 9948: p*Pꜣ-n-pj*, pCologny-Geneva CVII; tombs of *Ḏḥwtj-mśw* TT 32 and *Nḫt.w-Ỉmn* TT 335);

d. – the body of the serpent has *four* bends (p*Tꜣ-wḏꜣ.t-Rꜥ* pCairo S.R. VII. 11496);

e. – the body of the serpent has a *closed-ring form (Ouroboros)* (p*Nḫt-ꜥ-Ỉmn* pBerlin P. 3002; pDublin 4 pTrinity College 1661; coffin of *Ḫꜣ-ꜥs.t* Cairo J.E. 29665);

f. – the body of the serpent has been *struck with the additional knives* (p*Nḫt-ꜥ-Ỉmn* pBerlin P. 3002; tomb of *Nḫt.w-Ỉmn* TT 335).

Furthermore, the location of the ***tree*** may vary:

a. the tree is behind the cat (pDublin 4; p*Mw.t-m-wjꜣ* pBerlin P. 3157; p*Nsj-tꜣ-nb.t-išrw* pLondon BM EA 10554 (Sh. 11, 76); p*ꜥnḫ=f-(n-)Ḫnśw* pCologny-Geneva CI; p*Ṯnt-imnt.t-hr-ib* pCologny-Geneva CII; p*Ns(j)-Ḫnśw* pTurin 1818; p*Ḏd-Ḫnśw* Hermitage 18587; p*Diw-sw-n-Mw.t* pLondon BM EA 9948; tombs of *Sn-nḏm* TT 1, *Nfr-ḥtp* TT 216, and *Ỉni-ḥr.t-ms* at El-Mashayikh);

b. the tree is behind the serpent (p*Hw-nfr* pLondon BM EA 9901; tomb of *Ḏḥwtj-mśw* TT 32);

c. the cat is on the background of the tree (p*ȝnj* pLondon BM EA 10470);
d. the serpent is on the background of the tree (p*Tȝ-wḏȝ.t-Rʿ* pCairo S.R. VII. 11496: tomb of *Ỉnj-ḥr-ḫʿw* TT 359);
e. both cat and serpent are on the background of the tree (coffins of *Ḫȝ-ʿs.t* Cairo J.E. 29665 (the snake is shown on the tree branches), and *Ḫnśw-mś* Turin 2238: CGT 10106b).

Late iconography of BD 17 vignette with the cat and serpent is not significantly beyond the scope of New kingdom tradition, depicting the same three main participants.[130] However, it is possible to point out several new iconographic variants.

1) The cat (without the knife) presses the serpent's head with his paw (p*Ns-Mnw* pNew Jersey University (***Figure 28***);[131] p*Nḥm-s-Rʿt-tȝwi* pLouvre N. 3149 (***Figure 29***);[132] p*Ỉw=f-ʿnḫ* pTurin 1791 (***Figure 30***).[133]

2) The cat presses the head of the coiled up serpent to the ground, and holds the serpent's tail with his other paw (p*Nḥm-s-Rʿt-tȝwi* pLouvre N. 3087 (***Figure 31***)).[134]

3) The scene is supplemented with a new participant and design, the falcon's image above the L-inverted composition and together with baboon image (p*Ỉrti-w-r-w* pChicago OIM 10486 (= pMilbank) (***Figure 32***);[135] p*Nfrt-ii* (*Nfr-ii-n-i*) pBerlin P. 10477 (***Figure 33***).[136]

FIGURE 28

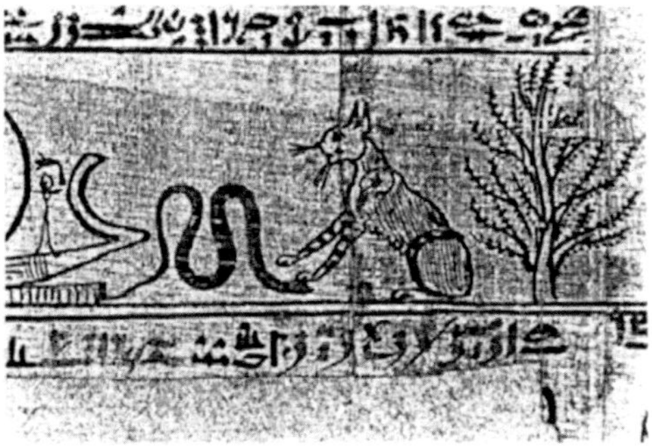

FIGURE 29

[130] See: Mosher 1990: 182; pl. 32–39. The Roman Period echo of this motif is possible to recognize on the fragment of painted cartonnage mummy case from Bahri Oasis showing a cat and tree (but without images of serpent and knife) as the personages of Judgment scene (Riggs 2013: 146, Figure 67).
[131] Clère 1987: pl. V.
[132] Broze 1991: 111, Figure 55.
[133] Lepsius 1842: Taf. IX.
[134] Broze 1991: 111, Figure 56.
[135] Allen 1960: pl. LXI.
[136] Lüscher 2000: Photo-Taf. 6.

FIGURE 30

FIGURE 31

FIGURE 32

FIGURE 33

Thus, the collected material summarized in **Appendix 1** gives data to focus on the semantic analysis of the considered vignette within a particular chronological period.

Chapter 2

Correlation between text and visual image

§ 2.1. The textual source for the vignette

Scholars unanimously[137] believe that the cat, serpent and sacred tree composition illustrates the following fragment of BD chapter 17 (= CT Sp. 335, IV: 282a–293a) (**Appendix 2, Text No. 1**):

(54) [...] *ink miw*(A) *pwy* (*ꜥ3*) (*ntj*) *pšnj išd* (55) *r-gś=f m Ꞽwnw grḥ pwy* [*n ꜥḥ3-ꜥ n iri.t ś3w.t sbj.w hrw pw n*](B) *ḥtm ẖftj.w niw nb-r-ḏr im=f* [*ptr r=f*] *św miw pwy* [*ꜥ3*] *Rꜥ pw* (56) *ḏś=f ḏd.*(*n.*)*tw n=f miw m ḏd Śi3 r=f miw św m nn* (*n*) *iri.n=f ẖpr rn=f pw n miw*(C) *ky ḏd wnn* (57) *Šw pw ḥr iri.t imj.t-pr n Gb n Wśir ir grt pšn išd r gś=f m Ꞽwnw wnn mś.w Bdšt pw ḥr m3ꜥ* (58) *ḥr*SIC. *iri.*(*t*)*n=śn ir grt grḥ pf n ꜥḥ3-ꜥ ꜥḳ=sn pw m i3b.tj p.t ꜥḥꜥ.n ꜥḥ3-ꜥ* (*ẖpr*) *m p.t m t3 r ḏr=f*

'(54) [...] I am that (Great) Cat, beside whom the *išd*-tree (55) was split in Heliopolis on that Night [of the Combat and repelling of the rebels; on that day] when the Enemies of the Lord of the Universe were executed. [What is] that? As for the '(Great) Cat' that it is Re himself. (56) He was called 'Cat' (*miw*) because the (god) Sia said about him: 'he is similar (*miw*) to made by him' (or, 'he is what he has done')(D). Thus came into existence his name of 'Cat' (*miw*). Otherwise said: it was (57) Shu, who gave the Will to Geb and Osiris. As for 'the *išd*-tree was split in Heliopolis', that are the Children of *Bdšt*, punished (58) for what they had done. As for this 'Night of the Combat' – it happened when they invaded the East of the Sky, and there was the Combat in the Sky and in the entire Land' (after p*Nb-snj* pLondon BM EA 9900).[138]

Comments

(A) In the CT the *miw* determinative 'cat' 𓃠 / E13 is frequently substituted by 𓄜 / F 27 / 'cow's skin' symbol (see CT IV: 282a–283a (except for B_3C, T_2Be and T_3Be)). Such a substitution was conventional for determining animals in this corpus. Such cases are noted in the BD too.[139]

[137] Allen 1974: 27, fn. 47 (No 15);30 (§ S 15); Hornung 1979: 424 (15); Mosher 1990: 182 (A15), 643; Milde 1991: 38 (Sc. XV); Quirke 2013: 67 (Part 4); Tarasenko 2014: 248 (Sc. 11).
[138] Urk. V: Abs. 22, 52–53 (54–58); Lapp 2006: 192–205.
[139] Lapp 2006: 192–193, 196–199 (cL1, pP5*, pC3, TT 82, pV1, pLe1, pLe2).

(B) Addition from the p*Jwỉ3* pCairo CG 51189.[140]

(C) Translation of this sentence is not ambiguous.[141] According to E. Otto, M. Heerma van Voss, P. Barguet and Cl. Carrier, in the CT and BD this sentence is interrogative, not a narrative.[142] E. Otto founds his opinion by the use of the preposition *ỉn* in nine out of sixteen versions of CT Spell 335 in A. de Buck's edition.[143] However, I believe that R. Faulkner is correct in seeing no traces of interrogation in this sentence: '*mỉw św*, adjectival predicate with dependent pronoun. In several cases the sentence is introduced by *ỉn*, the full form of *n* 'because'. BH_1Br has corruptly *mywy nn ỉr.n.f*, omitting *św m*'.[144]

(D) The mythological etymology of the name *mỉw* 'Cat' is brought here to homonymy with *mỉw* (= *mỉỉ* (*j* – *w* = 'Auslaut')) – 'similar', 'like', 'identical', etc. ('Ein Gleicher')[145] derived from the preposition *mỉ*.[146] Such homonymous interpretation of the etymology is first found in the *Pyramid Texts* in the so-called *Namensformeln,*[147] where one can find an example of the living myth creation (or early example of a 'reflection'). A number of scholars are inclined to analyze *Namensformeln* as only 'the first steps towards mythology'.[148] However, I believe that such an approach underestimates the depth of mythological concepts existing in that era.[149] The play on homonyms is frequent in later religious and mythological texts, and even in the literary texts.[150] The usage of homonymic techniques can be found in Ptolemaic times, such as in the so-called Theban cosmogony of Khonsu who travelled ('He traveled (*ḫnś* – lit.: 'had traveled')[151] to Thebes in his form of Khonsu ((*Ḫnśw*) ... Thus came into existence his name of Khonsu the Great in Thebes'),[152] where the verb *ḫnś* – 'travel' and the name of the god *Ḫnśw* are played on, with similar etymology ('Traveler', 'Wanderer')[153] related to his lunar functions.

140 Budge 1910 I: 68 (line 65–66); Munro 1994 I: Taf. 48 (line 91); Lapp 2006: 194. Cf. Shorter 1938: 110 and CT IV, 282a–285a.
141 See: Otto 1956: 66; Allen 1960: 90 (15, 14); Piankoff 1962: 56; Hornung 1979: 69; Rößler-Köhler 1979: 224, Z. 56; Verhoeven 1993 I: 102 (10, 8); Malek 2000: 79; Faulkner 2001: 48; Quirke 2013: 60 ('that is how (Miu) he is, by what he has done').
142 Otto 1956: 66; Heerma van Voss 1963: 45; Barguet 1967: 61; 1986: 568; Carrier 2009a: 87.
143 Otto 1956: 66.
144 Faulkner 1994 I: 269, fn. 68; cf. Speleers 1922: 647. As to the meaning of the preposition (*i*)*n* see: Gardiner 1958: 126–127 (§ 164), comp.: 128–129 (§ 168); Borghouts 2010 I: 112–113 (§ 29.d.4).
145 Edel 1955: § 142; Otto 1956: 66.
146 Wb. II: 38.15; Otto 1956: 65–66.
147 Sander-Hansen 1946: 1–22.
148 Большаков 2003: 12; cf. Ассман 1999: 134–140.
149 See: Baines 1996: 363, 374–377, Goebs 2002: 27–59; Hellum 2014: 123–142.
150 Cf. Тарасенко 2007: 53–58.
151 Wb. III: 299.5.
152 Lesko 1991: 105.
153 Wb. III: 300.13.

Based on this text, the vignette depicts the cat, identified as *miw ꜥꜣ* – 'the Great Cat', the *i̓šd*-tree and the snake, not named directly in the text and, therefore, the most controversial character to be identified. Thus, the iconographic 'legend' of the scene is the 'Great Cat' (according to the gloss it is the image of Re), cutting off a serpent's head with the knife under the shadow of the sacred *i̓šd*-tree.

§ 2.2. Participants of the scene: the problem of identification

Let's consider the first two members of the vignette composition:

1. The 'Great Cat' ( – *miw ꜥꜣ*) is identified as the serval (*Felix serval* or *Leptailurus serval*)[154] (***Figure 34, 34a***).[155] This animal is known as a specific zoomorphic 'manifestation' of Re, his *Erseheinungsform.*[156] There is an inscription in the tomb of *Nḫ.t-tw-Ỉmn* TT 335 in Deir el-Medina, next to the image of the cat in a picture identical to BD 17 vignette (***Figure 22***): 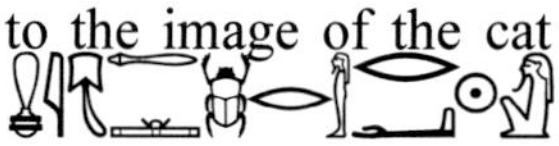 – *miw ꜥꜣ ḫprw Rꜥ* – 'The Great Cat, the image of Re'.[157]

In mythology, Re is quite frequently associated with various divine cat representations. Moreover he had relations with various lion-goddesses.[158] These goddesses embodied the Eye of Re, i.e. power and sacred energy, the visible manifestation of which was sunshine.[159] The Eye of Re, identified with the goddesses-lioness, could be endowed with a punitive function, attacking his enemies. The *Book of the Heavenly Cow* says that once the Eye of Re was directed against humanity.[160] On the other hand, the disappearance of the Eye was an unbearable disaster for humans and gods. This is narrated in the 'Legend of return of Hathor-Tefnut from Nubia' (the myth was restored from the number of later papyri: pLeiden I 384; pBerlin 21443 etc.).[161] Here the Eye is the lioness.

In Heliopolis, as early as the Old Kingdom Atum was identified with Ruty – 'double' lion-god of Leontopolis (*Rw.tj* – dual from *rw* 'lion'). In several texts Ruty claims the 'seniority' over Atum (Pyr. § 446a–447d; CT Sp. 173, III, 56a and Sp. 438, V, 290b, d, k).[162] Apparently syncretization of Atum-Re and Ruty

---

[154] Malek 2000: 84; Meyrat 2010: 87–92.

[155] Photos of serval are taken from the open Internet resources (http://www.naturephoto-cz.com/serval-photo-12476.html; http://hq-oboi.ru/wall/koshka_serval). Cf. with the colours of the animals in the tombs of *Sn-nḏm* TT 1 (***Figure 17***) and *Ỉnj-ḥr-ḫꜥw* TT 359 (***Figure 23***).

[156] Otto 1956: 65–66; Dondelinger 1987: 80; LGG III: 241.

[157] Saleh 1984: 18; Bruyère 1926: 171, Figure 113, 172.

[158] Rössler-Köhler 1980: Kol. 1080–1090; Bonnet 1952: 427–429; Kees 1977: 6–11.

[159] Bonnet 1952: 733–735.

[160] Hornung 1982.

[161] Smith 1984: Kol. 1082–1087.

[162] Altenmüller 1973: 123; Zandee 1992: 171–173.

FIGURE 34

FIGURE 34A

(in this case, as a single deity) was facilitated by the geographical proximity of the cities. BD 17 text and vignette provide convincing evidence that Re could be identified with the cat family even without 'intermediaries'. It can be assumed that the local cult of the solar Cat (as serpent's killer manifestation) could have really existed in Heliopolis.

The *miw ꜥꜣ* character is known in Egyptian texts from Middle Kingdom onwards: in addition to the BD 17 prototype – CT Sp. 335 (IV, 282a, 293f), *miw ꜥꜣ* is mentioned in CT Sp. 294 (IV, 47e) and Sp. 674 (V1, 303l). More occurrences are preserved from the New Kingdom and the Third Intermediate Period, although these data are very vague in terms of deciphering the mythological BD 17 plot.

There is a text in p*ꜣnj* pLondon BM EA 10470 vignette of BD 151, placed next to the deity figure in the bottom right register, which refers to *miw ꜥꜣ*: [...] *ink bꜣ iḳr imy-m śḥt pn n.t ꜣbḏw ink miw ꜥꜣ imy-m ś.t mꜣꜥ.t n.t wbn Šw im=f* – '[...] I am a magnificent *bꜣ*-soul, placed in this *ꜣbḏw*-fish. I am the Great Cat in the Place of Truth, when Shu appears in it'.[163]

Another description of *miw ꜥꜣ* can be found in the *Litany of Re*, where the 56th Glorification starts with *ḥknw n=k Rꜥ ḳꜣ sḫm miw ꜥꜣ nḏ.w nṯr.w* – 'Glory to Re of

[163] Faulkner 1998: pl. 33; Lüscher 1998: 101.

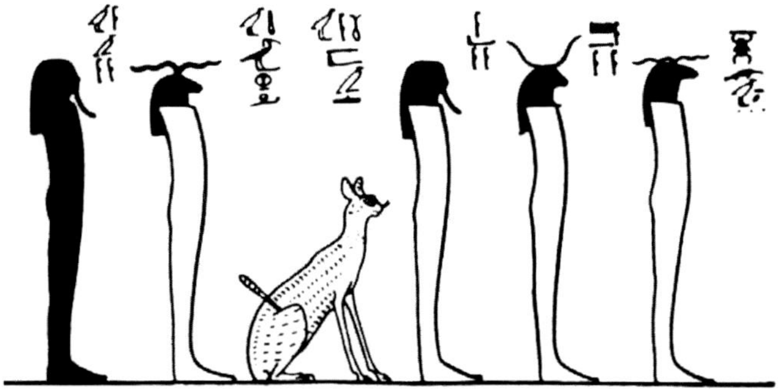

FIGURE 35

great manifestation (or 'power'), the Great Cat – the Avenger of the gods'[164] (cf. Glorifications 33 and 55).[165] Among the illustration of the so-called 'Great Litany of Re' in the tomb of Thutmose III (KV 34) there is the picture of this 'Great Cat', in its zoomorphic form, rather than anthropomorphic one, as in the cases of other deities (***Figure 35***).[166]

FIGURE 36

In the mythological p*T3-ḥm-n-Mw.t* pWarsaw Mus. Nat. No. 199 628 (21st Dynasty) are also preserved the picture of that divine Cat and the corresponding inscription – *miw ꜥ3* (line 35).[167] In the same scroll the cat is shown 'protecting' Osiris.[168] The stele Oxford Ashmolean Museum 1961. 232 (Deir el-Medina, 19th Dynasty) has a prayer to 'Great Cat' and Re, and the upper register depicts two cats, one is labeled as *miw ꜥ3*, and the second as *miw nfr* (***Figure 36***).[169]

S. Hodel-Hoenes associates the studied BD 17 vignette with the scene of the 7th Hour of *Amduat,*[170] where the anthropomorphic deity with cat ears (or the cat's head) and a knife over three decapitated figures is placed in the upper register[171]

[164] Budge 1904 I: 345; Speleers 1922: 648; Langton 1938: 54; Schott 1958: Taf. 11; Piankoff 1964: 27: pl. 6; Hornung 1977 I: 64.
[165] Budge 1904 I: 272; II: 297.
[166] Piankoff 1964: 14, Figure B, reg. 5 (67); Cf. Hornung 1999: 147, Figure 90; Malek 2000: 82, Figure 49 (coloured, but incomplete reproduction).
[167] Andrzejewski 1959: 46–47.
[168] Andrzejewski 1959: 59, Figure 3: pl. 4; Niwiński 1989: 169, Figure 55.
[169] Sweeney 2009: 556, Figure 10; for photo see: Malek 2000: 88, Figure 56.
[170] Hodel-Hoenes 2009: 282, 313, fn. 41.
[171] Karlshausen 1991: 102.

FIGURE 37

FIGURE 38

(***Figure 37***).[172] The inscription next to the deity, however, states  *mds-ḥr* – 'Evil-faced', and there is postscript near the headless figures *ḫfty.w Wśir,*[173] i.e. portrayed here is the execution of the 'Enemies of *Osiris*', but not the Enemies of *Re*, as in BD 17. This fact contradicts the connection between the vignette BD 17 and given image from *Amduat*. In this context it is necessary to recall the image of cat defeating the figure of enemy on the Middle Kingdom' 'magical knife' New York MMA 15.3.197 (***Figure 38***).[174]

2. The *išd*-tree,  – lit.: 'fruit tree'; *Perseabaum.*[175] At present time the *išd* is often identified as the *Balanites aegyptiaca* (L.; Del.), the tree of the *Zygophyllaceae* Family[176] (***Figure 39, 39a***).[177]

In Egyptian mythology the *išd*-tree, along with 'the tree of Hathor', was considered sacred in Heliopolis, and is known as a fetish-symbol of Benu bird.[178] 'The House of *išd*' (*pr-išd*), that is, in fact, the temple of *išd*, had previously existed in Heliopolis in the Old Kingdom.[179] Apparently, *išd* was revered as the Heavenly Tree. On the other hand, *išd* was also a symbol of fate, a sort of Tree of Life. Thot, Seshat and Atum wrote royal lifetime events on the *išd* leaves defining years of reign and life and, moreover, they recorded the most significant

[172] Hornung 1963 I: Taf. 7; Karlshausen 1991: 103, Figure 51; Hornung, Abt 2007: 214.
[173] Hornung 1963 I: 120, No. 492–495; Hornung, Abt 2007: 222 (537, 495).
[174] Altenmüller 1965 II: 119, Abb. 13.
[175] Bonnet 1952: 83; Kákosy 1980: Kol. 182–183; Baum 1988: 263–273; Corteggiani 1995: 141–151.
[176] Germer 1985: 298–300; Baum 1988: 268–273; Koemoth 1993: 20.
[177] Photos of the *Balanites aegyptiaca* (L.; Del.) are taken from open Internet resources (http://bg-aqaba.ju.edu.jo/pages-tree/Balanites%20aegyptiaca.aspx; http://agroforesttrees.cisat.jmu.edu/tree_detail. asp?id=20).
[178] Kees 1977: 87, 232.
[179] Urk. I:197, 10; Helck 1958: 117.

FIGURE 39

FIGURE 39A

historical events.[180] The best known scene of this type is depicted on the Karnak temple north side of the Seventh Pylon.[181] In the Theban temples of the 18th Dynasty the *išd*-scene was usually included into the composition associated with the coronation ritual (legitimization of power), and from the 19th Dynasty onwards *išd* can be also found on scenes of the receiving royal *sd*-festivals from the gods.[182] The mythem of 'splitting of the *išd*-tree' is known in CT Sp. 335 / BD 17; *Amenophis-Ritual* 25, 1; BD 125 (*iw m33.n=i pšn išd m-ḫnw R3-šṯ3w* – 'I saw the split of the *išd*-tree in *Re-Setau*') and inscription in the New Year crypt (*wʿb.t*-sanctuary) in the Hathor temple at Dendera.[183]

3. The Serpent is the most mysterious character of the vignette. Its iconography corresponds to the Hieroglyphic sign for 'snake':  / I14 (p*Ḳnn3* pLeiden T 2 (***Figure 3–3a***), p*Mw.t-m-wi3* pBerlin P. 3157 (***Figure** 7*) and p*Nsj-t3-nb.t-išrw* pLondon BM EA 10554 (***Figure 8***); p*Ini-pḥ=f-nḫt* pCologny-Geneva C (***Figure 13***) etc.). M. Mathieu,[184] based on comparative analysis of BD 17 and the '*The Book of Repelling the Evil*' describing the festival ritual of Osiris in Abydos temple (19th Dynasty, pParis pLouvre 3129F and pLondon BM EA 10252), suggested identifying the serpent from the BD 17 vignette with *Imj-*(*w*)*hn=f* (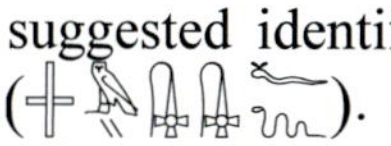). According to '*The Book of Repelling the Evil*' the serpent litigated with Re (anthropomorphic in the text) for the division of Heliopolis.[185] However, transliteration of the reptile name in the text made by S. Schott[186] and

180 Bonnet 1952: 84; Helck 1958: 117–140; Kees 1977: 87, 212, 215.
181 Quirke 2001: 108.
182 Costa 2003: 193–204.
183 Helck 1958:130–131; Rößler-Köhler 1979: 224, Anm. 1.
184 Матье 1956: 33–34 = 1996:172–173.
185 Urk. VI, 63 (17, 21), 65 (18–19).
186 Urk. VI, 62 (21–22).

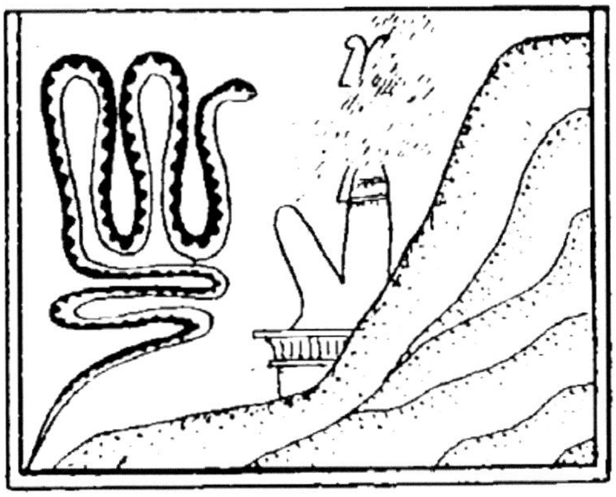

Figure 40

M. E. Mathieu as *ỉmj-(w)hn=f* is controversial and it can be read as *ỉmj-ẖt / sḏt=f*,[187] or, as suggested by J. F. Borghouts, as *ỉmy-nsrsr*[188] – 'The-one-in-his-own-flame'. Obviously, the same name as an epithet to Apophis is mentioned in the texts of the temple of Edfu: *Jmy-nsr=f*.[189] Interpretation by M. E. Mathieu was not supported by the majority of scholars (although it was accepted by M. A. Korostovtsev).[190] BD 108 also refers, apparently, to the same the serpent: – *ỉmj-(w)hn=f* (?), inhabiting *ḏw n(j) Bꜣḫw* – 'Mountain of Sunrise', shown in the vignette of p*Ḳnnꜣ* pLeiden T 2 (***Figure 40***).[191] This name is consonant with the other snake's name in the same spell: *tpy ḏw / ỉmj-(w)hm=f* – 'The-one-who-is-on-his-mountain'.[192]

However, no mention of the trial in Heliopolis and cat-Re was found in this text. Reported is another solar myth, where the key role is played by Seth: $_{(4)}$ […] *ỉw ḥfꜣw ḥr wp.t n(j).t ḏw pf n sw mḥ* 30 *m ꜣw=f mḥ* 8 *m ḥꜣ.t=f* $_{(5)}$ *m ds wbḫ(w) n bšw* (?) – $_{(4)}$ […] 'There is a Serpent on the top of that mountain; the length of him is 30 cubits, the first 8 cubits of his body are covered $_{(5)}$ with flint (?) (scales?)'[193] (after p*Nww* pLondon BM EA 10477).[194] In the afternoon the serpent is trying to stop the motion of the solar bark by drinking seven cubits of heavenly waters, but Seth strikes it with an iron harpoon (*bjꜣ spd*) from the bow of the ship of Re, making it vomit all the swallowed waters (lines 6–8).[195]

Traditional is the identification of the snake in BD 17 as *Apophis*.[196] M. Broze associates this character with serpent mythology, believing that the picture depicts the 'scene of triumph' of good forces, personified in Re, over the chaos

[187] Тарасенко 2003: 216, прим. 138.
[188] Borghouts 1973: 115, fn. 7.
[189] Edfu, I, 62, 9; Borghouts 1973: 115, fn. 7;125.
[190] Коростовцев 1976: 68.
[191] Naville 1886 I: Taf. CXIX; Quirke 2013: 238.
[192] Borghouts 1973: 114–115, fn. 7.
[193] Or 'flowstones (?)' by St. Quirke (Quirke 2013: 238).
[194] Lapp 2004: pl. 22.
[195] Borghouts 1973: 114–115 (§ 2); Quirke 2013: 238–239.
[196] Mercer 1927: 220; Kees 1977: 36; Bonnet 1952: 371; Dondelinger 1987: 80; Faulkner 2001: 48; Malek 2000: 84; Kákosy, Bács, Bartos, Fábián, Gaál 2004 I: 199.

and darkness, embodied in Apophis.[197] P. Koemoth shares his hypothesis.[198] A similar interpretation was offered by O. Goelet: 'Instead we have a more generic snake type often used to depict harmful creatures, such as Apophis, the enemy of Re and the chief representative of the forces of chaos and nonexistence', further identifying it with Apophis.[199] Precise description of the picture meaning were given by R. Faulkner[200] and E. Hornung.[201] W. Westendorf also highlights *nḥḥ* and *ḏt* eternities in confrontation of the cat-Re and the snake.[202]

Special attention should be paid to the interpretation of the theme proposed by H. Goedicke, where he expressed his disagreement that the cat should be understood as the embodiment of the sun god and 'in particular in his active aspect of overcoming the negative'.[203] The grounds for this opinion is the following: 'cats are not known to use knives, nor do they have habit to kill snakes'[204] (!). Further, the scholar focuses on the onomopoetical consonance between *mỉw* 'cat' / *mỉ(w)* 'like, similar' (see above) in the sentence *mỉw św m nn (n) ỉrỉ.n.f ḫpr rn.f pw n mỉw*, where he sees an indication that 'man is in the likeness of the divine' and, accordingly, a 'man should emulate in his actions, i.e. his model ... man should try to carry out the divine example'.[205] Thus, the main idea is to ensure that a person, as a 'likeness of divine', simulated the behavior of god, in this case, 'in the overcoming of chaos, for which snake is a symbol'.[206]

The most controversial in H. Goedicke's opinion is the point of 'similarity' between a man and a deity in the Egyptian world view.[207] In Ancient Egypt, as pointed by A. E. Demidchik 'the notions of kinship between man and god, apparently never existed'.[208] It can be explained by the fact that direct 'likeness' of god on earth has, according to Egyptian ideas, only the king, who had the 'direct' blood and genealogical kinship with the solar creator-god.[209] 'Mere mortals' were united

[197] Broze 1991: 109–115.
[198] Koemoth 1993: 19–31.
[199] Faulkner 1998: 160.
[200] 'The cat of Re cuts up the evil serpent Apophis before the sacred *ished*-tree of Heliopolis') (Faulkner 2001: 48).
[201] 'Der Sonnengott als 'Großer Kater', der bei seinem Aufgang den *Ished*-Baum spaltet und über alle seine Feinde triumhiert' (Hornung 1979: 426).
[202] Westendorf 1975: 181–208. For more information on these temporal terms see: Thausing 1934: 35–42; Bakir 1953: 110–111; 1974: 252–254; Otto 1954: 135–148; Žabkar 1965: 75–87; Hornung 1965: 334–336; Assmann 1975; Servajean 2007; Тарасенко 2009: c. 147–179; Assmann 2011: 13–86.
[203] Goedicke 1998: 43.
[204] Goedicke 1998: 43.
[205] Goedicke 1998: 43.
[206] Goedicke 1998: 43.
[207] The very idea of displaying the notion of similarity between the creator-god and his creatures in this BD 17 fragment was already expressed in 1956 by E. Otto (Otto 1956: 65–66).
[208] Демидчик 1999: 108.
[209] See: Berlev 2003: 19–35.

with the divine world through the magic that is well illustrated, in particular, by the so-called *Gliedervergottung* texts.[210]

The mythological component of the BD 17 vignette with the cat and snake was ignored by H. Goedicke, even though it is, in my opinion, the main content both of the text and the picture. Actually, the same inaccuracy appears in the initial sentence of his commentaries, where he claims that the cat in the Egyptian religion was not associated with the use of the knife or with serpent-killing – the vignette BD 17 itself, to which the author refers, with its generally stable iconography, testifies to the opposite.

In reality, the situation is quite different, even on the earliest monuments, where the cat appears in the mytho-religious and magical context, it already has both attributes. This is the graphic plot of the so-called 'magic knives' (*Zaubermeßer*) of the Middle Kingdom,[211] which were magical 'amulets against snakes'.[212] Thus, the 'knife' from the Moscow Pushkin State Museum of Fine Arts No. 6736 has an image of a seated cat with a knife in his paws (***Figure 41***).[213] Shown with a knife is a cat on the 'knife' Petrie Museum London College UC 16379; the objects London College UC 16380 and Berlin No. 142 (***Figure 42***)[214] depict the cat holding both knives and snakes in its paws, and on the fragment London College UC 35309 the animal, though without a knife, is holding a snake in his mouth[215] (***Figure 43***).[216]

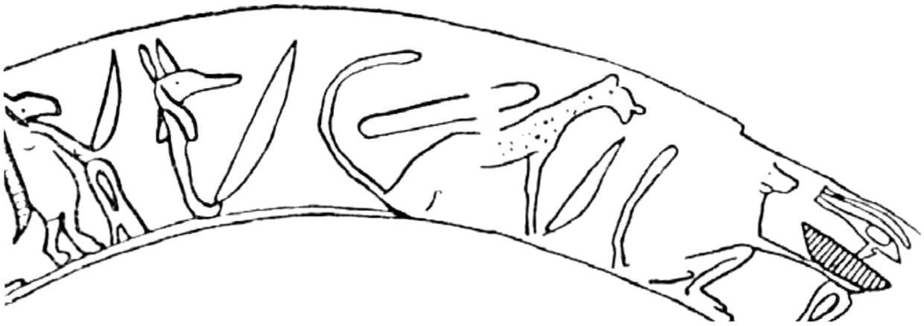

Figure 41

[210] Ranke 1924: 558–564; Massart 1959: 227–246; Altenmüller 1977: Kol. 624–627; Assmann 2002: 182–188 (§ 37); DuQuesne 2002: 237–271; Тарасенко 2009: 209–240.
[211] See: Altenmüller 1965.
[212] Ходжаш 1960: 255.
[213] Ходжаш 1960: 247. There is a false label to the monument in the edition under the picture: 'BM EA 2736', compare photo above (Ходжаш 1960: 244).
[214] Ходжаш 1960: 249.
[215] Similar images see also: Altenmüller 1965 II: 117, Abb. 9; 124, Abb. 26 (Boston MFA 12.1519); Delvaux 1991: 94, Figure 47 (Liverpool; Luzern; New York MMA 22.1.154).
[216] © Petrie Museum London College (photo by: http://www.petrie.ucl.ac.uk).

FIGURE 42

FIGURE 43

More examples of cats with knives and snakes are evidenced in New Kingdom art. Given below are some of them:

- The scene of the upper register of the 7th Hour of the *Book of the Amduat* – the image of an anthropomorphic deity shown with cat ears and a knife above three decapitated figures of Osiris's enemies (***Figure 37***);
- The illustration of the 12th Hour of the *Book of Gates* (lower register) – the god with the cat's head named *Mjwtj* is shown with a snake in his right hand and *wꜣs*-scepter in his left (***Figure 44***);[217]
- The picture illustrating BD 145 has the image of a cat-headed gate guardian called *Mi͗w* with knives in his hands in the Sethnakht tomb (KV 14, corridor 'D', 20th Dynasty)[218] and many others.

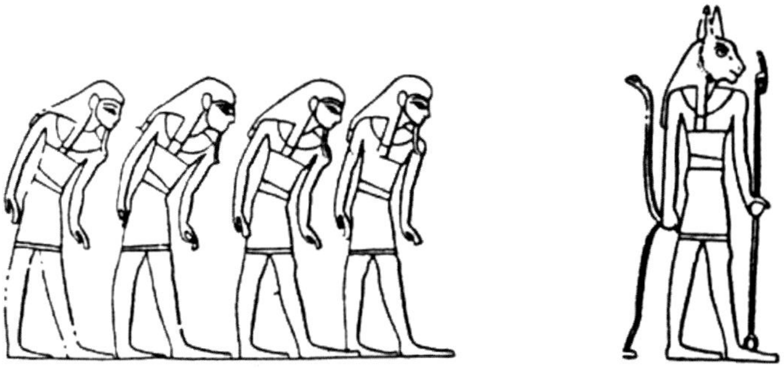

FIGURE 44

In the Late Period the cat in the snake-killing image is frequently represented on the magical stelae – the so-called 'Sippy of Horus', specially designed to protect against snake and scorpion bites. One should consider the spell in this particular context directed to the cat (called 'daughter of Re') on the *Metternichstele* (New York, MMA Fletcher Fund 1950 (50.85)) and aimed against the snake's poison

[217] Hornung 1979–1980 II: 285, 286 (Szene 100), Taf. 12 (Zwölfte Stunde); Karlshausen 1991: 103, Figure 52.
[218] See *Theban Mapping Project* Photo archive (http://www.thebanmappingproject.com).

(Sp. III).[219] Similar in meaning is the utterance represented on the Cairo statue of *Ḏd-Ḥr(w)*,[220] where the text is given in the form of *Gliedervergottung* list on behalf of the same divine cat (*miw.t*): 'glorious (*ȝḫ*) daughter of Re', who was the goddess Bastet, according to J. F. Borghouts.[221] The image depicting two cats with knives on the iconography close to BD 17 scene, can be found in a series of BD 146 vignettes of the Ptolemaic Period, such as p*Ꞽw=f-ꜥnḫ* pTurin 1791 (***Figure 45***)[222] or the mummy shrouds Vleeshuis Fr. 5 No. 4946 2/2 (Antwerp) (***Figure 46***).[223]

FIGURE 45

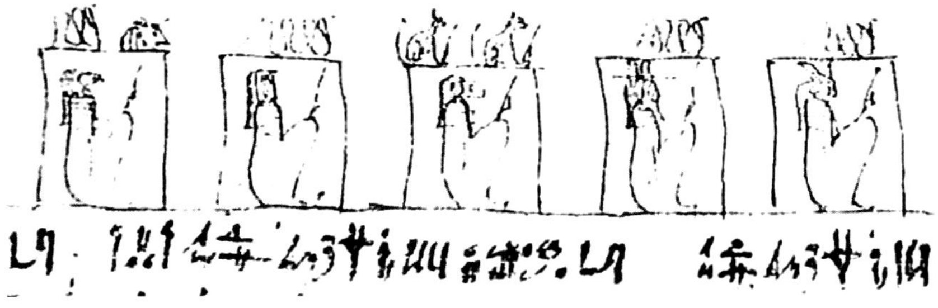

FIGURE 46

Thus, H. Goedicke's arguments can not change the generally accepted interpretation of the serpent image on the BD 17 vignette as an Apophis. But what is the proof for such a confident identification of the snake with Apophis? Indeed, there are very scarce sources where the serpent form in the vignette is explicitly named as *ȝꜥpp* – Apophis.

[219] Sander-Hansen 1956: 20–28; comp.: Sp. IV and Sp. XII.
[220] Jelinkova-Reymond 1956; Translation: Borghouts 1978: 56–58 (Text 87).
[221] Borghouts 1978: 108, fn. 211.
[222] Lepsius 1842: Taf. LXVI.
[223] Caluwé 1993: 205; pl. XIX.

1) In the p*Tꜣw-wḏꜣ.t-Rꜥ* pCairo S.R. VII. 11496 the single BD 17 vignette has the prescription: *śmꜣ ꜣꜥpp i͗n mi͗w ꜥnḫ prt m Dwꜣ.t i͗ri͗ rwd i͗mj ẖrt-nṯr* – 'Killing of Apophis by the living cat (who) came out of the Netherworld (*Duat*) (and who) is prosperous in the Necropolis'[224] (***Figure 12***).

2) In the tomb of *Nḫ.t-tw-I͗mn* TT 335 there is a postscript found on the picture, identical to the vignette of BD 17 (***Figure 22***), above the image of a snake: *ꜥꜣpp ḫftj n Rꜥ* – 'Apophis, the enemy of Re'.[225] Below the 'extermination' of Apophis by the 'Great Cat', the 'image' of Re' is mentioned.[226] However, this spell, as indicated by M. Saleh, is closer to the title and the meaning of BD 7, aimed directly against Apophis.[227]

3) In the tomb of *I͗nj-ḥr-ḫꜥw*, TT 359, the picture of the cat, snake and the sacred tree (***Figure 23***) is followed by the accompanying text which aims to defeat Apophis, but it does not belong to the BD corpus.[228]

4) In the tomb of *I͗ni͗-ḥr.t-ms* at El-Mashayikh there is a damaged inscription over the BD 17 scene (***Figure 24***) which reports on 'cutting' (*šꜥd*) of Apophis: [*mi͗w*?] *pw i͗ri͗.t šꜥd ꜥꜣpp* – '[The cat?] who cuts Apophis'.[229]

Thus, the evidence base for confident identification of the serpent on the BD 17 vignette as Apophis is rather insignificant and in all cases it is based on indirect sources with specific representations. H. Milde cautiously suggests an acceptable solution to the problem: 'Not a word about any serpent, however. But there are enemies mentioned to be destroyed. The serpent cannot be other than the personification of those enemies'.[230] The text of spell mentions only 'enemies', appearing in connection with this mytheme: *mś.w Bdšt* – 'Children of Weakness'. There are here sufficient reasons to scrutinize these characters.

---

224 Piankoff 1957 I: 137 (vignette 6); Malek 2000: 84.
225 Bruyère 1926: 171, Figure 113; Saleh 1984: 18; Milde 1991: 23, fn. 23; Malek 2000: 84.
226 Saleh 1984: 18–19.
227 Saleh 1984: 19, Anm. 1.
228 Saleh 1984: 19; Hodel-Hoenes 2000: 282; Cherpion, Corteggiani 2010 I: 226–227.
229 Ockinga, al-Masri 1988: 8 (Scene 5, Text 104).
230 Milde 1991: 38.

Chapter 3

Mś.w Bdšt – the sources and the plot

One of the numerous deities in the ancient Egyptian pantheon, whose nature and function in religion and mythology is still vague and obscure, are *mś.w Bdšt* – ‘Children of Weakness’.

The starting point of any research on Egyptian mythology representations is the choice of the basic sources that provide the most informative data as to its role and functions. In the case of *mś.w Bdšt* the pertinent source is the BD 17 text (= CT Sp. 335) which has the most extensive and lengthy exposition of the myth with characters entailing one of the most interesting and controversial interpretation of the mythological content of the whole utterance.

Mś.w Bdšt are twice mentioned in semantic relation to BD 17: in lines 3–5 and 54–58 (*Abschnitt* 1 and 22 after H. Grapow),[231] i.e. in the first and last *Abschnitt* of the first part of spell, BD 17^{A} allegedly artificially connected with the other, originally independent spell – BD 17^{B} (CT Sp. 335^{A-B}, IV, 188–326).[232]

Thus the text of BD 17 contains *two* versions of the myth with *mś.w Bdšt.*

Version I (Appendix 2, Text No. 2): $_{(3)}$ […] (*ink*)**(A)** *Rʿ m ḫʿ.w[=f]***(B)** *m* $_{(4)}$ *š3ʿ=f ḥk3.t iri.t.n=f ptr r=f sw Rʿ pw m š3ʿ=f***(C)** *ḥk3.t iri.tn=f m š3ʿ Rʿ pw ḫʿj.t m nswt iti ir.tn=f***(D)** *m wnn***(E)** $_{(5)}$ *ḫpr.t sts.w Šw iw(=f) ḥr=f k33 imj Ḫmnw ist rdi n=f mś.w Bdšt im.jw Ḫmnw*

‘$_{(3)}$ [...] (I am) Re at his (first) rising, $_{(4)}$ (when) he began to reign over his creation. What is that? It is Re, (when) he began to reign over what was created by him. It is Re, who ascended to the kingship over what was created by him before $_{(5)}$ the Supports of Shu appeared, when he was on a Hill, which is in Hermopolis, (and) when the Children of *Bdšt***(F)** were given to him in Hermopolis’ (after p*Nb-snj* pLondon BM EA 9900).[233]

---

[231] Urk. V: 6–7, 50–54.

[232] A contrary hypothesis was orally explained to me by U. Rößler-Köhler (Bonn), according to which the BD 17 is a *single utterance*, dating back to CT Sp. 335, and initially could have had even greater volume, as it could include CT Sp. 337 / BD 18 which is very close in style. The direct continuation of CT Sp. 335 was CT Sp. 336, containing the description of the ‘Gates of the *Duat*’ (*sbḫ.t Dw3.t*) and their guardians, with reminiscences to CT Sp. 335, fixed, however, only on the coffin B1L, and not included in the BD corpus (Borghouts 1988: 12–22). The semantic unity of CT Sp. 335–337 / BD 17–18 is also proved by the text on the coffin of queen *Mntw-ḥtp* BM EA 10553 (Second Intermediate Period) (Geisen 2004), with the earliest known version of BD 17, where the text of BD 18 continues it directly, without any introductory rubric, indicates that this was another independent spell (Ibid: 43, 79). See also: Lapp 2009: IXff; Quirke 2013: 69, 73–74.

[233] Urk. V: Abs. 1, 6–7 (3–5); Naville 1886 I: Taf. XXIII, 3–5; Lapp 2006: 12–19.

Comments

[(A)] In p*Nb-snj* independent pronoun *ỉnk* is omitted by error.[234]

[(B)] In *pNb-snj* hieroglyph for 'cobra' is written by mistake instead of the 'horned viper' (𓆑 / I 9 / *f*), i.e., suffix pronoun = *f*, masc., 3rd person.

[(C)] U. Rößler-Köhler suggests reading *ḫꜥ=f* rather than *šꜣꜥ=f*.[235]

[(D)] Part of the manuscripts makes it clear that accession to the kingship took place in Heracleopolis (for example:  – *ḫꜥj(.t) m Nn-nśwt m nsw* – p*ꜣnj* pLondon BM EA 10470).[236]

[(E)] Some scrolls have *Ỉwnw* – Heliopolis, written by mistake instead of *wnn*.[237]

[(F)] Part of the documents of the New Kingdom after *Bdšt* can have either *ḥr ḳꜣꜣ n ỉm.jw Ḫmnw* – 'on the Hill which is in Hermopolis',[238] or *m nṯr.w ỉm.jw Ḫmnw* – 'as gods, who are in Hermopolis'.[239]

For transliteration, translation and comments of ***Version II*** *see previous Chapter.*

For the Ancient Egyptian spiritual culture J. Assmann distinguishes three 'levels', 'dimensions' or 'semantic horizons' of the 'contact with the sacred' (i.e. 'religious activities and religious experience'): *the cultic, the cosmic* and *the mythic.*[240] According to J. Janák, this separation is applicable to the analysis of religious texts semantics, where one can easily single out several levels, when 'a single event can be described as a cosmic phenomenon, a ritual act or mythic event'.[241] For my research on *mś.w Bdšt* in BD 17 and related documents the main interest focuses on the *mythological level*, since it was obviously the primary one, giving grounds both for the ritual, and for cosmological contextual use of *mś.w Bdšt* image in the various texts.

Thus the key element for the mythem, represented in the abovementioned fragment of BD 17 is the subject of the cosmic battle, the 'night of the Combat' (*grḥ n ꜥḥꜣ-ꜥ*), which occurred in Hermopolis, and / or Heliopolis between Re,

---

[234] Lapp 2006: 12–13.
[235] Rößler-Köhler 1979: 165, Anm.7*.
[236] Lapp 2006: 15 (pLe1, pL5, pL13, pDu).
[237] Lapp 2006: 17 (pL4, pLe2, pLe13).
[238] See also in p*ꜣs.t-m-ꜣḫ-bit* pLondon BM EA 9904: 21st Dynasty (Shorter 1938: 111).
[239] Lapp 2006: 18–19.
[240] Ассман 1999: 25–26.
[241] Janák 2003: 5. Along with three Assmann's 'dimensions' J. Janák also adds 'anthropological' one and divides it into subgroups: 'pre-humous' and 'post-humous' (Janák 2003: 5).

depicted in the snake-fighting image of the 'Great Cat' (*miw ꜥ3*), with 'enemies' (*ḫftj.w*) and 'children' (*mś.w*) of the creature named *Bdšt*.

Firstly, it is pertinent to find *subject parallels* between this mythem and *mś.w Bdšt* image that would give matter to clarify the meaning of the whole myth. Apart from BD 17, the list of *mś.w Bdšt* references is sufficient. 'Lexikon der ägyptischen Götter und Götterbezeichnungen' (LGG) presents the most comprehensive form of it. It outlines ***eight functions*** of *mś.w Bdšt:*[242]

A) *As a participant of ritual scenes* (in late temple inscriptions):

a. *Philae,* 81, 11;[243]
b. *Edfou* IV, 306, 3;
c. *Urk.* VIII, 5d (Monthtor) + *Edfu* VI, 149, 2 = *MamEdfu,* 173, 3–4, 5–6 ('*Book of Protection of the House*').[244]

B) *In relation to the funeral rites*:
Text on the coffin of *ꜥnḫ=ś-nfr-ib-Rꜥ* London BM EA 32, IXa, 383 (26th Dynasty).[245]

C) *As those who must being punished*:

a. The 11th Hour of the *Book of Gates*: scene No. 69, 356, 359–360;[246]
b. BD 17;[247]
c. *Edfou* II, 11;
d. BD 140:
   – p*Iꜥḥ-t3i-ś-nḫt* pCologne P. Colon Aeg. 10207 (26th Dynasty);[248]
   – p*Iw=f-ꜥnḫ* pTurin 1791: 67, 10–11;[249]
   – p*P3-šrj-n-t3iḥt* (*ḏd Psmṯk*) pVatican 48832;[250]
   – p*Psmṯk* pLeiden T 17;[251]
   – p*Ḥr* pCologny CV (*mś.w Btš.w* form);[252]
e. Text on the coffin of *ꜥnḫ=ś-nfr-ib-Rꜥ* London BM EA 32, IXj, 384;[253]
f. Tanut[h]amun's 'Dream Stela' (25th Dynasty, 663–656/5 B. C.);[254]

[242] LGG III: 422–423.
[243] Borghouts 1973: 136.
[244] Jankuhn 1972: 79. Not included in the LGG.
[245] Sander-Hansen 1937: 120–121.
[246] Hornung 1979–1980 I: 246–247, 248–249 (24–29).
[247] Urk. V: Abs. 1, 7, 12.
[248] Verhoeven 1993 I: 264; II: 98* (67, 3).
[249] Lepsius 1842: Taf. LVII; cf. Budge 1898: 316 (8).
[250] Gasse 2001: 243 (86, 11). Index of names at the end of the edition erroneously states lines 86, 4 (Ibid: 355). Not included in the LGG.
[251] Quirke 1999: pl. 21. Not included in the LGG.
[252] Munro 2009: Photo-Taf. 16; Taf. 18 (Col. 388), 21. Not included in the LGG.
[253] Sander-Hansen 1937: 141–142.
[254] Urk. III: 67, 17; Grimal 1981: 11, col. 17.

g. The 'Great Hymn to Re-Horakhty', pBerlin P. 3050: III, 8 – IV, 1 (21st Dynasty);[255]
h. pBremner-Rhind (pLondon BM EA 10188), 24, 22;[256]
i. BD 18:[257]
   – p*Jwiꜣ* pCairo CG 51189;[258]
   – p*Nb.sni* pLondon BM EA 9900;[259]
   – p*Ỉw=f-ꜥnḫ* pTurin 1791: 12, 16,[260]
   – p*Pꜣ-šrj-n-tꜣiḥt* pVatican 48832[261] etc.

D) *As a type of* snake:
'Ophiological treatise', pBrooklyn 47.218.48 / .85, §20, §48a, §80b (30th Dynasty – beginning of the Ptolemaic Period).[262]

E) *In relation to a geographical* toponym:
Tôd I, 153, 5; *Tôd* II, 188 A, 1 (here is reported that the temple was built on the (Primeval) Hill, where Re fought against *mś.w Bdšt*).[263]

F) *In calendar inscriptions*:
Data from the so-called 'Cairo Calendar' of the New Kingdom[264] (for details see below) and pBrooklyn 47.218.84, IV, 4 – V, 4 (30th Dynasty – beginning of the Ptolemaic Period).[265]

G) *As a part of the ship or fishing equipment*:
a. CT Sp. 409, V, 233g;
b. CT Sp. 477, VI, 35o (for details see below).

H) *Other functions*:
a. CT Sp. 335, IV, 290a–291a = BD 17;[266]
b. p*Bremner-Rhind* (pLondon BM EA 10188), 25, 18;[267]

---

[255] Sauneron 1953: 85–86.
[256] Faulkner 1933: 51.
[257] Urk. V: 126, 10; Naville 1886 II: 80 (Aa, see also: Pt, Ta, Bc annd Ia a); Lapp 2009: 80–81 (BD 18g – totally in 18 documents of the New Kingdom).
[258] Munro 1994 II: Taf. 48 (94–95).
[259] Budge 1898: 74 (13); Lapp 2004: pl. 46.
[260] Lepsius 1842: Taf. XII.
[261] Gasse 2001: 173 (17, 3) (? – A. Gasse version of probable restoration of incomplete writing is  (Gasse 2001: 173 (17, 3), 52)). Not included in the LGG.
[262] Sauneron 1989: 14, 74, 108–109.
[263] LGG III: 423.
[264] Leitz 1994.
[265] Meeks 2006: 10–12. Not included in the LGG.
[266] Urk. V: Abs. 22, 54–58.
[267] Faulkner 1933: 54.

c. the text of the High priest of Amun Osorkon, the son of Takelot II, on the 'Bubastite (southern) Portal' of the Karnak temple (mention of the revolt (*wd ḥꜣꜥyt*) of *mś.w Bdšt*, 22nd Dynasty);[268]
d. *Deir Chelouit* II, 84, 1 (it is reported that Isis protects Osiris from *mś.w Bdšt*).[269]

The collection of late records of *mś.w Bdšt*,[270] unregistered in the LGG, should be enriched by the Hymn to Amun in pBerlin P. 3055: XIX, 2 (Third Intermediate Period),[271] *Edfu* IV, 305, 306,[272] and *Esna* 576 – ritual scene on the exterior of the southern facade of the Columned Hall (the western scene, the second register), depicting the king before Khnum (Roman Period):[273] *smꜣ* [*ṯs*]*ty nti ꜥꜣpp ḥnꜥ mś.w bdš.w*.[274]

Chronologically, the **first mentions** of *mś.w Bdšt* date back to Middle Kingdom:[275] *Coffin Texts* spells **60** (I, 253f), **335** (IV, 290a-291a, 290c (T1S$^{\underline{b}}$) (not in LGG), 412h (Sq7Sq) (not in LGG)), **409** (V, 233g) and **477** (VI, 35o). Surprisingly, from the start, there are contradictions between utterance and image. Thus, CT Sp. 60 states that *mś.w Bdšt* are the 'Supports of the sky' (*ꜥꜣw*) and the 'protection of Osiris'; in CT Sp. 409 *mś.w Bdšt* are the equipment of mast on the Osiris's *nšm.t*-bark;[276] and in the CT Sp. 477 they are represented as floats (*ḏbꜣ.w*) of Sobek's fishing net. According to R. Faulkner, such strange assertions on the enemies of Re appeared in these texts by mistake.[277] However, this case is not unique. The same is true for the personification of Evil such as *Ꜣꜣw*-deity, acquiring quite a positive function in a number of spells.[278]

The mention of *mś.w Bdšt* also occurs in **pRamesseum XV verso** I, 5 preserved in an extremely fragmentary condition, which dates back to the late Middle Kingdom (***Figure 47***).[279] Part of the scroll germane to our subject, unfortunately, is badly damaged. We can only assume that it mentions some connection (?) with human fingers and *mś.w Bdšt* – '[...] *ḏbꜥ.w=j m m.św n* (?) *Bdšt* [...], translated by A. Gardiner: '... Then will he die; he does not die for them a second time .... My fingers with (?) the Children of Impotence ... To me my arm and my fingers'.[280]

---

268 The Bubastite Portal 1954: pl. 21, 7; LGG III: 423.
269 LGG III: 423.
270 See also: Wb., Belegstellen I: 79.
271 Moret 1902: 135.
272 Borghouts 1973: 129.
273 PM VI: 117 (38–39).
274 Derchain, Recklinghausen 2004: 36, fn. 107.
275 LGG III: 422–423; Hannig 2006 I: 829–830, 1132.
276 Lavier 2007: 1085.
277 Faulkner 1994 I: 55, fn. 13; II: 120, fn. 10.
278 Frandsen 2000: 9–34. It should be noted that the resume of P. J. Frandsen was critically reviewed by M. Kemboly, who does not sees signs of divinity in *Ꜣꜣw*, hardly having negative function (Kemboly 2005: 89–103).
279 Gardiner 1955: pl. XLVII.
280 Gardiner 1955: 15.

FIGURE 47

The image of *mś.w Bdšt* is further found in the sources up to the end of the Greco-Roman Period. Significantly, indications on the very essence of *Bdšt* as a separate image are rare.[281]

The **first mention of** *Bdšt* dates back to Old Kingdom when it occurs only once. It is Spell 343 of *Pyramid Texts* (**Pyr. § 558a-b**) represented in a short sacrificial formula, unfortunately, absolutely non-comital as to the essence of the character (**Appendix 2. Text No.3**).

ḏd mdw ii Bdšt i3m[(A)] *ʿẖ ʿẖʿ imjw-ś.t-ʿ.w rdj ẖt t ḥnk.t k3.w n* NN

'Pronouncing the words: *Bdšt* comes, the (sacrificial) *ʿẖ*-brazier[(B)] is lighted; ritual assistants stand up[(C)], a (meal) offering is done for NN (king)[(D)]'.

Comments

[(A)] See for *i3m*: Wb. I: 31.13.

[(B)] 'Berlin Wörterbuch' gives the following explanation of *ʿẖ*: 'Feuerbecken, als Gerät zum Brandopfer'.[282]

[(C)] Here I use the notion of *Imjw-ś.t-ʿ* given by D. Meeks as 'les ritualistes de service'[283] (his full translation of the spell is given below). Whereas, R. Faulkner in his 'Dictionary' gives *Imjw-ś.t-ʿ* the meaning of 'helpers',[284] but in his own

281 LGG II: 844.
282 Wb. I: 223.6.
283 Meeks 2006: 201; fn. 254. He proceeds: Quaegebeur 1994: 163–166.
284 Faulkner 1999: 19.

translation of the *Pyramid Texts* he calls them 'servants'.[285] S. Mercer gives explanation: 'The expression *'imi.w ś.t-ʿwi*, is the same which occurs as a title of helpers in 398b... It is the priests, with ready hands, who are there to give an offering to N, 'Those with (ready) hands' are priests'.[286] According to J. P. Allen *Ỉmjw-ś.t-ʿ* means 'assistants'.[287] 'Berlin Wörterbuch' gives two meanings: 'ein Titel' and 'Name eines Schmucksütcks'.[288]

(D) K. Sethe gives the following translation: '(558a) Es kommt die Ohnmächtige, es brennt das Feuerbechen. (558b) Die zu Händen seinded stehen da, damit das Mahldem NN. Gegeben werde'.[289] S. Mercer translates '(558a) To say: *Bdš.t* comes; the fire-pan burns. (558b) Those with (ready) hands stand to give an offering to N'.[290] R. Faulkner translates in the following way: 'Here comes the feeble one; the brazier burns, the servers stand up, and a meal is given to me'.[291] J. P. Allen translates: 'Come, weak goddess! Burn, brazier! Stand up, assistants! Let a meal be given to me'.[292] Cl. Carrier proposes: '– *Formule à reciter* – Viens, Bédéchet (et) offre un braséro (puisque) les aides sont là (et) qu'un repas est preparé pour N'.[293] D. Meeks provides a different and more accurate understanding of Pyr. §558b: '(558A) L'Impuissance (*Bdš.t*) vient, le brasero est allumé, (558b) les ritualistes de service se tiennent debout: offrande alimentaire est faite au roi'.[294]

This utterance can be found in three pyramids. In the earliest version, in Teti's pyramid (T) the word *Bdšt* is not determined at all, in Merenra I's pyramid (M) and Pepi II' pyramid (N) there is a symbol G7 ('falcon on the standard'): ; in the pyramid of Merena I a sharp object (thorn?) is thrust into the bird's head: 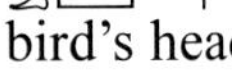 (Pyr. § 558a). As noted by K. Sethe in his comments on this spell, here *Bdšt* is most likely represented as a goddess.[295] The following explanation is given: '*Bdšt* – 'Die Ohnmächtige', eine Benennung wie sie für fendliche Wesen üblich ist nach der Muster 'der Wunsch ist der Vater des Gedankens, wie die Determinierung bei M. zeigt, die die Verletzung der Gottheit nach der Art des 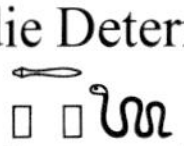 u.ä. Wesensdarsellt'.[296] The scholar suggests that the fire in the *ʿḫ*-brazier was intended precisely for *Bdšt*, who supposedly had to be sacrificed.[297] This interpretation is disputable: I fully agree with D. Meeks, who

285 Faulkner 1969 I: 110.
286 Mercer 1952 II: 271.
287 Allen 2005: 75 (Teti 156).
288 Wb. I: 75.6; but see also: Hannig 1995: 67.
289 Pyr. Komm. III: 51–52.
290 Mercer 1952 I: 117.
291 Faulkner 1969 I: 110.
292 Allen 2015: 78 (Teti 343).
293 Carrier 2010b: 221 (Teti); 2010c: 1331 (Pepi II); 2010d: 1917 (Merenre).
294 Meeks 2006: 201.
295 Pyr. Komm. III: 51–52. The same idea with reference to BD 17 was also given by S. A. B. Mercer: 'The word *bdš.t* occurs in BD 17 as mother of the serpent-enemy of the sun-god…' (Mercer 1952 II: 270).
296 Pyr. Komm. III: 52.
297 Pyr. Komm. III: 52. As for the S. A. B. Mercer, *Bdšt* is 'an unfriendly being – a being who is bound to be

noted that, firstly, the verb 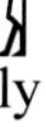 *ii* – 'come', 'get closer' and derivatives,[298] implies that she 'comes' completely independently, and not brought by using force, which is true if it had been the case of sacrifice.[299] And, secondly, the hypothesis of K. Sethe based on the abovementioned determinative , found in Merenra's pyramid, which, according to D. Meeks: '(indique) à la fois sa nature divine et son caractère maléfique'.[300] Presumably, K. Sethe proceeds from the later 'negative' understanding of *Bdšt* and *mś.w Bdšt* image in the mythology, but to claim its established form in Old Kingdom times is questionable. R. Faulkner sees here no god or goddess, and understands *bdšt* in this spell as an epithet of the deceased king: 'the king, limp in death and needing sustenance',[301] but similar royal epithet does not appear elsewhere in the *Pyramid Texts*, therefore this interpretation is doubtful. The conclusion of D. Meeks that 'le rôle de ce personnage dans le rite d'offrande demeure donc énigmatique'[302] is safer.

D. Meeks, on the assumption of his hypothesis (which I will consider below), based on data of pBrooklyn 47.218.84 (30th Dynasty – early Ptolemaic Period), that *mś.w Bdšt* is the incarnation of the four fingers (if taken wider – the whole hand) of the creator-god, offers the explanation that *Bdšt* is the image of the hand operating the sacrifice: 'Il y est apparemment question d'un sacrifice qui va permettre l'offrande alimentaire. *Bdš.t* pourrait ne pas être la victime, mais l'incarnation de la main qui sacrifie et qui se retrouve sans force, son geste de mauvais augure une fois accompli. Il s'agit là d'une explication que l'on avancera, bien sûr, avec d'extrêmes précautions'.[303]

Further the name of *Bdšt* as an independent deity (the enemy to Re and the king), in a formula akin to Pyr. § 558a occurs (again, only once) in the text of the papyrus pBrooklyn 47.218.50 of the Saite Period: 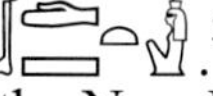.[304] This relatively small text (20 columns) clearly represents a copy of the New Kingdom original that, seemingly, originated in Heliopolis.[305] In the liturgical form the text describes the ceremony of enthronement of pharaoh, which took place during *epagomenai* (five extra days of the New Year) and the next nine days.

rendered helpless, faint, as the determinative of the word in M. shows' and 'the fire-pan (*ʿḫ*) is ready, which symbolizes the destruction of the serpent; for which reason the text may be considered a charm against those who would make offerings to the deceased king' (Mercer 1952 II: 270–271).

[298] Wb. I: 37.1; Hannig 1995: 27–28; Faulkner 1999: 10.

[299] Meeks 2006: 201 ('le verbe *iy* 'venir' implique une venue sans contrainte; la déesse n'est ni amenée, ni traînée, et cela s'accorde mal avec la proposition de Sethe').

[300] Meeks 2006: 201–202.

[301] Faulkner 1969 I: 110, fn. 1.

[302] Meeks 2006: 201. As for S. Mercer it is '*bdš.t* with a tooth or nail in head' (Mercer 1952 II: 270).

[303] Meeks 2006: 201–202.

[304] LGG II: 844; Goyon 1972: pl. V–VI (III: 11, 18).

[305] Assumption has been made on the basis of special role of Re in the ritual.

Another indication of probable close association between *Bdšt* and a group of deities (?) can be found in the Middle Kingdom:  *Bdš(y).w* (masc., pl.).[306] According to the editors of LGG, *Bdšt* is 'Impotent' ('die Ohnmächtig'; deity) and *Bdš(y.)w* is 'Weakned' ('die Schwachen'; group of the Netherworld inhabitants) – they are various characters of the pantheon; the last is the 'Gruppe von Leuten, die der Verstorbene im Totenreiche zusammehält (*s3ḳ*)'.[307]

This insignificant list should be supplemented with the mention of a creature *Bdš* in p*Bremner-Rhind* (pLondon BM EA 10188), 25, 19: ,[308] which was not taken into account in LGG, and whose name was translated by R. Faulkner as 'Rebellious',[309] and which is written as masculine and determined by the sign of 'serpent'; this feature shall be considered below.

Despite a relatively large number of *mś.w Bdšt* mentions in the Late Period, there are no close parallels or semantic additions to the BD 17 text plots. In general we can only assert that the brief reminiscences in temple ritual texts, where frequently *mś.w Bdšt* are represented, they are a collective image of the god's or the king's enemies, who are defeated, executed, punished, beheaded, etc. In a number of cases *mś.w Bdšt* appears with Apophis.[310]

As to the relationship between myth and ritual in archaic concept, it is stressed that myth itself is the basis of ritual action, as a rule, reproducing certain mythological event that took place in the mythical past. According to T. Apinyan, ritual is the 'reproduction, dramatization of the plot of the myth',[311] in ritual 'people deliberately repeat action, performed by the gods, heroes or ancestors to restore, to nourish cosmic existence with their targeted energy, the part of which is the world and human life'.[312] This mainly explains the inclusion of certain myths plots into ritual practice.

But in the case of *mś.w Bdšt* there was another important factor, which contributed to introduce this image as a personification of the kings' enemies, especially in Late Period. This is the ideology of the royal power – according to O. Berlev,[313] the monarch was perceived as a 'Young Sun', while Re is an 'Elder Sun'. They represent two forms of a sole nature and flesh, connected into a single unit after the death of pharaoh, and his ascension to Heaven (*Sinuhe* B 3. 5–8; Urk. IV, 54).

306 LGG II: 844. Cf. Leitz 1994: 94 (S. VI: 3).
307 LGG II: 844.
308 Faulkner 1933: 54.
309 Faulkner 1938: 171.
310 For more information see: Esna V: 323–330; Yoyotte 1981: 88ff; Wilson 1997: 339–340; cf. Meurer 2002: 222.
311 Апинян 2005: 196.
312 Апинян 2005: 83. This definition is very close to M. Eliade's understanding of the ritual. Cf. Routledge 2001: 13–27.
313 Berlev 2003: 19–35.

Variety of notions about the solar god and the king was very close: the enemies of the king were perceived as the enemies of the Sun-Re, and *vice versa*, i.e. shifting the epithets of mythical enemies of the sun god to the enemies of the monarch was quite understandable, given that enemies of the king, and enemies of Re, in fact, are opposed phenomenon unified for human and divine spheres – the socio-cosmic principle of World order – *mꜣꜥ.t*.[314]

Certain proximity to the messages of BD 17 is demonstrated by data of the so-called '**Cairo Calendar**' of the New Kingdom (pCairo J.E. 86637: pSallier IV and pLondon BM EA 10474),[315] where various forms of *mś.w Bdšt* destruction is reported in six cases:

- Month 2, *ꜣḫ.t*-season, day 7;[316]
- Month 2, *ꜣḫ.t*-season, day 24;[317]
- Month 2, *ꜣḫ.t*-season, day 25;[318]
- Month 4, *prt*-season, day 22;[319]
- Month 1, *šmw*-season, day 14;[320]
- Month 3, *šmw*-season, day 24.[321]

Extremely curious is the reference to the localization of the *mś.w Bdšt* destruction place (along with *ḫnṯyw*-demon) in the northern district of Sais at Delta ( *Sꜣw(t) mḥw*) in month 2, *ꜣḫ.t*-season, day 24 (according to pSallier IV):[322]

ꜣbd 2 ꜣḫt sw 24 ꜥḥꜥ ꜥḥꜥ ꜥḥꜥ
im n=k pri m ṯꜣw nbt r ḥtpw Rꜥ
hrw pwy pri n[(A)] *ḫnṯyw m [Sꜣw(t)]*[(B)] *mḥw r ḥsśt*
[mś.w][(C)] *[Bdšy.t]*[(D)] *m wnw*[(E)] *m rdw m wꜣḏ-wr in*[(F)] *mꜣi(w)*
nb ṯḥn[(G)]*=śn r=f ꜥḥꜥ=f ḫpw ḥr-ꜥwj fj*[(H)]
'Month 2, *ꜣḫ.t*-season, day 24. Very unfavourable day.
Do not leave the house in any wind until the sunset[(I)].
This is the day when the *ḫnṯyw*-demons go out in the Northen Sais
in search of the Children of *Bdšt* when they are in the Ocean[(J)].
Any lion they meet (/ find) will immediately retreat[(K)]'.

---

[314] See: Smith 1994: 67–88; Assmann 2001.
[315] Bakir 1966: 146.
[316] Bakir 1966: 19; pl. IXa; Leitz 1994: 72–73; Brier 1981: 230.
[317] Bakir 1966: 21; pl. XIa; Leitz 1994: 94–96; Brier 1981: 231.
[318] Bakir 1966: 21–22; pl. XIa–XIIa; 146, 102–103; Brier 1981: 230.
[319] Bakir 1966: 39; pl. XXIXa; 146, 321–322; Brier 1981: 243.
[320] Leitz 1994: 341–342.
[321] Leitz 1994: 392; Brier 1981: 249.
[322] Bakir 1966: 21; pl. XIa; Leitz 1994: 94.

Comments

(A) The sign  is written instead of *n* as in pCairo J.E. 86637: *pri͗ n* is added to it.

(B) Restored after pCairo J.E. 86637: p*Sallier* IV has *ḏ*(*r*)*t* written by mistake.

(C) Restored after pCairo J.E. 86637: omitted in p*Sallier* IV.

(D) Spelling after pCairo J.E. 86637: *bškyw=f* is by mistake given in p*Sallier* IV. In antithesis of *ḥnṯyw* and *mś.w Bdšt* Chr. Leitz sees opposition of Eastern and Western winds, which can be confirmed by zoomorphic images of winds of the four cardinal points on the relief in the temple of Sobek at Kom Ombo, where the Western wind is personified by the four-headed serpent, close to the image of *mś.w Bdšt* in the 11th Hour of the *Book of Gates* (***Figure 44, 45,*** for more details see below in Chapter 5).[323]

(E) pCairo J.E. 86637 has *wn=f*.

(F) pCairo J.E. 86637 has *i͗r*.

(G) pCairo J.E. 86637 has *gmḥ=ś*, translated by Chr. Leitz as 'den sie (= *Bdšt*?) erblickt'.[324]

(H) Omitted in pCairo J.E. 86637.

(I) Literally: '(before) conciliation (*ḥtpw*) of Re'.

(J) Literally: 'Great Green' (*wꜣḏ-wr*).

(K) Chr. Leitz translates it as follows: 'Jeder Löwe, auf den sie stoßeng, der ist sofort dahingegangen'.[325]

The same locality – *Sꜣw mḥw* – is mentioned in Ptolemaic Period *texts* in the Horus of Behdet temple at Edfu as a place of the 'Great Combat', where the solar falcon Horus (it is important that he is described in four appearances) defeated the serpent-like enemies – the host of *mś.w Bdšt*.[326] J.-C. Goyon attributes the origin of this myth to Heliopolis (in contrast to other traditions, where victory was assigned to Atum or Re), noting that these serpent-like enemies might,

[323] Leitz 1994: 95–96 (2–3). For *ḥnṯyw* see also: Gourlay 1979: 374–375.
[324] Leitz 1994: 95, Anm. 'g'.
[325] Leitz 1994: 94.
[326] Goyon 1985: 9.

like Horus, take quaternary form.[327] Previous to the publication of J.-C. Goyon appeared, E. Jelinkova-Reymond had assumed the origin of these traditions to be in Heliopolis and Hermopolis.[328]

Consequently, it appears obvious that these two versions of the myth were reflected in the fragments of BD 17, in one case reporting about the annihilation of *mś.w Bdšt* on the Primeval Hill in Hermopolis, and in the other – about the combat with them in the Eastern Sky, the split of the *išd*-tree and a future trial in Heliopolis. The first, 'Hermopolitan version' is not recorded in the CT Sp. 335 – it is the New Kingdom gloss, while the second, 'Heliopolitan version', on the contrary, is given in the CT,[329] while here one can infer insertion of the typical solar implications into the plot – an indication to the sunrise area. These two versions are united by obvious cosmogonical context. To distinguish these close, but apparently local versions of the myth, it is appropriate to introduce the following terms:

Version I = Urk. V: Abs. 1 – '*Hermopolitan version*';
Version II = Urk. V: Abs. 22, respectively, – '*Heliopolitan version*'.

[327] Goyon 1985: 154.
[328] Jelinkova-Reymond 1956: 42, 43, fn. 3.
[329] CT IV: 290–291a.

Chapter 4

Mś.w Bdšt in the context of BD 175A, BD 123, CT Sp. 409, pBrooklyn 47.218.84 and the *Book of Heavenly Cow* – the Cosmogonic myth dénouement

Despite a number of similarities, all of the above mentioned evidences of *mś.w Bdšt* are extremely fragmentary and contradictory. Consequently, the meaning of BD 17 myths in its two versions need to be clarified. And therefore, for an adequate interpretation it is necessary to involve additional sources of contextually-close content. Fortunately, such sources are at hand.[330]

In particular, what is important is the description of the rebellion (*śbỉ*), initiated by *mś.w Nw.t* – the 'Children of Nut' ( (p*Ḫꜥ*);  (p*ꜣnj*)), placed in the initial part of **BD 175** (the so-called **175A**). This spell appears in nine documents.[331]

1. p*Ḫꜥ* pTurin A, Suppl. 8438: 18th Dynasty (Thutmose IV / Amenhotep III) (***Figure 48***);[332]
2. p*Mn-ḫpr*(*-snb*) pCairo, Grabung DAI, TT 79, 18th Dynasty (Amenhotep II).[333]
3. p*ꜣnj* pLondon BM EA 10470: 19th Dynasty (***Figure 49***);[334]
4. p*Rꜥ* pLeiden T 5, 19th Dynasty (***Figure 50***);[335]
5. p*Ptḥ-mś* pKrakow MNK IX–752 (+ pParis Louvre SN 2), 19th Dynasty[336] (***Figure 51***);[337]
6. p*Ỉmn-n-nỉwt-nḫt* pCairo S.R. VII 10224: 21st Dynasty (Hieratic, unpublished);[338]
7. p*Ḏd-Ỉmnt-ỉw=f-ꜥnḫ* pMarseille 292, Third Intermediate Period (Hieratic);[339]
8. pLondon BM EA 10081 (34, 24 – 36, 21), 30th Dynasty – Ptolemaic Period (Hieratic) – text of the rituals of protection of the king.[340]
9. pSękowski (pKrakow), 1st century AD (Hieratic);[341]

[330] See also: Hornung 1982: 91–95.
[331] Cf. Otto 1962: 249–256.
[332] Schiaparelli 1937: 59–60; Cf. Hornung 1982: 81, 92.
[333] Guksch 1995: 168–171, Taf. 45, 49.
[334] Faulkner 1998: pl. XXIX.
[335] Naville 1886 I: Taf. CXCVIII.
[336] Luft 1977: 46–75, Taf. I–III; van Es 1982: 97–121.
[337] Luft 1977: Taf. III.
[338] Niwiński 1989: 274–275 (pCairo 61).
[339] Meeks 1993: 290–299, Figure 1–5, pl. 14–15.
[340] Schott 1956: 181–189; Bommas 2004: 95–113, Taf. IX–XII.
[341] Szczudlowska 1963: 123–142.

Figure 48

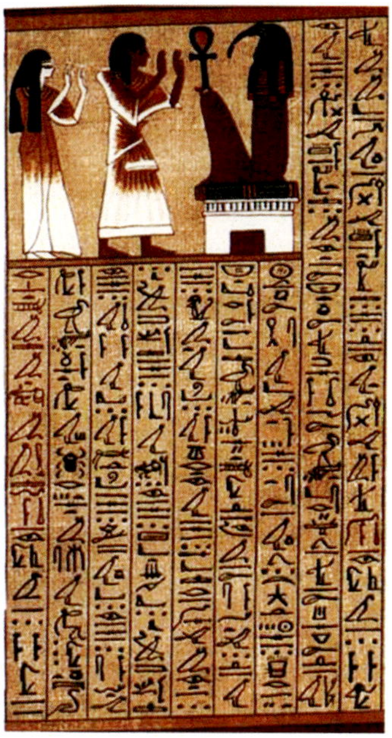

Figure 49

Figure 50

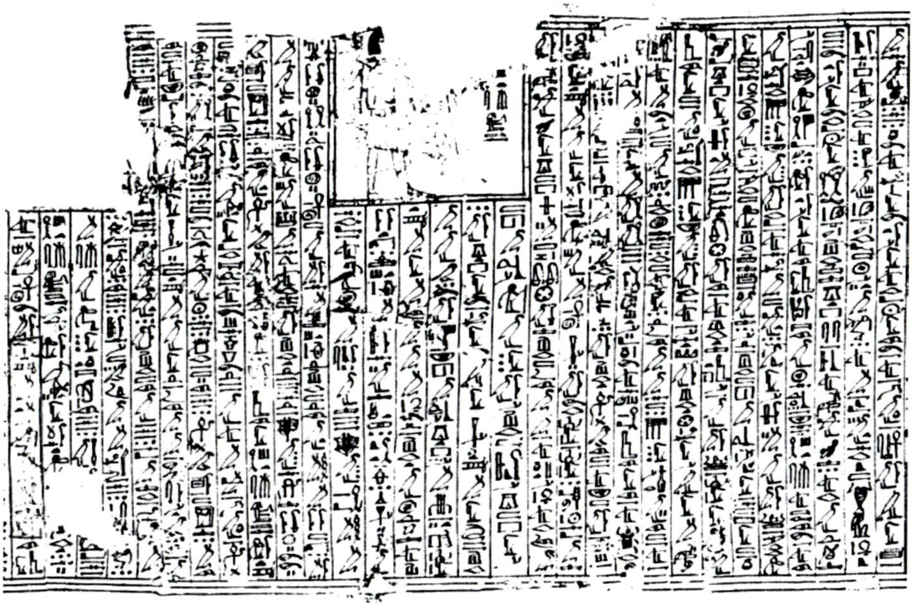

Figure 51

The section BD 175A is known in four scrolls (while in other documents[342] the text begins with section 175B). They are p*Ḫꜥ* pTurin A, Suppl. 8438; p*ꜣnj* pLondon BM EA 10470; p*Rꜥ* pLeiden T 5; p*Ptḥ-mś* pKrakow MNK IX–752 (**Appendix 2. Text No. 5**).[343]

p*Ḫꜥ* ————
p*ꜣnj* – (1) *r n tm m(w)t(w) m wḥm ḏd mdw ỉn Wśir ꜣnj mꜣꜥ-ḫrw*
p*Rꜥ* – (1) *r n tm m(w)t(w) m wḥm m ḫrt-nṯr ḏd mdw ỉn Wśir sš wdḥw Rꜥ* [////]
p*Ptḥ-mś* (1) *r n tm m(w)t(w) m wḥm ỉn Wśir* (2) *Ptḥ-mś mꜣꜥ-ḫrw ḏd=f*

p*Ḫꜥ* – (1) *ỉ Ḏḥwtj ỉšst pw ḫpr=t(y) sy m mś.w Nw.t*
p*ꜣnj* – (2) *ỉ Ḏḥwtj ỉšst pw ḫpr=t(y) s.t m mś.w Nw.t*
p*Rꜥ* – (2) *ỉ Ḏḥwtj ỉšst pw ḫpr=t(y) s.ty r mś.w Nw.t*
p*Ptḥ-mś* – *ỉ Ḏḥwtj ỉšst* [*pw ḫpr=t(y)*] *sy* (3) *m mś.w Nw.t*

p*Ḫꜥ* – *ỉr.n=sn ḫrwy.w* (2) *šd.n=sn ḫnnw ỉr.n=sn ỉśf.t*
p*ꜣnj* – (3) *ỉr.n=sn ḫrwy.w ỉw šd.n=sn ḫnnw ỉr.n=sn ỉśf.t*
p*Rꜥ* – *ỉw ỉr.n=n* [*ḫr*]*w*(3)*yw ỉw šd.n=sn ḫnnw ỉr.n=sn ỉśf.t*
p*Ptḥ-mś* – *ỉr.n=sn ḫrwy.w ỉ*[*w š*]*d.n=sn* (4) *ḫnnw ỉr.n=sn ỉśf.t*

p*Ḫꜥ* – *ḳmꜣ.n=sn śbi.w ỉr.n=sn šꜥ.t* (3) *ḳmꜣ.n=sn sꜣwt(y).w*
p*ꜣnj* – (4) *ḳmꜣ.n=sn śbi.w ỉr.n=sn šꜥ.t ḳmꜣ*(5)*.n=sn* (5) *sꜣwt(y).w*
p*Rꜥ* – *ḳmꜣ.n=sn śbi.*(4)*w ỉr.n=sn šꜥ.t ḳmꜣ.n=sn sꜣwt(y).w*
p*Ptḥ-mś* – *ḳmꜣ.n=sn śbi.w* (5) *ỉr.n=sn šꜥ.t* [*ḳm*]*ꜣ.n=sn sꜣwt(y).w*

p*Ḫꜥ* – *ỉw grt ỉr.n-sn ꜥꜣ r nḏś ỉr.n=sn ḥḏ*(4)*t*(SIC.)*ỉmn.t m ỉr(w).t.n=k nbt*
p*ꜣnj* – *ỉw grt ỉr.n-sn ꜥꜣ r nḏś m ỉr(w).t.n* (6) *nbt*
p*Rꜥ* – *ỉw grt ỉr.n-sn* [////] (5) *m ỉr(w).t.n=ỉ nb(t)*
p*Ptḥ-mś* – *ỉw grt ỉrw.n-sn ꜥꜣ r nḏś m* (6) *ỉr(w).t.n=ỉ nb(t)*

p*Ḫꜥ* – *di* (/ *ỉmi*) *ỉr=kwi* (?) *ꜥꜣ Ḏḥwtj ḫrw=fy Tm*

p*ꜣnj* – *di* (/ *ỉmi*) *ỉr=k ꜥꜣ Ḏḥwtj ḫrw=fy sy Tm*
p*Rꜥ* – *di.t* (/ *ỉmi.t*) *ỉr=k Ḏḥwtj ḫrw=fy st Tm*
p*Ptḥ-mś* – *di* (/ *ỉmi*) *ỉr=k ꜥ*[*ꜣ Ḏḥw*]*tj ḫrw=fy st Tm*

p*Ḫꜥ* – *nn mꜣꜣ.n=k ỉś*(5)*f.t nn wḫd(w)=k*
p*ꜣnj* – *nn mꜣꜣ.n=k ỉśf.t nn w*(7)*ḫd(w)=k*
p*Rꜥ* – *nn mꜣꜣ=k ỉśf.t* [*nn*] (6) *wḫd(w)=k*

[342] Unfortunately, I do not have a copy of p*Ỉmn-n-niwt-nḫt* pCairo S.R. VII 10224. See: Bonn Totenbuchprojekt, TM 134492 <totenbuch.awk.nrw.deobjekttm134492>.
[343] Text: de Buck 1950: 86–88; Luft 1953: Taf. III. Translations: Barguet 1967: 260–261; Allen 1974: 183; Faulkner 2001: 175; Ockinga 1988: 518–522; Hornung 1979: 365–366, 517–518; Stadler 2009: 370–371; Carrier 2009a: 779–780; Quirke 2013: 437.

p*Ptḥ-mś* – *nn m33.n=k iśf.t nn w*(7)*ẖd(w)=k*

p*Ḫ*ᶜ – *sḥwᶜ rnp.wt=sn stkn 3bd.w=sn ḏr-ntt* (6) *ir.n=(s)n*[344] *ḥḏ.t*(SIC.) *imn.t m ir.t.n=k nbt*
p*3nj* – *śḥwᶜ rnp.wt=sn śtknw 3bd.w=sn ḏr-nty* (8) *ir.w.n=sn ḥḏi imn.t m ir.t.n=k nbt*
p*R*ᶜ – *śḥwᶜ rnp.wt=sn śtkn 3bd.w=sn ḏr-nty ir.n=sn [ḥḏi]* (7) *imn(.t)*
p*Ptḥ-mś* – *śḥwᶜ rnp.wt=sn stknw 3bd.w=sn ḏr-nty ir.t.n=k ḥḏi imn.t m ir*(8)*.t.n=k nbt*

p*Ḫ*ᶜ – *ink gstj=k Ḏḥwtj sᶜr.n=i* (7) *p3s=k*
p*3nj* – *ink gstj=k Ḏḥwtj śᶜr.n=i n=k p3s=k*
p*R*ᶜ – *ink gstj=k Ḏḥwtj śᶜr.n=k p3s=k*
p*Ptḥ-mś* – *ink gstj=k Ḏḥwtj (ś)ᶜr.n=i n=k p3s=k*

p*Ḫ*ᶜ – *nn nw n nw n(y) ḥḏ.t*(SIC.) *imn.t nn ir(w)=tw ḥḏ.t*(SIC.) *im=i nn śẖm* (8) *m(w) t(w) sin im=i*
p*3nj* – *nn nw*(9)*=j m-m nw n(y) ḥḏi imn.t=sn nn ir(w)=tw ḥḏi im=i*
p*R*ᶜ – *nn* [////] (8) *gs*(SIC.) *nw ḥḏi imn(.t) nn ḥḏi im=k*
p*Ptḥ-mś* – *nn nw=j m-m nw n(y) ḥḏi* (9) *imn.t=sn nn ir(w)=tw ḥḏ im=i*

Rubric (only in pḪᶜ):[345] … (8) *ḏd mdw ḥr twt n* (9) *Ḏḥwtj ir.w m ṯḥnt di n s r ḏrt=f w3ḥ pw tpyw-t3* (10) *tm m(w)t(w) n śin nḥm=f pw n nw.*

(1) '<u>Spell for not dying a second time, words spoken by Osiris N, true of voice</u>**(A)**.

(2) – O Thot, what will happen (/ to be done)**(B)** with the Children of Nut?

(3) They**(C)** have initiated war, they have raised fuss**(D)**, they have created injustice, (4) they have started rebellion, they have organized slaughter, and they have put on guard. (5) Indeed, they have turned great into small in all that I**(E)** have done**(F)**.

(6) Reveal your**(G)** greatness (/ come closer – ?)**(H)**, Thot, – says Atum.

(7) – You shall not see injustice, you shall not suffer.

Their years**(I)** are shorted**(J)**, their months are counted because**(K)** (8) they have created**(L)** hidden destruction**(M)** in all that you have done.

---

344 By mistake it is given ⊂⊃ *t3* instead of —⊶— *s*.
345 de Buck 1950: 88.

I am your writing-palette, (O) Thot! I have brought for you your water-vessel[(N)]. (9) I am not among those who have (created) (their) hidden destruction[(O)]! No destruction shall not be arising in me[(P)] '(after p*ꜣnj* pLondon BM EA 10470).

Rubric (only in p*H̱ʿ*): '... (8) To mention above the statue of (9) Thot[(Q)] made of faience. It should be placed in the hand of a man. It will extend his age among the living (and) (10) save from imminent death. This will save him'.

Comments

[(A)] In p*H̱ʿ* the introductory sentence is missing; p*Rʿ* gives the following form '<u>Spell for not dying a second time, to be said</u> by Osiris N, true of voice ...'.

[(B)] According to A. de Buck,[346] adopted by T. G. Allen,[347] the verb *ḫpr* here should be read as 'done', i.e.: 'O Thot, what is to be done with the Children of Nut?'[348]

[(C)] p*Rʿ* has suffixal pronoun 2nd person, plural, masculine =*n*, i.e. 'We created ...'. Apparently, this is a mistake made by the scribe.

[(D)] 'Tumult, uproar',[349] also 'Störung', 'Unordnung' – 'trouble, hindrance, disorder',[350] but *ẖnnw* / 'Störung' – derivative from *ẖnw* / 'Lärm' – '(violent) noise, fuss, uproar'[351] i.e. translation as 'fuss' or 'noise' will be more precise.

[(E)] p*H̱ʿ* has suffixal pronoun 2nd person, masculine=*k*. p*Rʿ* and p*Ptḥ-mś* give suffixal pronoun 1st person, masculine =*i*. In p*ꜣnj* the pronoun is omitted by mistake.

[(F)] It is added in p*H̱ʿ*: 'they have created hidden destruction!'

[(G)] In p*H̱ʿ* for the pronoun =*k* the New Egyptian graphic  =*kwj* is given. A. de Buck sees here pronoun 1st person singular =*w*(*j*).[352]

[(H)] All the scrolls give different spellings, thus A. de Buck refrained from translating this phrase, noting that it is 'an unknown idiomatic expression'.[353] P. Barguet offers the following reading: 'Fais montre de puissance (?), Thot',[354] R. Faulkner translates: 'show greatness, O Thot!',[355] T. G. Allen: 'Give thou effective (help,

346 de Buck 1950: 83, fn. 7.
347 Allen 1974: 183.
348 Allen 1974: 183.
349 Faulkner 1999: 203.
350 Wb. III: 383.5; Hannig 1995: 637.
351 Wb. III: 383.5.
352 de Buck 1950: 80, fn. 14.
353 de Buck 1950: 80, 84, fn. 14.
354 Barguet 1967: 260.
355 Faulkner 2001: 175.

O) Thoth',[356] Cl. Carrier: 'Fais donc preuve d'excellence, Thot!',[357] E. Hornung: 'Gib doch wirksame (Hilfe), o Thot',[358] M. Stadler: 'Veranlasse doch (Großes), Thot'[359] St. Quirke: 'Give then a great (decision), Thot'.[360] The main difficulties with transliteration and reading are:

1. Sign 𓂞 (D 37, 'give', 'put') can mean *di*, and *imi;*[361]
2. Determinative to *ꜥ3* 𓂝 differs: in p*Ḫ*ꜥ it is the sign 𓈐 (N 31); in p*3nj* and in p*Ptḥ-mś* (this part of the papyrus would be partially destroyed) – 𓏛 (Y 1); in p*R*ꜥ the word *ꜥ3* is absent. Spelling *ꜥ3* with the determinative of 'papyrus' (Y1) assumes translating 'greatness',[362] and with the determinative of the 'road' (N 31) has the meaning 'here' ('hier, hierher'),[363] this understanding of *ꜥ3* is also supported by B. Ockinga: 'Begib dich hierher, Thot'.[364] This reading, could be backed up by the spelling 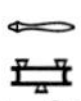 as  in BD 39 (column 19) after p*Ms-m-nṯr* pParis Louvre E. 21324; SN 1 (18th Dynasty).[365]

(I) 'vorzeitig abbrechen';[366] 'cut short (*time or activities*)'.[367]

(J) 'verküzen (*Jahre, Lebenzeit*)'.[368]

(K) *ḏr-nty* / *ḏr-ntt* may be also translated as 'because' or 'since'.

(L) In p*3nj* passive construction *ir.w.n=sn* is used by mistake. In other documents active voice is used: *ir.n=sn* – 'they created…'.

(M) Expression *ḥḏi imn.t* 'hidden destruction' can also be translated as 'secret damage, spoiling'. The noun *ḥḏi* has a meaning of 'destruction, extermination'.[369] The sign of the (false) plurality, ending *.t* and determinative 𓏛 of the adjective *imn* ('hidden, secret')[370] indicate an abstract concept.[371] The form *ḥḏ.t imn.t* in p*Ḫ*ꜥ, first suggests a gender accord, however rather questionable because of a

---

356 Allen 1974: 183.
357 Carrier 2009a: 779 (6).
358 Hornung 1979: 365.
359 Stadler 2009: 370.
360 Quirke 2013: 437.
361 See: Gardiner 1958: 454; 217, § 289, 1; 257–258, § 336.
362 Wb. I: 163; Faulkner 1999: 36.
363 Wb. I: 164.2.
364 Ockinga 1988: 519.
365 Naville 1886 I: Taf. LIII; Cf. Allen 1974: 46 (13) ('come hither').
366 Hannig 1995: 782.
367 Faulkner 1999: 254. For the analysis of the verb forms see Stadler 2009: 377–380.
368 Hannig 1995: 735.
369 Wb. III: 212–213.16; Faulkner 1999: 182.
370 Faulkner 1999: 21.
371 Gardiner 1958: 60–61, § 77.

spelling mistake in the suffix pronoun in front of it in column 6 and is probably is incorrect. Translators are not unanimous in their understanding of this sentence: 'hidden destruction';[372] 'destruction secrete';[373] 'hidden damage';[374] 'verborgene Störung';[375] 'l'anéantissement dissimulé';[376] 'heimlich gestört';[377] but '... was du geschaffen hast, im Verborgenen gestört haben';[378] 'a mockery secrecy'[379] and 'harm to the hidden'.[380]

(N) *p3s* – 'water-vessel', writing materials;[381] A. de Buck and R. Faulkner translate it as 'inkpot'.[382]

(O) T. G. Allen translates: 'I am not among these who betray their secrets'.[383] But the identical writing *ḥḏi imn.t* in the previous columns (even twice in p*Ḫ*ʿ) specify that it is the very same 'hidden destruction'.[384]

(P) p*R*ʿ has: *nn ḥḏ im=k* – 'there is no destruction in you'. In p*Ḫ*ʿ the conclusion is added: 'Let the quick death not overtake me'.

(Q) This ritual proclamation in front of a god is illustrated by the vignette preserved in p*3nj* (***Figure 49***).

Vignette: In p*3nj* the BD 175 vignette (***Figure 49***) shows the deceased and his wife in adoration pose in front of the ibis-headed Thot figure with the *ʿnḫ*-sign in his hands that corresponds well to the chapter's rubric, ordering to read the spell before figure of Thot. In the p*Ḫ*ʿ the BD 175 chapter is illustrated with two vignettes. On the first, placed over section 175B, is shown the god Thot with a *w3s*-staff and *ʿnḫ*-sign. On the second picture, placed over section 175C, is shown the falcon-headed deity with the same attributes. Its silhouette is painted in a black (***Figure 50***). Originally, the illustration accompanied the BD 175A text in p*Ptḥ-mś*, but it didn't survive, while over section 175B is placed the vignette representing deceased with a *w3s*-staff[385] (***Figure 51***).

372 de Buck 1950: 80, 83, fn. 12.
373 Barguet 1967: 260.
374 Faulkner 2001: 175.
375 Stadler 2009: 370.
376 Carrier 2009a: 780.
377 Ockinga 1988: 519.
378 Hornung 1979: 366.
379 Allen 1974: 183.
380 Quirke 2013: 437.
381 Wb. I: 499.5; Faulkner 1999: 88; Allen 1974: 183; Hornung 1979: 366.
382 de Buck 1950: 80; Faulkner 2001: 175.
383 Allen 1974: 183.
384 Cf. de Buck 1950: 80, 84, fn. 23; Faulkner 2001: 175; Hornung 1979: 366.
385 Luft 1977: 50; Taf. III.

LGG ignores the earliest mention of *mś.w Nw.t* for BD 175A in p *Ḫ*ʿ.[386] BD 175A is also not given in two editions of the text of the spell.[387] However, in 1950 A. de Buck published BD 175A on the basis of three scrolls.[388] Originally, all three sections of BD 175 seem to be independent spells,[389] considering the fact that two sections have separate title rubrics. BD 175A is a dialogue between Atum and Thot (at certain moment the deceased joins the dialogue), and it describes the myth 'Children of Nut'. BD 175B is an eschatological dialogue between Atum and Osiris, originating, as noted above, from CT Sp. 1130. It is interesting because of the pessimistic description of the Netherworld, reminiscent for J. Assmann of the Jewish notion of Sheol, the Greek notion of Hades, etc.[390] This text represents the so-called 'skeptical' attitude of the Egyptians towards the Afterlife, reflected in a series of texts, which have been attracting attention of Egyptologists for a long time,[391] and associated with the notion of the Theodicy or the so-called texts of 'Reproaches to God' (*Vorwurf an Gott*), initiated in Middle Kingdom.[392] The essence of these attitudes is summarized in the formula on the statue of *Nḫt=f-Mw.t* Cairo CG 42206; J.E. 36704 (22nd Dynasty, Osorkon II) (**Appendix 1. Text No. 5**):[393]

ꜣḫ ꜣt n mꜣꜣ stwt ỉtn r ḏt m ḥḳꜣ ỉgr.t[394]
'It is better to see (one) moment of sunlight[395] rather than spend eternity as the Lord of the Netherworld.'

According to A. de Buck, this idea is reflected in the eleventh song of Homer's 'Odyssey'[396] – in the words of Achilles, addressing Odysseus in the underworld of Hades:

> 'Nay, seek not to speak soothingly to me of death, glorious Odysseus. I should choose, so I might live on earth, to serve as the hireling of another, of some portionless man whose livelihood was but small, rather than to be lord over all the dead that have perished'.

386 LGG III: 423.
387 Kees 1930: Pl. 1* (Jl) (H. Kees begins reading BD 175 in p*Ḫ*ʿ from sheet 15, while the beginning of the spell has seven columns on the previous sheet (it follows BD 155); Szczudlowska 1963: 128 (Jl) (in pSękowski section BD175A is missing).
388 de Buck 1950: 79–88.
389 de Buck 1950: 79.
390 Assmann 2003: 197, 213–216; 2005: 122–123, 134–137.
391 Assmann 2003: 186–204; 2005: 113–127.
392 Ассманн 1999: 256–274; Assmann 2002a: 189–193.
393 Jansen-Winkeln 1985 I: 25–34 (Text A 2) (note: 27; 30, Anm. 80); II, S. 441 (b, 3); Assmann 2003: 198; 2005: 122.
394 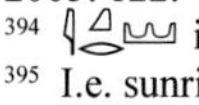 is a late form of writing  – *igr.t* (Wb. I: 141.2).
395 I.e. sunrise, morning.
396 de Buck 1958: 74–96.

> 'Glorious Odysseus: don't try to reconcile me to my dying. I'd rather serve as another man's labourer, as a poor peasant without land, and be alive on Earth, than be lord of all the lifeless dead' (*Hom.*, Od., XI, 488–491).[397]

Passages close to the description of the Netherworld in BD 175^{B} / CT 1130 appear in the tomb of *Nfr-sḫrw* at Zaviet el-Sultan (Tomb No. 1, 19th Dynasty):[398]

št3y n3 n ỉmntt ḳsnw sḫr=sn wdf wj r šm n=sn
bw sḏd=f ḫrt=f ḥtp=f m ś.t-f w3t nḥḥ (ỉ)r=f m kkw
'Those who are in the West are in a predicament, their state is nasty. Motionless are those who get to them. He can not reveal his state. He rests in his one place (and) and the *nḥḥ*-eternity is before him as darkness'.[399]

The last section – BD 175C – sets forth the Herakleopolitan Osirian myth studied in details by H. Kees[400] (p*3nj* doesn't have this part). As correctly indicated by M. Stadler, the formation period of all three BD 175 sections can be attributed to First Intermediate Period – Middle Kingdom.[401]

The fundamental fault of the 'Children of Nut' in BD 175A is the creation of 'hidden destruction' (*ḥḏỉ ỉmnt*), a kind of 'damage' or 'curse' to the ideal Universe of Atum, a consequence of their rebellion and rioting. This is what entailed punishment, proclaimed by Thot: shortening of life and emergence of 'imminent death' – *m*(*w*)*t*(*w*) *sỉn* – and against which BD 175A was directed. Noteworthy are the following BD 175 sections directed against the 'second death' (*m*(*w*)*t*(*w*) *m wḥm*) – i.e. the 'final' death, happening in the Netherworld, and giving no hope for a posthumous revival.[402] In addition to BD 175, the motive for avoiding 'second death' is found in Middle and New Kingdoms funeral rubrics and texts, namely: CT Sp. 83, II, 47b; Sp. 156, II, 312b; Sp. 423, V, 261; BD 64, 5; BD 130, 8–10; BD 135, 2; BD 176.

It is quite significant that longevity in BD 175A is directly associated with such a fundamental idea for the Egyptian worldview as loyalty to the authority of the god and, therefore, the king, as Atum appears in the text exactly as an earthly ruler (but of mythical times), while Thot played the role of his advisor or vizier.[403] This correlates well with the lines from the 'Teaching for Merikare': *ỉr*(*ỉ*) *m3ʿ.t w3ḥ=k tp t3* – 'Make Justice (*m3ʿ.t*), (and) you shall stay on the earth (for a long

---

[397] Translation by A.T. Murray after Homer, The Odyssey, I–II, London 1919.
[398] Kees 1927: 76; KRI I: 305; Osing 1992: 55.
[399] As a rule, *nḥḥ*-eternity is associated with solar representations. In this case, it would not imply comparison of *nḥḥ* with Darkness (*kkw*), but the inaccessible 'solar (daylight) eternity' for the deceased in the darkness of tomb.
[400] Kees 1930: 65–83.
[401] Stadler 2009: 371–380.
[402] Zandee 1960: 186–188; Hornung 1968: 33, 35; Westendorf 1980: 953; Meurer 2002: 230.
[403] Stadler 2009: passim.

time)' (*Merikare*, 46–47; list 'P', pHermitage 1116A verso), as well as with the 'Teaching for Ptahhotep'[404] (**Appendix 2. Text No. 6**):

(637) *mi pḥ=k wj ḥʿw=k wḏ3(w)*	'(637) Than you will reach me,[405] your body will be safe,
(638) *njśwt ḥtp(w) m ḫpr.t nb.t*	(638) (and) the king will be satisfied with what is happening,
(639) *iṯ(i)=k rnp.wt m ʿnḫ*	(639) you will spend[406] your lifetime.[407]
(640) *nn šr(j) irt.n=i tp t3*	(640) A lot has been done by me on earth.
(641) *iṯ(i).n=i rnpt* 110 *m ʿnḫ*	(641) I have spent 110 years of my life,[408]
(642) *n dd n(=i) njśwt*	(642) given to me by the king.
(643) *ḥswt(=i) ḫnt tp(j) w-ʿwi(=i)*	(643) (My) blessing is grater than one of (my) predecessor,
(644) *m-ʿ jrt(.n=i) m3ʿ.t n njśwt r st im3ḫ*	(644) because I have made[409] Justice (*m3ʿ.t*) for the king till the place of honour[410]'[(F)] (Prisse 19,6–19,8; 637–644).[411]

Data from BD 94 and BD 123 (= BD 139)[412] are among the closest parallels to the plot of BD 175A. In the first spell – **BD 94** – the deceased identifies himself with Thot and asks him to bring the water-vessel (*p3s*) mentioned in BD 175A and writing palette (*gstj*) of Thot, along with all its 'secrets' (*št3w*) (**Appendix 1. Text No. 7**)[413] (after p*Nww* pLondon BM EA 10477):

[…] (4) *ini n=i p3s gstj m ḫrt-ʿ-ṯwy n.t Ḏḥwty št3w.w im(yt)=sn*[414] *mk wi m sš in n=i ḥw3.wt Wśir sš=i im*

[404] A. de Buck, who studied this fragment in BD 175A context, does not go beyond stating the fact that the Egyptians feared premature death reflected in these texts (de Buck 1950: 81).
[405] I.e. 'reach my age'.
[406] For translation of the verb *iṯi* as 'to spend' see: Wb. I: 149.10.
[407] I.e. either 'long lifetime' (lit. 'years of life')', or 'my years of life'.
[408] Lit. 'years in life'. See: Gardiner 1958: 356, § 442, 5. Period of 110 years of life was considered ideal by the Egyptians (Janssen 1950: 33–43).
[409] Lit. 'did'. To complement pronouns see line 640.
[410] My translation follows the transliteration and translation of M. Sokolova (Moscow) (published on www.egyptology.ru).
[411] Prisse d'Avennes 1926: pl. XIX.
[412] Stadler 2009: 373–374.
[413] Naville 1886 II: 212; Budge 1898 I: 199–200; Lapp 1997: pl. 35. Translations: Barguet 1967: 129; Allen 1974: 77; Faulkner 2001: 88; Hornung 1979: 186, 473; Stadler 2009: 382; Carrier 2009a: 329; Quirke 2013: 213.
[414] In p*Nb-imn* pLondon BM EA 9964 (18th Dynasty) and p*Ḫnśw-mś* pParis BN 20–23 (21st Dynasty) *nṯr.w* is added (Naville 1886 II: 212).

[...] ‘(4) Bring me a water-vessel and writing palette which are in the hand of Thot (and) the secrets that are in them. Look, I am a Scribe![415] Bring me the remains of Osiris, that I may write with them’.[416]

The second source – **BD 123** – once again display Atum and Thot. The text is arranged as an appeal of Thot to Atum, where Thot indicates that he had stopped the Combat and reconciled the ‘Two Comrades’ (*Rḥ.wy*), and also ‘liberated’ (*šdi*) *ꜥdw*-fish, performing the commands of Atum (**Appendix 2. Text No. 8**)[417] (after p*Nww* pLondon BM EA 10477):

(1) *r n ꜥḳ r ḥw.t-ꜥꜣ.t ḏd mdw in* NN *inḏ-ḥr=k Tm ink Ḏḥwty wḏꜥ Rḥ.wy*

(2) *iw dr.n=i ꜥḥꜣ=sn šk.n=i iꜣkbw.w=sn šdi.n=i ꜥdw m ḥm=f iw ir.n=i wḏ.t.n=k*

(3) *r=f šḏr.n=i [m-ḫt]*(A) *m-ḫnw ir.t=i [ink šw m sḏb.w ii.n=i mꜣꜣ.n=k wi m ḥw.t Wḥm-ḥr]*(B) *m wḏ[=i]*(C) *mdw.w iꜣw.w ḫr sšm=i ny-ink šrryw.w*

(1) Spell for entering the Great House(D). Pronouncing the words by N.
– Hail, Atum! I am Thot, who judged Two Comrads(E). (2) I have stopped their Combat. I have finished their plaints. I have liberated *ꜥdw*-fish on his(E) return. I did (what) you commanded to do (3) for him(F). [Then] I spent the night inside of my Eye(G). [I am free of evil thoughts; I have come, and you see me in the House of *Wḥm-ḥr* (Herald?)(H)], when [I] give the commands(I). The Aged are under my control (and) I possess the Children(J)’.

Comments

(A, B, C) The text in square brackets is restored from pParis Louvre 3073.[418]

(D) The Temple (‘Residence’) of Atum at Heliopolis.[419]

(E) The epithet of Horus and Seth during their trial for the right to rule over Egypt.[420]

(F, G) In the Egyptian the name of the *ꜥdw*-fish is masculine.[421]

(H) Reference to the lunar features of Thoth.[422]

---

415 I.e. Thot.
416 The *ḥwꜣ.wt Wšir* used by the deceased seems to act as a metaphor for Thot’s writing-kit (Тураев 1898: 135, прим. 2), which is thus called to give a verdict for the soul of the deceased at the Netherworld Court of Osiris, the results of which are recorded by Thot.
417 Naville 1886 II: 269; Budge 1898 I: 242–243; Lapp 1997: pl. 43. Translations: Barguet 1967: 156; Allen 1974: 95–96; Faulkner 2001: 114; Hornung 1979: 230–231, 489–490, 473; Stadler 2009: 200; Carrier 2009a: 423; Quirke 2013: 266.
418 Naville 1886 II: 269; Budge 1898 I: 242–243.
419 Wb. III: 4, V.
420 LGG IV: 703. Cf. BD 17, 30–32 (Urk. V: 32, 12).
421 More about this image in the mythology see: Stadler 2009: 201–203.
422 Stadler 2009: 203ff.

(I)  – understanding of the meaning of the name is rather difficult (not mentioned in LGG). T. G. Allen, E. Hornung and U. Verhoeven[423] believe that the incorrect form of title  *wḥmw* wrote – 'herald, messenger'.[424] R. Faulkner translates the name as 'Him of the double face'.[425] P. Barguet and Cl. Carrier leave the name without translation,[426] but P. Barguet notes that it literally means 'Celui qui renouvelle le visage', and perhaps it is an epithet of Thot.[427] M. Stadler rejects the 'incorrectness' of writing and understands the name as 'Changing / Repeating face' ('des Gesicht erneuert / an Gesicht Wiederholtem'), where is rightly seen a lunar aspect of Thot.[428] The same understanding of *Wḥm-ḥr* is given by St. Quirke: "Temple of the repeating of face' would denote the temple of the moon, reflecting the lunar aspect of Thot, complementing the sun'.[429]

(I) The sentence in p*Nww* is translated by St. Quirke as 'I have slept within my eye by the command'.[430]

(J) St. Quirke translates: 'The elder gods are under my guidance, the lesser ones are mine'.[431]

As for the case of *mś.w Bdšt*, the question of how *mś.w Nw.t* can be understood in BD 175A remains disputable. Among the various interpretations, the most popular one is that initially a group of people, gods or demons hostile to the Demiurge was created. The first interpretation is given, in particular, by E. Hornung who understands the 'Children of Nut' as epithet to a rebellious mankind parallel to myth 'about the destruction of mankind' in the *Book of the Heavenly Cow* (see below).[432] This interpretation is approved by M. Stadler, who believed that 'human' appearance is more acceptable for the 'Children of Nut' in BD 175A and finds confirmation of this in the final lines of BD 123, where the power of Thot over the elderly people and children is mentioned as an echoe of the same myth.[433]

G. Meurer suggested that the 'unrest' quelled by the 'Children of Nut' in BD 175A displayed a conflict of Horus and Seth for the throne of Osiris, and this resulted in Atum's trouble.[434] This, however, does not explain the need for Thot to reduce

423 Allen 1974: 96; Hornung 1979: 231; Verhoeven 1993 I: 225.
424 Wb. I: 344.4; Faulkner 1999: 67
425 Faulkner 2001: 114.
426 Barguet 1967: 156; Carrier 2009a: 423.
427 Barguet 1967: 156, fn. 4.
428 Stadler 2009: 200, Kom. 3.
429 Quirke 2013: 266.
430 Quirke 2013: 266.
431 Quirke 2013: 266.
432 Hornung 1979: 517; 1982: 90–95.
433 Stadler 2009: 373.
434 Meurer 2002: 193.

the period of their life, even if one recollects the thesis of the eschatological 'finiteness of life' of the gods in texts of BD 175B and CT Sp. 1130.

Chr. Leitz focuses on the astral semantics of the 'Children of Nut' image (he doesn't touch upon the data of BD 175A) as stars or deans, and personifies them as deities of the latest generation of the Heliopolitan Ennead, whose birthdays were celebrated in *epagomeny*.[435] In a number of astronomical texts the stars without compulsory divine identification were understood to be the notion of the 'children' of the celestial goddess Nut.[436] In particular in the cenotaph of Seti I at Abydos an interesting myth reports that in the morning Nut, under the image of a pig, devours her children-stars to give them birth in the evening again and places them in the sky.[437]

Finally, P. Barguet expresses his objection to the correlation between the 'Children of *Bdšt*' and the 'Children of Nut' and considers the latter to be the deities of Ennead: Osiris, Isis, Seth and Nephthys, conflicting with the Horus.[438] But similar to the interpretation of G. Meurer, still unclear is the destructiveness of their rebellion, and the inexplicable choice of the punishment by the god-creator and Thot, given that the latter is well known as a god, who reconciled 'Two Comrades' (*Rḥ.wy*) – Horus and Seth (cf. above BD 123).

It is significant that the majority of 'Children of Nut' texts bear positive features and one should note that they are first appear in the *Pyramid Texts* (PT 519, Pyr. § 1213c).[439] In the 'Cairo Calendar' the 'Children of Nut' are mentioned twice. On the 28th day of the first month of the *ꜣḫt* season ('very favorable'): *iw ntr.w hrw m rꜤ pn mꜣꜣ=śn mś.w Nw.t ḥtpw hrw* – 'The gods enjoy this day when they see the Children of Nut being pacified (and) happy'.[440] On the 21st day of the second month of the *šmw* season ('dangerous'): *hrw pwy n mnmn.tj Ꜥnḫ(t) (n) mś.w Nw.t* – 'The day, when land of the West[441] trembles (due to) the 'Children of Nut'.[442] In BD 1 (= CT Sp. 314, IV, 94–96) the 'Children of Nut' act as defenders of Osiris, defeating his enemies: *ink wꜤ m nw n nṯr.w mś.w Nw.t smꜣyw ḫfty.w Wśir ḫnriw śbi.w ḥr=f* – 'I am one of these gods, the Children of Nut, who killing enemies of Osiris, repelling the rebel against him'.[443] In the version of BD 1

435 Leitz 1994: 366–368.
436 LGG III: 423.
437 Frankfort 1933 I: 82–86; II, pl. 84–85; Leitz 1994: 366.
438 Barguet 1967: 260, fn. 2.
439 Pyr. Komm. V: 95 ('Kinder der Nut sind es, die auf dish herabsteigan'); Faulkner 1969: 193; Allen 2015: 166 (519); 207, fn. 94.
440 Bakir 1966: 18 (4); Leitz 1994: 59.
441 Or 'Western (Necropolis)'; see: Wb. I: 205.16; for the spelling of *Ꜥnḫ* in the sense of 'West' without determinative see: Urk., IV, 33, 3; 366, 12.
442 Bakir 1966: 44 (5–6); Leitz 1994: 366. I'm thankful to Dr. M. Panov (Novosibirsk) for the consultation with the translation.
443 Lüscher 1986: 20–23.

on the first shrine of Tutankhamun the *mś.w Gb* – 'Children of Geb' is written instead of *mś.w Nw.t,*[444] but this case is a unique exception.

It should also be stressed that if one assumes that *Bdšt* is not a name but an epithet, then, considering the parallelism with the BD 175A mythem, it is possible to perceive *Bdšt* as the sky goddess Nut, whose children rebelled against the creator-god. But this interpretation has a number of disputable issues, namely: significant discrepancy in time between the epoch of *Coffin Texts*, where the name of *Bdšt* is determined by the sign of 'goddess' and middle of the 18th Dynasty, the time of creation of pḪᶜ with the earliest record of BD 175A. On the other hand, as noted above, similarity with BD 175B narration can be found in CT 1130 (CT VII, 467–468),[445] moreover BD 175C describes the Herakleopolitan version of the myth of Osiris's accession to this center, and may date back to First Intermediate Period state theology.[446] Based on views expressed by a number of scholars about representations of the plot of the *Book of the Heavenly Cow* in the 'Teaching for Merikare', and definite association with the latest BD 175A (see below), M. Stadler also reasonably assumed an early origin of BD 175A.[447]

Moreover, the parallelism between BD 175A and BD 17 plots can be confirmed by data, unfortunately fragmented in passages germane to our subject, **CT Sp. 409 (Appendix 2. Text No. 9):**[448]

[in]ḏ-ḥr=ṯn šnw nw ẖt n n[šm.t] iw N *pn rḫ=ṯn m rn.w=ṯn m ḫpr.w n=ṯn n im mś.w Bdšt* [//////////][449] *pw irjw šᶜ.wt ᶜ3.wt r* [/////////////////] *Nw.t*

'Hail to you, the equipment of mast on the *n*[*šm.t*]-boat![450] This N knows [you] in your name (and) your image in which you appeared; [You are] *mś.w Bdšt* [/////////], those who have arranged great slaughter to [//////////////] Nut'.

Attention should be paid to the existing *varia leclio* of *mś.w Bdšt* in CT Sp. 335 IV, 290a. On the coffin M4C 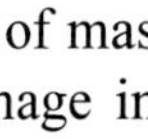 *Išd.t* is spelled out instead of *Bdšt*.[451] But even a more curious writing, somehow ignored by M. Heerma van Voss, appears on coffin T3Be, where 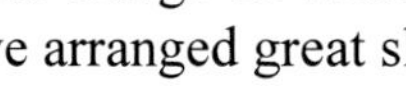 *mś.w ir.t.n=śn pw* – 'Children of their Eye' is written instead of *mś.w Bdšt*.[452] Perhaps this is an allusion to the human

[444] Lüscher 1986: 22.
[445] Backes 2005: 427; Stadler 2009: 374–375.
[446] Kees 1930: 65–83; Stadler 2009: 373–374.
[447] Stadler 2009: 373–375.
[448] CT V, 233e-g (T1Cb); Faulkner 1994 II: 62; Barguet 1986: 372.
[449] In this place G. Maspero saw demonstrative pronoun  *nw* – 'this, these' (Gardiner 1958: § 110; 511, 3), but A. de Buck reports when he has been working with the coffin, these signs could no longer be identified (CT V: 233, fn. 5 *).
[450] The boat of Osiris. See: Lavier 2007: 1083–1089.
[451] Heerma van Voss 1963: 46.
[452] CT IV: 291a.

essence of these creatures, since it was people in the Egyptian mythological antropogony who were represented as 'originating from their Eye' – 'tears' of the creator-god Atum. This plot is attested in Egyptian sources.[453]

It is possible that akin to the images of *mś.w Bdšt* and *mś.w Nw.t* are creatures 'Children of Apophis' –  *mś.w ꜥ3pp*, mentioned on naos Ismailia J.E. 2248 of el-Arish (Late Period). These are the Western Desert rebels who attacked Egypt from the road Saft el-Henna, and were defeated (*sm3*) by god Shu:[454] *jsk r=f mś.w ꜥ(3)pp śbj.w [...Wšr]w dšr.t iw=sn ḥr mṯn (i)w 'I3t-nbs ḫnd ḥr Km.t m wḫ3* – 'And the Children of Apophis, the rebels [... of *Usher*] came to *Iat-nebes* from the Desert and entered Egypt at night' (line 24–25 recto).[455]

There is another indirect parallel to the mytheme with *mś.w Bdšt* and *mś.w Nw.t* – data from **pBrooklyn 47.218.84**. The papyrus belonged to the collection of manuscripts from the Wilbour's collection, donated to the Brooklyn Museum. Like other scrolls from this collection, the document in question, apparently, originated from a priestly library in Heliopolis and dates back from Saite Period to 30th Dynasty – Early Ptolemaic Period. The text of the scroll contains a description of the various local calendar festivals and related mythological events (**Appendix 1. Text No. 10**).[456]

§ 10 (IV, 4) *3bd 1 šmw wnn nbtt nṯr ḏrt nt Rꜥ bk3.t*
(IV, 5) *[w m] Šw Tfnw.t śḫpr=śn m 3bd pn wn in ḏb3w nt nṯr pn ḫpr r=sn m mś.w Bdšw m sḫtw snḥmy ntt rsj n*
(IV, 6) *Ḥtp.t ḫpr*(A)*=śn m ḥf3.wt ir śbiw r nb=w m 3bd pn sii=tw n3 i3w.w ḥr nn ḳnw=śn n nb=śn m ḥb ḏrt*
(IV, 7) *ḫft ḥb Ḫnśw iw it.tw bd m ḥb pn m ḏd ḏrt pw 3m.tw ḥr mtwt nṯr śḥb=tw Nbt.t m ꜥmꜥ.w(t) m ḏd pw mitt wn.in=tw ḥr*
(IV, 8) *s3ḳ ḫt pn ḥnꜥ rdit r mw ir irw ir.tw m Ḥtp.t m ḥb 3bd* 1 *šmw ḫft ḥb ḏrt wnn ḏb3* 4 *nt Ḥr-3ḫ.tj ḫpr=śn m*
(IV, 9) *mś.w Bdšw wnn=śn ḥr ii r=ś m bw wꜥ ḫft ḫpr=śn m mś.w Bdšw iw ḏrt nṯr tn ḫpr.ti m s.t nfr.t ꜥn m ḏg3*
(IV, 10) *iw ir=tw n3 i3w.w m Ḥtp.t ḫr-ś.t-ḥr n ḏb3* 4 *pn iw ir.tw n=śn ḥb ḏrt wḫr.tw m ḥts ḥb iw sb=tw trtw m ꜥrḳ=*
(IV, 11) *śn dmt=śn ḏr ḳnw=śn iw ḥś.tw n Nbt.t m ꜥmꜥw m ḏrt.wj ḏrt nṯr pw Nbt.t ḏd.tw ṯꜥi m rn n Nbt.t*
(V, 1) *tn ḏrt nṯr n Ḥr-3ḫ.tj wnn ḏbꜥ* 4 *śḫpr m* (?) [/////] [*m*]*ś.w bdšw k3=tw r=śn m3wt rꜥ-nb* [//////] *ḳm3.n=f*

[453] See e.g.: CT Sp. 80, II, 33b–h; Sp. 714, IV, 344b–g; Sp.1130: VII, 465a; stelae Berlin 7313 and Cairo J.E. 28569: The *Book of Gates*, 4th hour, middle register, pBremner-Rhind 27, 2–3, etc.
[454] LGG III: 422.
[455] Griffith 1890: pl. 24.
[456] Meeks 2006: 10–12 (§ 10).

(V, 2) *iś m mś.w Bdšw pri=śn im=f k3[y ḫp]r=śn m sḫtw śnḥmy wn.y(n)=śn ir.w r-gs* [/////] *ś.t=śn*
(V, 3) *r-gs rsw ḏrt=śn ḥb.tw n=śn m 3bd* 1 *šmw ḏd[.tw i3]w ḥr ḥr=śn ḫwi.tw r nṯr* 4 *ḏd* 4 *ḏbʿ* 4 *ḫwi* [////] *wʿt ḏd*
(V, 4) *ʿnt n Nbt.t tn ḏrt n nb t3 ḏri iw=ś im r-mn hrw pn*

'(IV, 4) The 1st month of the *šmw* season. Golden divine hand of Re comes into being, pregnant (IV, 5) with Shu and Tefnut. They appeared**(B)** in this month. The fingers of this god turned for them into Children of *Bdšw* in the Fields of Grasshoppers, located to the south of (IV, 6) Hetepet**(C)**. They turned into snakes. (They) arranged the rebellions against their Lord in this month. The Elders assembled (?)[457] because of their fault**(D)** to visit their Lord in the Feast of Hand (IV, 7) during the Feast of Khonsu. The shape (of the Hand) is made in this Feast, and it is said: 'This hand squeezes the divine semen'. The Golden is honoured with the (wooden) sticks[458] and it is said: 'It is also the Hand'. Then**(E)** it is followed to (IV, 8) gather the amulet**(F)** and to place**(G)** it into the water.

As for the ceremony taking place in Hetepet during the celebration of the 1st month of the *šmw* season, during the Feast of Hand, there were four fingers of Re-Horakhty, and they turned into (IV, 9) Children of *Bdšw*. They confronted her all together, when they turned into Children of *Bdšw*. This divine Hand turned into a beautiful woman. (IV, 10) The Elders instituted**(H)** the control for Hetepet over these four fingers. The Feast of the Hand is established for them and they are taken care of[459] during the entire ceremony. The willow is brought**(I)** when they put an end[460] to (IV, 11) their slaughter**(J)**, the limit of their torment (?)**(K)**. The Golden is praises with applauses. This is the divine Hand, the Golden. It is called 'man' in the name of this 'Golden', (V, 1) the divine hand of Horakhty.

Four fingers turned into the [serpents]**(L)** Children of *Bdšw*, as they are called**(M)**. Re, the Lord [/////], planned this.[461] He created (V, 2) them as Children of *Bdšw*. They originated from him. He planned this (so) that they appeared in the Fields of Grasshoppers. All together they appeared near the [Hetepet]**(N)**, their place (V, 3) to the south of her hand. They are honoured during the first month of *šmw* season. They are call[ed 'the Eld]ers'. The four gods, named 'Four fingers' are defeated. One is protected [////] who is named (V, 4) the 'Thumb of the Golden' – hand of the Lord of the whole land. It exists even today' (pBrooklyn 47.218.84, § 10 (IV, 5 – V, 4).

[457] See: Meeks 2006: 68, fn. 119.
[458] See: Wb. I: 167.18; 186.2.
[459] See: Wb. I: 355.7–9.
[460] See: Wb. I: 211–212.
[461] For translation see: Meeks 2006: 71, fn. 141.

Comments

(A) The form  is given; the similar graphics for *ḫpr* or *ḫpi* is known starting from the Middle Kingdom (CT II, 334c; IV 184b (B1Y)).[462]
(B) I.e. 'were born'.[463]
(C) The mythological region of Hetepet was located in the north of Heliopolis.[464] In BD 125B the 'Fields of Grasshoppers' are situated to the north of Heliopolis: *ḥtp. n=i m niw.t mḥty.t m sḫtw snḥm.w* – 'I found rest in the northern city, in the Fields of Grasshoppers',[465] whereas in our text they are located to the south of Hetepet. But in pBrooklyn 47.218.84 they are placed to the south of Hetepet.[466] Thus, in the sacred topography of the Heliopolis environs, the Fields of Grasshoppers could be located between Hetepet and the central part of the city.
(D) Substantive from *ḳn* 'guilt, harm, damage'.[467]
(E) Pseudoverbal construction *iw.in=f* is used.[468]
(F) Lit. 'thing'.
(G) The *infinitive* + *ḥnʿ rdi.t* construction.[469]
(H) Lit. 'made'.
(I) Temple (sanctuary) of *Nb.t-Ḥtp.t* ('Mistress Hetepet') in Heliopolis is mentioned on the label Turin 2682 (Late Period) with a list of inventory and plan of the temple in Heliopolis.[470] Documented here is the 'Chapel of the willow establishing',[471] which confirms the existence of a religious festival at Heliopolis, the same as described in the text of Brooklyn papyrus.
(J) D. Meeks translates *dmt* as 'combat',[472] but it may be the derivative noun form *dmt* 'knife', i.e. 'slaughter'.
(K) The verb *ḳn* is not mentioned in the 'Berlin Wörterbuch'. D. Meeks translates 'souffrent',[473] contextually correlating it with the preceding derivative form of 'combat', which originated from *dm(.t)* – 'cut, wound'.[474]
(L) D. Meeks offered to restore in the lacuna *ḥfꜣw* – 'serpents'.[475]
(M) D. Meeks translates 'on les appelle les Enfants de l'Impuissance'.[476]

462 Meeks 2006: 68, fn. 117.
463 See: Meeks 2006: 67, fn. 113.
464 For more information see: Vandier 1964: 55–146 (especially 61–65); 1965: 89–176. Concerning the mythological localization of the 'Fields of Grasshoppers' (*sḫtw snḥmy*) see: Meeks 2006: 67–68, fn. 116.
465 Lapp 2008: 198–201.
466 See also: Vandier 1964: 62–63.
467 Wb. V: 48.
468 Gardiner 1958: 390, § 470.
469 See: Gardiner 1958: 130, § 171, 3.
470 Ricke 1935: 111–133.
471 Ricke 1935: 120–122; Meeks 2006: 70, fn. 135;72, fn. 145;206.
472 Meeks 2006: 11.
473 Meeks 2006: 11.
474 See: Wb.V: 451.4–5; Meeks 2006: 71, fn. 137.
475 Meeks 2006: 71, fn. 140.
476 Meeks 2006: 11.

(N) The restoration of lacuna by D. Meeks.[477]

The narration set out here, unfortunately, does not detect direct parallels with the data of BD 17 and BD 175A, though it makes it clear that *mś.w Bdšt* rebelled against the creator-god. Probably the text displays another local Heliopolitan version of the myth, which will be considered in detail further down.

However, interesting is the information that *mś.w Bdšt* were born out of the fingers of the Demiurge, identified with the goddess with name/epithet *Nbt.t* (= *Nbw.t*) – 'Golden'[478] and interrelated with the region *Ḥtp.t*.[479] It should be said that the title *Nb.t-Ḥtp.t* (in pBremner-Rhind, 19, 22)[480] belonged to the Heliopolitan incarnation of the goddess Hathor,[481] according to a detailed study of Chr. Leitz, before the publication of the Brooklyn papyrus.[482] Hathor, as well as Nut, was closely associated with the concept of celestial domain.

The connection between *mś.w Bdšt* and the fingers of the creator-god (?) is indicated, as noted above, by the Middle Kingdom pRamesseum XV recto I, 5, testifying the ancient nature of the myths. Thus, D. Meeks doubts the parallelism of these sources.[483] Although fragments of the myths in these documents differ significantly from the BD 17 and BD 175 plot, but they could complement a number of details to the interpretation of their content.

Close to BD 17 and BD 175A plots is also the text of the so-called 'Myth of destruction of mankind' in the ***Book of Heavenly Cow***, known from records in four New Kingdom royal tombs: Seti I, Ramses II, Ramses III, and Ramses VI (short versions also appear in pTurin 1982:[484] and on the first shrine of Tutankhamun (Cairo J.E. 60664).[485] Comparison of the data from these sources allows, as indicated by H. Grapow[486] to assume the similarity of their mythems, which has been repeatedly highlighted by specialists.[487]

477 Meeks 2006: 12, 72, fn. 144.
478 LGG IV: 180–182.
479 Meeks 2006: 10, IV, 6; 11, IV, 6.
480 Faulkner 1933: 38.
481 Vandier 1964; 1965; LGG IV: 111–112.
482 Leitz 1994: 100, fn. 41.
483 'L'état très fragmentaire du texte ne permet de saisir que quelques bribes, mais celles-ci sont suffisantes pour comprendre que les faits relatés devaient être assez proches de ceux rapportés par notre papyrus. Un dieu dont le nom est perdu, de toute évidence le dieu créateur, parle à la première personne de ses doigts et des Enfants de l'Impuissance, de sa main et de ses doigts, de sa copulation et d'un combat mené contre Apopis' (Meeks 2006: 200).
484 Hornung 1999: 148.
485 Maystre 1941: 53–115; Hornung 1982 (review of the sources: 33–36).
486 Grapow 1931: 36, Anm. 1.
487 Hornung 1979: 517; 1982: 90–95; Ockinga 1988: 518; Stadler 2009: 375–380.

In general, the central leitmotif of the myth in the *Book of the Heavenly Cow*, as well as BD 17 and BD 175A, is conspiracy (lit.: *k3t md.wt* – 'evil deeds') of mankind against creator-god. Already the first sentence brings us back to a mythical time when Re reigned over gods and men (**Appendix 1. Text No. 11**):

ḫpr [s]w[t w]bn Rꜥ nṯr ḫpr ḏs=f m-ḫt wnn=f m niśwtj rmṯ.w ntr.w m ḫt wꜥti(.t) wn in rmṯ.w ḥr k3t md.wt r ḫftiw ḫw Rꜥ(w) iśtw r=f ḥm=f ꜥnḫ wḏ3 śnb i3ww ḳs.w=f m ḥd ḥꜥ.w=f m nbw šnnw=f m ḫsbḏ m3ꜥ.t wn.in ḥm=f ḥr śi3 mdwt nt k3t [r=f] in rmṯ.w

'It happened (that) Re[488] shines, the god who create himself, after he has reigned[489] over the people and the gods together.[490] And people planned to do evil things against Re,[491] when His Majesty, alive, safe and healthy, aged; his bones turned to silver, his parts of body – to gold, and his hair – to true lapis lazuli.[492] And His Majesty revealed the evil deeds against him planned by the people' (*Book of the Heavenly Cow*, 1–2, after the text in the tomb of Seti I (KV 17)).[493]

Structurally the text of the *Book of the Heavenly Cow* can be divided into four semantic parts:

1. *Destruction of mankind* ('Vernichtung des Menschengeschlechts').
    a. Revolt. People organize a rebellion against the aged Lord. Re consults the gods of the Ennead and Nun, and decides to destroy mankind.
    b. Punishment. Re sends his divine Eye, the goddess Hathor (in the image of the lioness-goddess Sekhmet) against the rebels in the desert, she quells the rebellion. Some people managed to escape to the south.
    c. Conciliation. Re decides to return Hathor and to forgive the survivors. His messengers make beer and colour it in red, which Hathor takes for blood, drinks it and gets drunk, therefore the survivors were rescued.
2. *Creation of the Sky* ('Einrichtung des Himmels').
    d. Consequences of rebellion. Due to these events, the 'time of sickness' comes, making Re leave this place and arise to the sky.

[488] Reading of lacuna as *wbn* is given after: Hornung 1982: 51, Anm. 1. M. Panov suggests the following version: *ḫpr [s]wt [wn.in] Rꜥ nṯr ḫpr ḏs=f* – 'It happened that Re existed, the god who created himself ...' (personal communication). But the meaning of *wbn* as 'to shine' is likely to correspond to etiological meaning of the text setting forth the myth of Re ascension into heaven.
[489] Lit. 'he acted as a king'.
[490] Lit: 'over the people and the gods taken together'.
[491] For translation see: Hornung 1982: 51, Anm. 4.
[492] Way of *M3ꜥ.t* writing is determined by the sign (Hornung 1982: 1), giving a possibility to read it as 'lapis lazuli of (goddess) Maat'.
[493] Maystre 1941: 58–59; Hornung 1982: 1.

   e. Creation of the Sky, its topography, inhabitants and support (Shu and Heh).
3. *Creation of the Netherworld* ('Einrichtung der Unterwelt').
   f. Protection against serpents and magic.
   g. Appointment of Thoth to the position of night assistant of Re in Heaven, i.e. the moon.
   h. The rubric to the text of the magical spell.
4. *The power of magic* ('Macht durch Zauber').
   i. Completion of the sky creation. Re and Nun ('*bꜣ*-Theologie'), magician and magic protection.
   j. Conclusion. Signs and instructions for the magician ('Apotheose des Zauberers').[494]

Thus, despite the victory over the rebels, Re encounters a certain weakness and sees the danger coming from the mankind (*ḥꜥ.w=i ꜣhdw m sp tpi nn jjj=i r pḥ.t wi kyy* – 'Parts of my body have weakened for the first time, I will not return to be defeated by others' (col. 29).[495] It is time for *tr pw in mr* – 'time of sickness / torment' that has something in common with the term *rk n mn* – 'time of illness' (103)[496] in the 'Teaching for Merikare' (*ḏd.tw=k hḏ rk n mn* – 'Let it be said about you (Merikare): 'who destroyed the time of illness''(*Merikare*, 142)), which acquires a cosmological shade in this light. The 'Teaching for Merikare' resembles the plot of the *Book of the Heavenly Cow* and BD 175A due to the passage mentioning the deeds of the creator-god: *śmꜣ.n=f ḫftiw=f ḥḏ.n=f mśw=f ḥr kt=sn m irt śbi* – 'He killed his enemies, he destroyed his children, because they have planned a rebellion' (*Merikare,* 133–134, according to the list 'M' (pMoscow 4658) and 'C' (pCarlsberg VI).[497]

In the *Book of the Heavenly Cow* the result of the people's rebellion is separation of divine (heavenly) and human (earth) worlds and creation of the Netherworld – the *Duat*. Creation of the Netherworld is caused by emergence of death in the world and thus a need to create a habitat of the dead. The opinion of L. Kákosy, recently approved by J. Assmann,[498] that death came into the world only with the death of Osiris[499] is not indisputable, since Osiris was *the first god to resuscitate,* to overcome death, and to show mortals the way to a life beyond the grave (here is his main essence), but the *death* itself up to this moment was already existing

[494] Hornung 1982: 75–79; 1999: 149–151.
[495] Maystre 1941: 76–77; Hornung 1982: 11.
[496] Wb. II: 67.17.
[497] See: Демидчик 2005: 226, прим. 242.
[498] 'Osiris' reign came to a violent end, for he was slain by his brother, Seth. Thus did death come into the world, confronting the gods with a great problem' (Assmann 2005: 24).
[499] Kákosy 1964: 212–214, 216.

– the rebels faced it in the *Book of the Heavenly Cow*, as well as *mś.w Bdšt* in the BD 17 mytheme and *mś.w Nw.t* in BD 175A.[500]

As shown by E. Hornung, creation of Netherworld had a deeper meaning due to separation of divine and human worlds – the death becomes a means to regain their initial merge.[501] However, it is impossible to provide details of this significant mythological event on the basis of the available data from Egyptian texts. Obviously, the myths associated with the emergence of death in the world, as well as the story about the death of Osiris, conceptually related to this phenomenon,[502] were considered to be a kind of taboo, preserved in oral tradition, and not recorded in writing. As noted by J. Assmann: 'This is a prehistory having no associated narration in the Egyptian texts',[503] V. Tobin, however, believes that the absence of a specific description of the death of Osiris is due to its 'solemnity' and 'awesomeness'.[504] It was natural that there were no images of death of Osiris[505] and, on the contrary, a considerable number of pictures display his resurrection.[506]

The first mention of Osiris's death mythem appears in the *Pyramid Texts.*[507] It is characteristic that the very name of the god was not usually mentioned directly,[508] simply using hints or metaphors, for example, *wr pw* – 'the great one',[509] etc. The very fact of Osiris's death (related with Seth)[510] is mainly expressed by verbs *ḫr* and *ndi* (and, apparently, between *ndi* and *Ndi.t*, the place of god's death)[511] and one can trace the homonymous play on words (e.g. *ḫr rf ty pw ḫr gś=f* ***ndi*** *rf imj* ***Ndi.t***).[512]

Theoretically the considered texts of the *Book of the Heavenly Cow*, BD 17 and BD 175A might be called an Egyptian *analogue* of the 'myth of the Fall', although, it is certainly far from the essence of the biblical tradition because of the lack of ethic nature. The majority of Egyptologists, who refer to the myth of the *Book of the Heavenly Cow*, diligently tended to abandon any parallels with the biblical tradition. Thus J. Assmann defines this myth with a term 'divided world' (*gespalten Welt*) (and believes it to be the main meaning[513] specially to

500 Cf. also the late replica of this myth in the Demotic pCarlsberg 462 (Smith 2000: 95–112).
501 Hornung 1982: 76–78.
502 Cf. Griffiths. 1960: 5; Assmann 1977: 41; Baines 1990: 16–17; 1991: 103; 1996: 369–370, 375–376.
503 Assmann 2005: 24.
504 Tobin 1993: 103, fn. 40.
505 Brandon 1961: 320.
506 See.: Тураев 1914: 415–422; Vassilieva 2010: 68–96.
507 See summary: Tobin 1993: 102–103; for the later texts see: Griffiths 1960.
508 Tobin 1993: 103.
509 Pyr. §§ 721a-b, 819a.
510 Pyr. §§ 972b-c, 1033b, 1256b, 1500a-b.
511 *Ndi.t* may originate from the verb *ndi* – 'niderwerhen' (Wb. II: 367), 'to fell' (Tobin 1993: 103).
512 Pyr. § 819a.
513 Assmann 2001: 215–216; cf. Assmann 2002a: 189–193.

avoid this analogy.[514] However, in recent years there are some scholars who recognize plot similarities between Egyptian and Old Testament myths on the appearance of Evil in this world. P. Frandsen, for example, notes: 'the Egyptians really distinguished good and evil in somewhat similar way to what we find in the Bible. Biblical analogy can be considered good both from the eschatological and soteriological points of view. This however does not mean that complete comparison is appropriate. Rescue and the means to achieve it significantly differed in Egypt and in Bible'.[515] E. Hornung considers acceptable to use biblical term 'Fall' in relation to the mytheme of the *Book of the Heavenly Cow,*[516] although he thinks that BD 17 does not correlate with it, specifying only the plot with the 'Children of Nut' in BD 175^{A},[517] which he understands as the epithet of rebellious mankind.[518]

In my understanding, the narration of the *Book of the Heavenly Cow* and parallel sources is a Thanatological myth of the origin of evil, death and 'sin' of the collapse of the *Golden Age,*[519] and the separation of the world of men and gods (i.e. the cosmogonic formation of celestial and terrestrial worlds, as well as the Netherworld) – is the final part of the myth of Creation.[520] It should be stressed that this myth has been preserved in Egyptian religious concepts for a very long time, originating in Middle Kingdom and enduring until Roman Period. Therefore, references to *mś.w Bdšt* rebellion are quiet numerous in Late Period, and the religious festival, with a ritual reproduction of this rebellion was celebrated in Heliopolis during the 30th Dynasty (pBrooklyn 47.218.84, § 10).[521] The myth set forth in the New Egyptian *Book of the Heavenly Cow* was reflected in the so-called '*Book of the Fayum*' of the Roman Period.[522] The 'Children of Nut' rebellion mythem, best known from the BD 175A, as proved by L. Kákosy, is reproduced in the Hermetic treatise 'Κόρη Κόσμου', which mentions a rebellion against the creator-god and that before suppressing it, the god consults Hermes (i.e. Thot).[523]

Thus, we have some reasons to believe that the BD 17 plots with *mś.w Bdšt* describe the mythical Combat with rebels, which resulted in the ascension of Re to heaven and completion of the Cosmogony process according to the *Book of the Heavenly Cow*.

514 Frandsen 2000: 10; cf. Goedicke 1998: 43.
515 Frandsen 2000: 12; cf. also: Morenz 2004: 205.
516 'Was dann ausführlich beschrieben wird, sind der 'Sündenfall' und seine Folgen' (Hornung 1982: 76).
517 Hornung 1982: 90–95.
518 Hornung 1979: 517.
519 Kákosy 1964: 205–216; Assmann 2002a: 386–388.
520 Hornung 1982: 74–78.
521 Meeks 2006: 10–12.
522 Beinlich 1991; Hornung 1999: 148.
523 Kákosy 1988: 258–261.

1. The Combat takes place in 'the eastern sky' – the place of sunrise. In Egyptian notions, as known, the eastern sky was considered to be a very dangerous place, since here was held the punishment of sinners, rebels and enemies of the sun (including Apophis) and a variety of places for these purposes were situated – 'trials', 'slaughters', 'prisons', etc.[524]
2. The text of the spell mentioned 'split' of the *išd*-tree, and as already noted, this displayed 'separation' of two trees on the eastern horizon (*ꜣḫ.t*), between which the sun rises.[525]
3. BD 17 contains a gloss, mentioning an *imj.t-pr* – lit. 'the content of the house', lit. 'will', 'heritage', 'property', etc..[526] The *imj.t-pr* could be understood as a special document certifying the right of the king to own land in Egypt. F. Friedman considers Old Kingdom origin under the rule of Djoser (3rd Dynasty).[527] Thus, in *imj.t-pr* in BD 17, may be an indication of hereditary kingship passed by Shu to Geb and Osiris, or about *imj.t-pr* of Geb passed by Shu to Osiris – *Šw pw ḥr irt imj.t-pr n Gb n Wsir*.[528] According to U. Rößler-Köhler, the name of Geb is written here incorrectly and should be read not as *Gb*, but as *sꜣ*,[529] i.e. in this plot he suggests transmission of *imj.t-pr* by the god Shu to Horus, 'the son of Osiris' (*Sꜣ Wsir*), without any participation of Geb.[530] However, the Horus accession (to the throne) plot is precisely described further down in the chapter,[531] therefore U. Rößler-Köhler's interpretation is questionable. The analogy with the *Book of the Heavenly Cow* shows that the gloss can voice a Cosmogonic notion of Shu, as the holder of the sky (when Re put the heavenly cow on his back, Shu supported her belly and ever since he has been 'assigned' as a 'support' of the sky). There is no doubt that the *first* sunrise (ascension of Re) and formation of the sky is meant in the *Book of the Heavenly Cow* and in BD 17. Correspondingly Shu acquires his cosmological role of the sky holder for the *first time*, and the necessity to transfer his *imj.t-pr* ('terrestrial heritage' = royal title) to the posterior representatives of the 'divine dynasty' on earth.[532]

Since the Old Kingdom Egyptians had imagined that initially the world was governed by the divine dynasty,[533] which was replaced by the legitimate dynasty

[524] Kees 1956: 59ff, 212.
[525] Bonnet 1952: 83; Helck 1958: 117; Gamer-Wallert 1975: Kol. 656; Kees 1977: 84–89; Rößler-Köhler 1979; 224, Anm. 1; Hermsen 1981: 88–95; Germer 1986: Kol. 113–119.
[526] Wb. I: 73; Gardiner 1958: 553; Logan 2000: 49–73. R. Hannig gives eight meanings (Hannig 1995: 49).
[527] Friedman 1996: 341.
[528] Cf. Allen 1960: 90 (15, 14–15); Piankoff 1962: 56; Barguet 1967: 61; Hornung 1979: 69; Verhoeven 1993 I: 102 (10,8–10,9); Faulkner 2001: 48; Quirke 2013: 59.
[529] Rößler-Köhler 1979: 189, 97*.
[530] Rößler-Köhler 1979: 224.
[531] Urk. V: Abs. 28–29, 82–84; Rößler-Köhler 1979: 164, 229; Lapp 2006: 266–275.
[532] Cf. Hornung 1982: 88–90.
[533] See: Helck 1956: 1–8; Gardiner 1959: pl. 1.

of pharaohs identified with Horus, successor of Osiris and the last god-king.[534] This is clearly reflected in the 'Teaching of Ptahhotep':[535] $_{(88)}$ *wr mꜣꜥ.t wꜣḥ śpd.t* $_{(89)}$ *n ẖnn.t(w)=ś ḏr rk Wśir* $_{(90)}$ *iw ḫsf=tw n swꜣ ḥr hpw* – '$_{(88)}$ The great is Justice (*mꜣꜥ.t*) (and) (its) continuous efficiency. $_{(89)}$ It has not been violated since the time of Osiris. $_{(90)}$ (Because) the one who violated the law shall be punished' (p*Prisse* 6, 5).[536] One can correlate the meaning of this fragment with the plot of the myth about the murder and resurrection of Osiris, but I believe that 'the time of Osiris' should be interpreted as reference to the period of the god's terrestrial reign.[537] This may be confirmed by the term used to identify 'time' in the 'Teaching':  *rk*, associated with the time of the reign, ruling etc.[538]

The 'divine' dynasty (as well as some semi-divine dynasty of 'spirits' and 'followers of Horus') was included in the annals of the Palermo stone.[539] It is significant that the *Book of the Heavenly Cow* expressly represented Re as a monarch, that presumably explains the particular importance of this text for earthly rulers, the 'sons of Re' (*śꜣ Rꜥ*).[540] Re is titled as *ḥmw=f* () and *nsw-bit*,[541] his name is enclosed in the cartouche,[542] and followed by *ꜥnḫ wḏꜣ śnb* formulae.[543] Given the analogy with the *Book of the Heavenly Cow* the considered New Kingdom's glosses of the BD 17 concerning the *imj.t-pr* inheritance may indicate the same idea.

534 See: Bolshakov 1999: 312–332.
535 Luft 1977a: 47–78.
536 Prisse d'Avennes 1926: pl. VI.
537 Cf. Junge 2003: 82–101.
538 Wb. II: 457; Luft 1977a: 75; Baines 1989: 135;. Faulkner 1999: 153; Hannig 1995: 479.
539 Gardiner 1959: pl. 1; Schott 1952: 70, Anm. 2; Baines 1989: 134.
540 Hornung 1999: 151. In tombs the content of this *Book* was reproduced in a special room adjacent to the burial chamber, where the sarcophagus was placed (Ibid: 148).
541 Hornung 1982: 1 (10), 7 (75).
542 Hornung 1982: 7 (75) 8 (83).
543 Hornung 1982: 1 (10, S I).

Chapter 5

Mś.w Bdšt in the *Book of Gates*

Another significant mention of *mś.w Bdšt* is given in the upper register of the 11th hour of the *Book of Gates.*[544] Here represented is its only extant picture (scene No. 69) (***Figure 52,***[545] ***53).***[546]

This composition depicts the large fist of the deity *ỉmnw-ḫ3.wt* – 'Those-who-hides-corpses', rising above the earth and clasping the rope (according to the text it is *ỉḥ nik.w* – 'the punishing rope'). On the left the rope controls the throat of Apophis and to the right – it extends over four serpents. In the tomb of Ramses VI (KV 9) they are painted in blue. On the extreme right the picture displays the head of the fifth serpent emerging from the earth. Scholars ignore this fact, but in the context of the above mentioned data from pBrooklyn 47.218.84, reporting that *mś.w Bdšt* came from the right hand fingers of creator-god (or goddess Hathor), presence of the fifth serpent is naturally explicable.

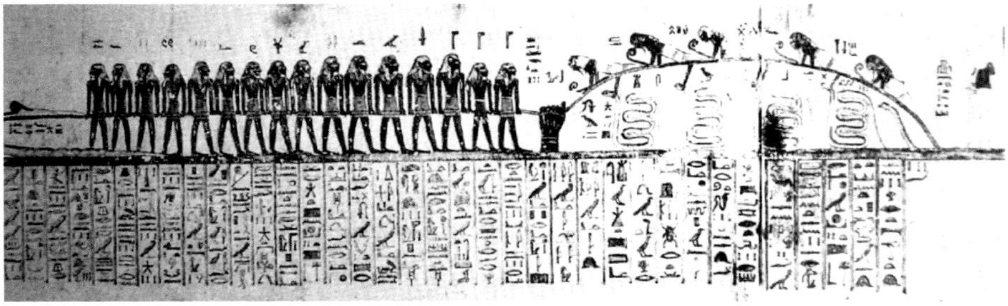

FIGURE 52

FIGURE 53

The picture shows that the main rope is connected to the serpents with four separate yellow ropes-fetters, tying together their necks. Shown above are five deities labeled as Geb and the Children of Horus, holding in their hands the other

[544] Piankoff 1954 I: 75–81; Zandee 1960: 127, 294–295; 1969: 318; Hornung 1979–1980 I: 356–360; II: 246–247; Zeidler 1999: 306–313; Wiebach-Koepke 2003 II: 334–337.

[545] Piankoff 1954 II: pl. 58–59.

[546] Hornung 1979–1980 II: 247; 1999: 75, Figure 39.

end of the ropes which binds the serpents. There is a postscript *Wꜣmmtj* next to the first serpent and *mś.w Bdšt* above the other three.[547]

The composition is complemented by a text under *Ỉmnw-ẖꜣ.wt*'s fist and sixteen gods, holding the rope, *Wꜣmmtj* and *mś.w Bdšt* (*Book of Gates* (KV 9, Ramses VI), 11th hour, upper register, scene 69, col. 25–51):[548]

40	*wnn=sn m sḫr pn*	'They exist in that form,
41	*m sꜣw.t nt mś.w Bdšt*	As the guard of Children of *Bdšt*.
42	*sꜣw=sn m ỉḥ nik.w*	They guard the punishing rope,
43	*ỉmi ḏr.t Ỉmnw-ẖꜣ.wt*	In the hand of 'Those-who-hides-corpses'.
44	*(r)dd.tw m(w)t.w m šmtw.t=f*	The deceased(E) are placed around him
45	*r sbḫ.wt Ḫntj-imntjw*	next to the Khentiamentiu gates.
46	*ỉn*(A) *nn (n) nṯr.w*	These gods say:
47	*kk.w n ḥr=k Wꜣmmtj*	– Darkness on your face, *Wꜣmmtj*!
48	*ḥtm n=ṯn mś.w Bdšt*	– Destruction to you, Children of *Bdšt*
49	*m*(B) *ḏr.t imn.t (r)di=s ḏw.t=ṯn*	In the Hiding Hand! It returns back your evil
50	*m ỉśh nik.w ỉm=f*	In the rope of punishment(F),
51	*Gb sꜣw=f ntt.w=ṯn*	Geb guards your shackles.
52	*mś.w ḳꜣs.w (r)di=sn ṯn (n) ỉḥ(k)w*	Children of Fetters(G), they give you to decrepitude (/weakness) (?)(H)
53	*sꜣw=ṯn m [śip (n) Ḫntj-]*(C) *imntj.w*	They are guarded under [the order of Khentiamentiu](I)!
54	*[wnn=śn]*(C) *m śḫr [pn*	[They exist] in [that] form,
55	*wdn]*(C)*=sn ḳꜣś.w*(D) *mś.w Bdšt*	They [puts] fetters on the Children of *Bdšt*.
56	*ỉw wiꜣ nṯr ꜥꜣ šꜣ(t)=f r h(ꜣ).w pn n ꜥꜣpp*	The boat of the Great God, it travels(J) across this outskirts of Apophis.
57	*nꜥꜥ=f m-ḫt wdi.t nt(n)ṯ.wj=śn*	It is going (forward) after he has put their fetters'.

[547] Hornung 1979–1980 II: 248–249 (24–29).
[548] Piankoff 1954 I: 75–81; Hornung 1979–1980 I: 358–360; 2005: 174–175; Carrier 2009: 259–260.

Comments

(A) In the tomb of Ramses VI the signs *i* and *n* are mixed, in the tomb of Seti I and 'Osireion' it is given correctly as *in*.[549]

(B) In the text of Seti I it is incorrectly written out 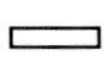 instead of , in the 'Osireion' it falls in a lacuna.

(C) In the tomb of Ramses VI the part of the text is destroyed, the restoration of lacunae is given according to the text in the tomb of Seti I.

(D) The word *ḳꜣś.w* 'fetters' in the tomb of Ramses VI is incorrectly written as 𓏏 *t* instead of 𓈎 *ḳ*. In the tomb of Seti I *ḳ* is written correctly, but instead of the sign for 'kite' 𓄿 (G1, phonet. *ꜣ*) is written the sign 𓅱 (G43, phonet. *w*).

(E) In Cl. Carrier's translation: 'C'est à la périphérie que l'on place les morts (?) vers lesportes qui sont devant l'Occident'.[550] E. Hornung gives the following translation "Mit verborgenem Liechman' ist Stricke warden um ihn berumgewunden beim Tor des Chontamenti'[551] / 'Ropes are wound around him at the Gate of Khentamenti',[552] believing that *m(w)t.w* should be understood as 'Stricke'.[553]

(F) Lit. 'The punishment is in the rope'.

(G) I.e. the Children of Horus.

(H) J. Zandee believes the word *ḏw.t* 'evil' is missing in the text and should be read as *rdi=śn ḏw.t=ṯn* – 'the fetters cause your evil'.[554]

(I) The text does not give a clear translation. J. Zandee translates: 'Take heed of the verdict of the First of Westerns';[555] E. Hornung: 'Hütet euch vor Verdammung (durch) Chontamenti'[556] / 'Beware of the sentence of damnation by Khentamenti!';[557] J. Zeidler: 'Möget ihr euch vor der Revision Chontamentis hüten!';[558] S. Wiebach-Koepke: 'Möget ihr euch vor der Prüfung des

549 Hornung 1979–1980 I: 359.
550 Carrier 2009: 260.
551 Hornung 1979–1980 II: 248–249.
552 Hornung 2005: 173.
553 Hornung 1979–1980 II: 250, Anm. 17.
554 Zandee 1969: 318; cf.: Hornung 1979–1980 II: 249 (36); 250, Anm. 21; 2005: 173; Wiebach-Koepke 2003 II: 337 (2242) ('Schwahen'); Zeidler 1999: 313, Anm. 4 ('Altersschwäche'); Carrier 2009: 260 ('(puisqu')ils vous ont donné la faiblesse').
555 Zandee 1969: 318.
556 Hornung 1979–1980 II: 249 (37); 250, Anm. 22.
557 Hornung 2005: 173.
558 Zeidler 1999: 313 (53).

Chontamenti';[559] Cl. Carrier: 'Gardez-vous de [la condamnation de Celui qui est à la tête de][560] l'Occident!'.[561]

(J) J. Zandee, however, understands that the boat of Re here runs aground, and continues to move after the fetters are imposed on Children of *Bdšt*: 'The boat of the great god runs aground in this neighbourds of Apophis, but it sails after they have been fettered'.[562]

FIGURE 54

Commenting on the scene, J. Zandee (with the reference to the old number as 10th hour)[563] and E. Hornung, literally understand that *W3mmtj* and three *mś.w Bdšt* are depicted in the form of serpents.[564] But the scene may have another explanation. In 1965: H. Altenmüller in his thesis suggested that the first fragment of BD 17 (version I) can depict an ancient form of Hermopolitan Cosmogony[565] (pre-existing before the Ogdoad's four pairs of deities of Primeval Chaos).[566] The Hermopolitan myth of Creation points out several phases: emergence of the Primeval Hill on the place of the city, emergence of Lotus on this Hill and the birth of a sun god-child – the creator of the world, people and gods, finishing the Cosmogony.[567]

559 Wiebach-Koepke 2003 II: 337 (2243).
560 Addition from the text in the tomb of Seti I.
561 Carrier 2009: 260.
562 Zandee 1969: 318; cf.: Carrier 2009: 260.
563 Zandee 1960: 127, fn. 2;295, fn. 1.
564 Hornung 1979–1980 II: 247; Zandee 1960: 127, 294–295.
565 Altenmüller 1965 I: 101–103.
566 Leitz 1994: 70, Anm. 18.
567 For Egyptian Cosmogony see.: Sethe 1929; Allen 1988; Bickel 1994.

Illustration to the Hermopolitan myth of Creation appears also on the coffin of *Mn-ḫprw-Rʿ* Cairo J.E. 29628; CG 6271 (21st Dynasty),[568] where in the middle of *Ouroboros* there is a 'hare' sign on the standard – the symbol of the goddess Unut (*Wnw.t*) and 15th Upper Egyptian (the so-called 'Hare') Nome (***Figure 54***).[569] Here we can see a graphical display of the Egyptian Cosmogenesis important feature, according to which the large Nome centers (their temples) claimed to be the region where the first rise of the Terrestrial Hill from the Primeval Ocean, perceived as the center of the world, occurred *in illo tempore*. Here the role of *Ouroboros* is related to the spatial perception of the world – in the mythological model of the Cosmos *Ouroboros*[570] serves as proven border of the created world (property of Re) in the endless waters of the Primeval Chaos of Nun, beyond which is Nothingness.[571] Thus, placing the Nome sign in the middle of the serpent surrounding the Universe may indicate that this region is the place where the act of Creation took place, the center of the Cosmos – its *axis mundi*.

A. Niwiński, one of the first scientist to focus on this picture, shows a direct relationship between graphic 'programs' of the sarcophagus design, with the body of the deceased (mummy) being the 'central axis' for placing the scenes aimed at the revival of the deceased Egyptian.[572] The scene with the *Ouroboros* (***Figure 54***) was placed in front of the feet of the mummy, i.e. in other words, the person put in vertical position is as if he was placed in the Center of the Universe.[573] It magically brought him back to the Act of Creation – to the primeval source of life.

According to H. Altenmüller, the battle described in BD 17 with the forces of Chaos, personified in *mś.w Bdšt,* takes place immediately after the birth of the Sun god-child from the Lotus, when creation was not yet over, and they had good (and unique) chance to prevent its completion while the divine child was not yet strong. H. Altenmüller points out a connection between this plot and the message of later texts[574] about the combat of young Re, who emerged from the Primeval Ocean, with four hostile gods or serpents in Hermopolis.[575] Similar conclusions, as it was noted, have been proposed by J.-C. Goyon and E. Jelinkova-Reymond, who paid special attention to the similarity of cosmogonies from Hermopolis and Edfu, where the second one seems to date back to an earlier prototype.

568 Niwiński 1988: 120 (89).
569 Niwiński 1989a: 56, Figure 3.
570 Egyptian *Mḥn(-tꜣ)* – 'Surrounding the Land' (Wb. II: 128.8–9; Altenmüller 1973: 82; Picione 1990: 43–52).
571 Hornung 1996: 161. For the ratio of the temporal and spatial elements in the image of *Ouroboros* see: Niwiński 1981: 41–53.
572 Niwiński 1989a: 53–66.
573 Niwiński 1989a: 58, Figure 5.
574 Altenmüller 1965 I: 103.
575 Jelinkova-Reymond 1956: 39.

FIGURE 55

Chr. Leitz developed and supplemented these ideas,[576] noting that in the picture of the *Book of Gates* the name *W3mmtj* is placed vertically, whereas *mś.w Bdšt* – horizontally, suggesting that *W3mmtj* here is not the name of the first snake, but rather a sign of the 'the leader' (*Anführer*) of all four serpents.[577] Thus, the four serpents, *mś.w Bdšt*, are here acting as manifestations of *W3mmtj*, who himself was identified as Apophis. Although *W3mmtj* was considered as one of the names or epithets of Apophis,[578] sometimes he could play an independent role, as in Medamud where he was placed among the four serpents hostile to Re: *Ḏw-ḳd, W3br, Hmhmti* and *W3m(m)t(y)*.[579]

Close parallels to this confrontation is shown on a fragment of p*Ḫnmw-m-ḥb* pLondon UC 32365 (Frag. 10) (19th Dynasty, Seti I) (***Figure 55***),[580] reporting

[576] Leitz 1987: 50; 1994: 99–101.
[577] Leitz 1994: 99.
[578] Wb. I: 251.15.
[579] Borghouts 1973: 118, fn. 4.
[580] Shorter 1937: pl. X; Quirke 2001: 60, Figure 23 (drawing).

on the destruction of four Apophis-snakes () by four gods of the solar circle.[581] It should be noted that there is a well-read signature on the fragment under consideration next to the figure of the scribe in the upper register of the picture: *Wśir Rꜥ-mś* – 'Osiris Rames'.[582]

In the quaternary image of Apophis in the p*Ḫnmw-m-ḥb* A. Shorter sees special forms of serpents, which opposed to Re in the most crucial phases of his daily motion – sunrise, noon, sunset and midnight,[583] which, however, is more a product of late, secondary Cosmogonic myths processing.[584]

There are numerous mentions of the combat with quaternary representation of evil. In p*Ns-Mnw* p*Bremner-Rhind* (pLondon BM EA 10188), the formula aimed against Apophis, enemies and rebels, with *mś.w Bdšt* among them, require quaternary repetition,[585] i.e. ⊚ |||| – *ḭfdw spw*: '(repeat) for four times':

(18) *ḭw Rꜥ mꜣꜥ-ḫrw=f*[(A)] *mꜣꜥ.t ḭrt n.w ꜥꜣpp mś.w Bdš wr.w Bdš mꜣꜥ-ḫrw Rꜥ r ḫftj.w=f ḭfdw spw*[(B)] […] (19) *ḭw śḫr.n=ḭ ꜥꜣpp śbḭ.w štyw Ḏw-ḳd mś.w Bdš m ś.t=ś n.w nb.t m bw nb.t ntj ḭw=śn ḭm*

(18) 'Re triumphs and (restore) justice over Apophis, Children of *Bdš* (and) *Bdš*-serpent[(C)]. Re triumphs over enemies – '(repeat) for four times […]. (19) I've overthrown Apophis, rebels, turtle, the Unhealthy (?)[(D)] (and) the Children of *Bdš* from each and every throne and place, wherever they have been' (p*Bremner-Rhind*, 25, 18–19).[586]

Comments

[(A)] Writing of *mꜣꜥ-ḫrw* in this context corresponds to 'triumphiren'.[587]

[(B)] Numerals were written after noun but usually pronounced before it.[588]

581 Shorter 1937: 36, pl. X.
582 St. Quirke labels this drawing as 'the scribe Ramose stands on the prow facing Osiris. Papyrus of Khnumemheb…' (Quirke 2001: 60, Figure 23). Fragments of p*Rꜥ-mś*, discovered in the 19th century along with p*Ḫnmw-m-ḥb* in Sedment are in the museum collection of the University of Cambridge (Cambridge, Fitzwilliam Museum E.2a.1922). Restoration of R. Velthem (2004–2005) and study of I. Munro (2005) demonstrate that part of the Cambridge fragments of p*Rꜥ-mś* may be the parts of London p*Ḫnmw-m-ḥb* and *vice versa* (personal communication of Dr. I. Munro), as well as in the case of this fragment. However, it is also possible that *Rꜥ-mś* was the son of *Ḫnmw-m-ḥb*, this would explain the presence of his image in the funeral scroll of his father.
583 Shorter 1937: 38.
584 Leitz 1994: 100, Anm. 36.
585 Faulkner 1933: 54 (25, 18–19); 1937: 171; cf. Parker, Leclant, Goyon 1979: 61–65; 62, fn. 9.
586 Faulkner 1933: 54–55.
587 Wb. II: 15.1 (II).
588 Allen 2014: 125 (9.4).

(C) R. Faulkner translates as ‘O, Apophis and Ye Children of Revolt, Ye Greatly Rebellious’,[589] however, a qualitative adjective, as definition in the sentence, written after the noun and agrees in gender and number.[590] In our case qualitative adjective-epithet *wr* – ‘great’ follows *mś.w Bdš* in plural form – *wr.w*, i.e. it may be associated with *mś.w Bdš*, rather than the name of serpent *Bdš* (singular) as R.Faulkner thought.

(D) R. Faulkner suggests that *ḏw-ḳd* is ‘Ill-disposed One’.[591] The same name is written underneath the twenty-nine names of Apophis.[592]

The same text[593] describes the procedure of producing and further destruction of four statues (*twt*) of enemies with faces of serpents (or birds),[594] labeled as *mś.w Btš* (= *Bdšt*),[595] embodying the king’s enemies:[596]

(46) [...] *iri.t n ky.w twt.w n ỉfdw ḫfty.w m ḥr.w n* [ ] (A) (47) *snḥ.w ntt ʿʿ.wt=śn n ḥ3=śn mś.w Btš* [...] (53) *tw ky twt(.w) n ỉfdw ḫfty.w m ḥr.w n 3pd ntt m ʿʿ.wt=śn rd.wt=śn* (54) *ḥ3=śn m-ʿ=śn nw.w (m) ḏd mś.w Btš.w*

‘(46) [...] Make other statues (*twt.w*) of four enemies with faces [of serpent], (47) their hands shall be tied with fetters – (these are) the Children of *Btš*(B). [...] (53) (And) other statues of four enemies with faces of birds (shall have) tied hands (and) their legs (54) with fetters in front of them (and) called ‘Children of *Btš.w*’’ (p*Bremner-Rhind*, 32, 46–47; 53–54).[597]

Comments

(A) We agree with the contextual restoration of R. Faulkner of the first illegible characters in the word[598] as *ḥf3w* – ‘serpent’.[599]

(B) I.e. *Bdšt*.

On the question of the fourfold repetition of magical destruction of the king and gods’ enemies it is interesting to recall the ritual of protecting the graves of Osiris. The defeat was acquired via shots from the bows of four balls symbolizing enemies

589 Faulkner 1937: 171.
590 Allen 2014: 51 (6.4).
591 Faulkner 1937: 171; Faulkner 1999: 282.
592 Faulkner 1933: 89 (32, 18); 1938: 52.
593 Faulkner 1933: 91 (32, 46–47); 1938: 52.
594 Faulkner 1933: 92 (32. 53–54); 1938: 53.
595 Faulkner 1938: 53, fn. 32.47.
596 LGG III: 422. This ritual is very similar to the rituals of damnation, also requiring statues, what will be considered in detail later.
597 Faulkner 1933: 91, 92.
598 Faulkner 1933: 91, fn. ‘e’.
599 Faulkner 1938: 52 (32, 46).

and traitors of four countries – Nubia, Asia, Libya and Egypt. In particular, it is displayed on the east wall of the chamber ‘E’ of the Taharqa’s cenotaph at Kom Jem (25th Dynasty) (***Figure 56***).[600]

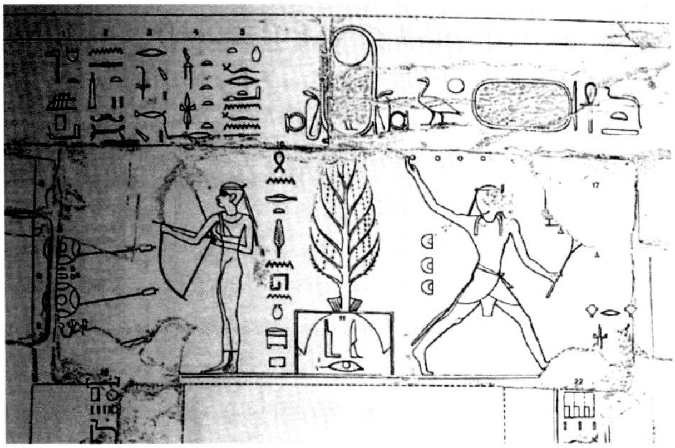

Figure 56

Moreover, of crucial importance is the correlation of *mś.w Bdšt* with the Supports of the Sky in CT Sp. 60, as it is known, there were four such Supports[601] (**Appendix 2, Text No. 12**):[602]

wr.t pr=k m ḥw.t-nṯr.w m ỉrỉ.t n Rˁ m ś3=[k] wn=k ỉm=ś r ḥḏt śbḫ.t(w) 3ḫ.t ḥśb.t ˁ3.w (pr)[(A)] *wnn.t m ś3 Wśir* (N *pn*)[(B)] [*ś*]*3 ˁ3.w=*[*ś* (*/ n*)][(C)] *mś.w Bdšt wnn m ś3* [*r*[*///*]*Wśir*[(D)] (N)[(E)] *pn*][(F)] *srḫt=ś ˁ.wy Nw.t* [...]

‘Your great house is in the temples, created by Re for your protection, (for you to be) here in the sunset. The horizon is closed (?)[(G)], the supports (of the house) are counted (?)[(H)], for protecting Osiris (N.)’, protection of his supports[(I)], – the Children of *Bdšt*, – existed for protecting Osiris (N); his beam is Nut’s hands [...]’.

Comments

(A) After $B_{10}C^{D}$.

(B) After $B_{1}4$.

(C) After $B_{4}C$ / $B_{10}C^{D}$.

600 Parker, Leclant, Goyon 1979: pl. XXV: 63–65.
601 Leitz 1994: 99.
602 CT Sp. 60, I, 253–254a ($B10C^{C}$).

(D)  is a rare form of writing the name of Osiris, found exclusively in the *Coffin Texts.*[603]

(E) Only in $B_{10}C^{B}$.

(F) After $B_{10}C^{B}$.

(G) Due to existing differences in reading of determinatives, *śbḫ.t ꜣḫ.t* can be understood as 'the gates of horizon'.[604]

(H) Possible translation: 'destroyed'.[605] P. Barguet reads the phrase: 'le porche (de l'horizon est l'evaluation de l'excès et) c'est la protection d'Osiris'.[606]

(I) As indicated by R. Faulkner, suffixal pronoun 3 person singular =*ś* here refers to 'horizon' (*ꜣḫ.t* – female) in CT I: 253d.[607]

It is typical that all six coffins, which recorded this spell, originate from the Hermopolitan necropolis (el-Bershe), which may indicate the local character of the notions set forth therein. Association of *mś.w Bdšt* with the Supports of Sky finds parallels in myths of Hermopolitan Ogdoad,[608] formed in the time of the Middle Kingdom, according to which each of the four pairs of the Eight (four male and four female deities whose names are formed as female forms of the god's name), often referred to as the Eight *ḥḥ*-gods, acted as preserver of one of the celestial supports in each four cardinal points, as described in CT Sp. 80.[609] This spell is known from five coffins from el-Bershe. Only two samples come from other regions ($G_{1}T$, $A_{1}C$). Therefore, its Hermopolitan origin, as well as for CT Sp. 60, seems plausible.

In general, the image of four enemies against the god is quite common in Egyptian religious art. In particular, the motif is placed in the mythological p*Ḏd-Ḫnśw-ỉw=f-ʿnḫ* II pCairo S.R. VII. 10266 (21st Dynasty) (***Figure 57***).[610] Here, the body of four beheaded creatures (obviously enemies of Re) are surrounded by *Ouroboros*-serpent, i.e. given the chthonic functions of the serpent devoted to the Underworld. In fact, the semantics of the composition, refer to the fate of *mś.w Bdšt,* according to the text of the aforementioned scene No. 69 of the 11th hour of the *Book of Gates*, reporting that Geb and the Children of Horus 'follow' the

603 Gardiner 1958: 467 (F51).
604 See: Faulkner 1994 I: 55, fn. 9.
605 Faulkner 1994 I: 55 and fn. 10.
606 Barguet. 1986: 199.
607 Faulkner 1994 I: 55, fn.14.
608 See: Sethe 1929.
609 CT II: 27–28; Allen 1988: 21–27; Bickel 1994a: 82–97; Willems 1996: 293–297, 469–473.
610 Piankoff 1957: 174, Figure 67.

fetters of *mś.w Bdšt*, held by 'Those-who-hides-corpses' (*Jmnw-ḫ3w.t*) (25–29)', i.e. according to J. Zandee: 'they (*mś.w Bdšt* – M. T.) are locked on earth'.[611] Therefore, attention must be paid to the reference in the *Pyramid Texts* about the reluctance of the king to be 'locked up' in Geb (i.e. earth).[612]

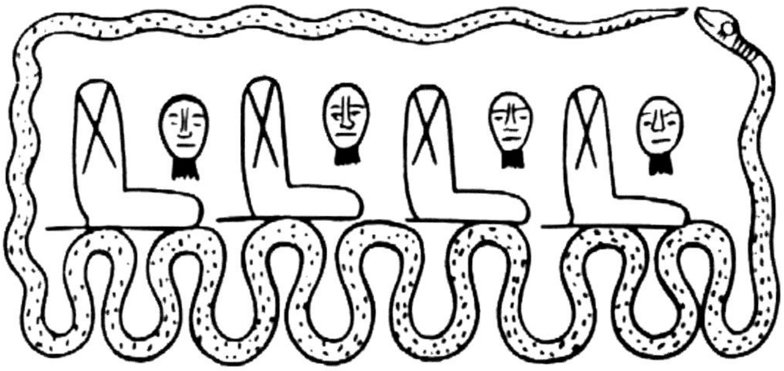

FIGURE 57

The Sons of Horus confront four *mś.w Bdšt,* as a quaternary form of *W3mmtj*/ Apophis in the *Book of Gates*, and Chr. Leitz rightly believes it to be the principle of symmetry, when Apophis, who takes the form of four serpent-like embodiments to fight Re, is opposed by equal number of deities – the Children of Horus (in Edfu mythology – four falcons) acting as a quaternary solar manifestation of the creator-god.[613]

The reminiscence of this myth can be a controversial image of **BD 30B** and **BD 125** vignettes (the so-called *Judgment scene* / *Totengerichtszene*) where the four Sons of Horus are depicted next to the throne of Osiris on a lotus flower growing out of the pond symbol.[614] The images identical in their iconography were widespread and found at other sites: painting of tombs[615] or stelae,[616] etc. From 18th Dynasty onwards this scenes became popular. Fr. Servajean collected forty-seven examples of them.[617] There present several iconographic types.[618]

1. The lotus flower grows directly from the pond symbol: p*Hw-nfr* pLondon BM EA 9901: 19th Dynasty (***Figure 58***),[619] etc.

---

611 Zandee 1960: 127.

612 Pyr. § 308.

613 Leitz 1994: 100–101.

614 B. Stricker sees in the image of the Sons of Horus the four primeval elements of the world – fire, air, water and land (Stricker 1992: 53, fn. 34).

615 See: Saleh 1984: 66, Abb. 77 (TT 296); 67, Abb. 79 (TT 305); Abb. 80 (TT 296).

616 See: Billing 2003: 394, Figure D.4 (BM EA 796);396, Figure D.8 (Naples 1000).

617 Servajean 2001: 280–289.

618 Cf. Servajean 2001: 293–294, Tab. IV.

619 © Trustees of the British Museum. See also: Milde 1994: 21, Figure 4; Stricker 1992: 52, Figure 9; Taylor 2001: 26, Figure 11.

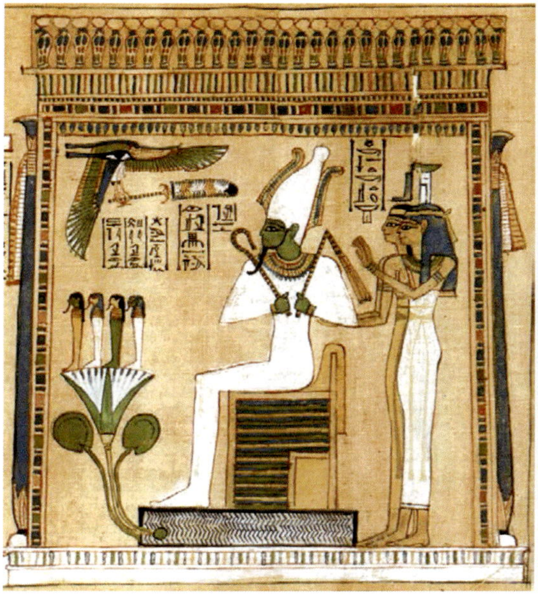

FIGURE 58

FIGURE 59

2. The lotus flower grows from beneath the throne of Osiris: p*ꜣnj* pLondon BM EA 10470: 19th Dynasty (***Figure 59***),[620] etc.
3. The lotus flower grows out of the floor in the palace in front of the throne of Osiris; p*Ns-Mnw* pHermitage No. 3531: Ptolemaic Period (***Figure 60***)[621] etc. The fact that the lotus grows out of the floor does not change the pictures' semantics, since the floor of the Osiris's palace was identified with waters of the Primeval Ocean of Nun.[622]
4. The lotus flower grows out immediately from the foot or under the foot of Osiris: p*ꜣnj* pLondon BM EA 10470 (***Figure 61***);[623] pectoral Museo Bologna (18th Dynasty),[624] painting in the tomb of *Nfr-sḫrw* TT 296 (19th Dynasty);[625] pectoral Florence № 1285:[626] etc.

According to Chr. Leitz, it is possible to find the illustration of the Hermopolitan myth of Creation in the composition under discussion – the scene of the sun god arising (in his 'warlike' quaternary form) from the Primeval Waters on the lotus flower.[627]

620 © Trustees of the British Museum. See also: Faulkner 1998: pl. 30.
621 Landa, Lapis 1974: pl. 135.
622 Milde 1994: 23.
623 © Trustees of the British Museum; cf: Milde 1994: pl. 4.
624 Servajean 2001: 280 (Doc. 3), 296, Figure 4.
625 Servajean 2001: 283 (Doc. 17), 297, Figure 8.
626 Servajean 2001: 289 (Doc. 47), 297, Figure 111.
627 Leitz 1994: 101.

FIGURE 60

FIGURE 61

In my view, this parallel can be supplemented with another illustration of this myth among the vignettes of the *Book of the Dead* – scene '3b' (or *Treppen-Szene*) in J. Gesellensetter's classification[628] in the lower register of **BD 110** (***Figure 62*** – p*Nb-snj* pLondon BM EA 9900).[629] This chapter represents the vignette-map of Egyptian 'paradise' – *sḫ.t-ỉ3r.w* ('Fields of Reed') and *sḫ.t-ḥtp* ('Fields of Offerings'),[630] dating back to the earlier prototype – drawing in the CT Sp. 465/6.

Depicted is the island (*wnm sw*) surrounded by channels, where figures of four deities are placed (***Figure 63*** (p*Nb-snj*);[631] ***64*** (p*Jwj3* pCairo CG 51189).[632] In p*Nb-snj* these gods are defined as *pśḏ.t ˁ3 ỉmj(.t) sḫ.t-ḥtp* – 'Great Ennead in the Fields of Offerings'.[633] Besides these two examples, the image of **four** deities in this segment of BD 110 also appears in pCairo S.R. VII. 10652;[634] pLondon BM EA 10472;[635] pLondon BM EA 9911;[636] pCairo S.R. IV. 981.[637]

However, the number of gods may vary. Many sources have **three** gods (pLeiden AMT 1-35, AP 52, relief from the tomb of *P3-jtn-m-ḥb*, Saqqara;[638] pLondon BM

[628] Gesellensetter 1997: 26, 178–192, 329, Taf. I.
[629] © Trustees of the British Museum; See also: Hummel 1983: 44; Milde 1994: 24, Figure 5.
[630] Gesellensetter 1997: 20–25.
[631] © Trustees of the British Museum; see also: Gesellensetter 1997: 178, Abb. 27.
[632] Davies 1908: pl. XVIII; Gesellensetter 1997: 184, Abb. 28.
[633] Gesellensetter 1997: 181; Zayed Abd El 1977: 14.
[634] Gesellensetter 1997: 335, Taf. 7.2.
[635] Gesellensetter 1997: 336, Taf. 8.1.
[636] Gesellensetter 1997: 337, Taf. 9.2; Taylor 2001: 34, Figure 16.
[637] Niwiński 1989: pl. 16a.
[638] Gesellensetter 1997: 330, Taf. 2.1.

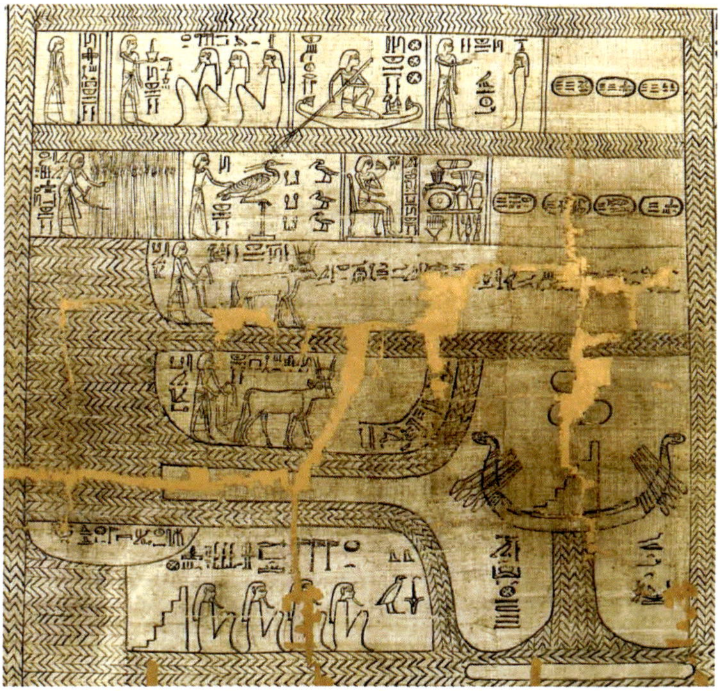

FIGURE 62

FIGURE 63

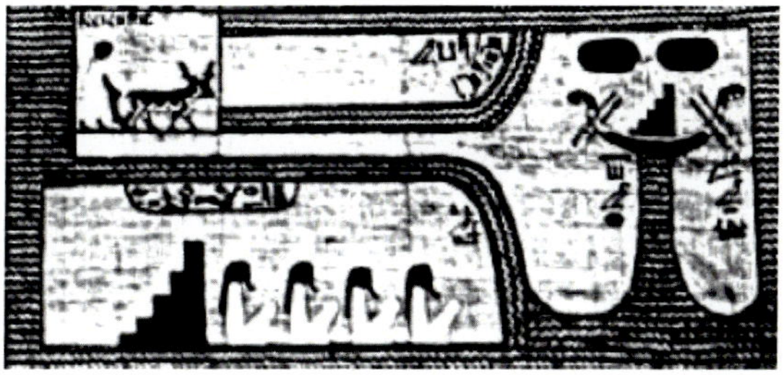

FIGURE 64

EA 10471+10473;[639] painting in tomb *Pn-Nw.t* in Anib;[640] relief in the mortuary temple of Ramses III at Medinet Habu;[641] pCairo S.R. VII 10249;[642] pChicago OIM 10486;[643] pParis Louvre E 3911;[644] pTurin 1791;[645] pHermitage No.3531;[646] pCairo S.R. VII. 10244; CG 10014.[647] In other case there may be **two** gods (pTurin 1837),[648] sometimes **one** (pLondon BM EA 10479;[649] pParis Louvre 3084:[650] or even **five**: pLeiden T 3.[651] In several papyri (especially in the later documents) there are no images of the gods in this segment of the vignette.[652]

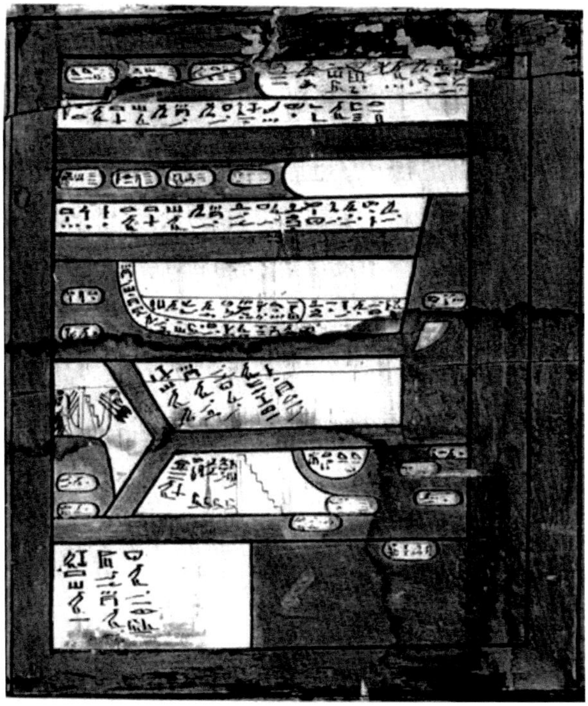

FIGURE 65

[639] Gesellensetter 1997: 331, Taf. 3.2.
[640] Gesellensetter 1997: 333, Taf. 5.1.
[641] Gesellensetter 1997: 333, Taf. 5.2.
[642] Gesellensetter 1997: 335, Taf. 7.1.
[643] Gesellensetter 1997: 337, Taf. 9.1.
[644] Gesellensetter 1997: 339, Taf. 11.2.
[645] Gesellensetter 1997: 340, Taf. 12.1.
[646] Матье 1956: табл. XXIV (not taken into account in the work of J. Gesellensetter).
[647] Niwiński 1989: pl. 24c.
[648] Gesellensetter 1997: 340, Taf. 12.2.
[649] Gesellensetter 1997: 338, Taf. 10.1.
[650] Gesellensetter 1997: 338, Taf. 10.2.
[651] Gesellensetter 1997: 335, Taf. 7.3.
[652] Gesellensetter 1997: 330, Taf. 2.2; 331, Taf. 3.1; 336, Taf. 8.3.

On the prototype picture of BD 110 in CT Sp. 465 the four Sons of Horus were believed to be inhabitants of the neighborhood (*ẖnww sw Jmst, Ḥpj, Kbḥsnw=f, Dw3mwt=f*)[653] (***Figure 65***).[654] The symbol / O40[655] is displayed in front of the deities, possibly symbolizing (as well as symbol / O41) the Primeval Hill (*ḳ33*).[656] But curiously two area names directly adjacent to this island (upper left),[657] are designated as *mśḫn* (*nṯr*) – 'Birthplace (of the god)'[658] and *ḳnḳn.t* – 'Battlefield' ('Kampfplatz',[659] 'Battle (field)',[660] from the verb *ḳnḳn* – 'züchtigen', 'prügeln', 'zerschlagen').[661] J. Gesellensetter perceives these images as more Cosmological than Cosmogonical and believes that *msḫn* (*nṯr*) and *ḳnḳn.t* should be understood as identification of eastern and western horizons – the place of sunrise and sunset.[662] But in my view, this area, according to the totality of its mythological nominations, undoubtedly going back to the Cosmogonic legend, and can be understood as a place of (self-) appearance of Primeval Hill, birth of the creator-god and cosmic battle of the four sons of Horus, displayed here with the forces of Chaos (possibly in the quaternary form of *mś.w Bdšt*?). Its semantics can be directly associated with the aforementioned subject.

In sum, the text and picture of the 11th hour of the *Book of Gates* (scene No. 69) contain crucial reference to *mś.w Bdšt*, which can be associated with the 'Hermopolitan' version of the myth according to BD 17. Characteristic for the visual display of this mythem is the representation of *mś.w Bdšt* in serpent quaternary form and contrasting them with four Sons of Horus. The reminiscences of this little-known Hermopolitan myth can be found in the semantics of vignettes BD 30B and 125, as well as on the one of the scenes of BD 110 / CT Sp. 465. This motif is also reflected in the plot of pBrooklyn 47.218.84, indicating that *mś.w Bdšt* were the four fingers of the creator-god, who rebelled against him (IV,5–V,4). Based on this, as well as data from pRamesseum XV verso I, 5, the presence of the fifth serpent, means the fifth finger of the creator-god. In the image of *mś.w Bdšt* in the *Book of Gates* this seems to be absolutely logical.

---

653 CT V: 357 (XVII), 361 (XVII).
654 CT V: 361 (B_1C); Piankoff 1972: Figure 1.
655 Gesellensetter 1997: 182–185.
656 Saleh 1969: 119; but cf. Zayed Abd El 1977: 13–14.
657 CT V: 358 (XXI); Gesellensetter 1997: 26 (scene '3b/1').
658 Cf. CT Sp. 465, V, 349–351.
659 Hornung 1979: 217.
660 Milde 1994: 25.
661 Wb. V: 55; Gesellensetter 1997: 40.
662 Gesellensetter 1997: 40.

Chapter 6

Mś.w Bdšt – the name and the image

This chapter examines the nomination of *mś.w Bdšt*. If the noun *mś.w* has no other meaning but 'children' ('Kinder', 'children', 'enfants'), *Bdšt,* more ambiguous has entailed various translations from scholars (although, considered in detail, they are synonyms). The word *bdšt* is formed from the noun *bdš*: 'weakness', 'impotence', 'fatigue', 'lethargy' and its derivative.[663]

One of the first attempts was read *mś.w Bdšt* as 'Kinder der Rebellen', so proposed by R. Lepsius.[664] His option was long followed in Egyptological literature. E. A. W. Budge approved it with a slight nuance: 'the children of Impotent revolt[665] / rebellion'.[666] B. A. Turaev in support of R. Lepsius and E. A. W. Budge, suggest *mś.w Bdšt* to be 'children of disobedience' and associate them with 'darkness'.[667] Similar translation was given by S. Sauneron and J.-C. Goyon: 'Enfants de la Révolte'.[668] B. Brier also suggests understanding *mś.w Bdšt* in the 'Cairo calendar' as 'Children of Rebellion'.[669] B. de Rachewiltz gives the old tradition 'Hijos de la Rebelión' already for BD 17.[670] St. Quirke, in his latest translation of BD 17 gives 'children of the rebel' for Version I[671] and 'the creatures of the evil one' for Version II.[672] Close is interpretation of *mś.w Bdšt* by P. Jürgens in CT Sp. 335,[673] but in a single word: 'die Rebellen'.[674] These interpretations would disregard the individual meaning of *mś.w* or imply a meaning close to the meaning of *mś.w Bdšt* in royal Late Period inscriptions, which, however, is not necessarily true in contexts of Middle Kingdom religious text. Noteworthy is M. Heerma van Voss suggestion 'Kinderen der Machteloze' for the same CT Sp. 335.[675]

---

663 Naville 1874: 60; Wb. I: 487.7; Budge 1911: 139; Gardiner 1958: 564; Faulkner 1999: 86; Hannig 1995: 266. Cf. usage of *bdš* in Pyr. § 1080, CT III: 346d; VI: 275v; VII: 66c, 98a.
664 Lepsius 1867: 28, 42.
665 Budge 1898a: 54 (21). However, in his 'Vocabulary' to the *Book of the Dead* E. A. W. Budge reads *Bdšt* as 'impotent fiends' (Budge 1911: 139), and *mś.w Bdšt* as 'malicious but powerless fiends' respectively (Budge 1911: 185).
666 Budge 1895: 80 (2).
667 Тураев 1898: 17.
668 Sauneron 1953: 68; Goyon 1985: 9. Though not for the *Book of the Dead*, but for the pBerlin 3050 ('Great (ritual) Hymn to Re-Horakhty') and the texts of the temple of Horus at Edfu.
669 Brier 1981: 230–231.
670 de Rachewiltz 2001: 53.
671 Quirke 2013: 55.
672 Quirke 2013: 59.
673 He correlates the fragment of CT IV: 252/3c–284/5b with the reference to *mś.w Bdšt* in his attributing CT Sp. 335 to *Abschnitt* 4 – 'Anrufung des Rechtfertigungsgerichts' (Jürgens 1999: 44).
674 Jürgens 1999: 44.
675 Heerma van Voss 1963: 45–46.

As well *Bdšt* was translated in accordance with its basic etymology 'Failure' (P. Le Page Renouf),[676] 'Feeble one' (T. G. Allen),[677] 'Weak one' or 'Feeble one' (A. Piankoff, J. P. Allen),[678] 'Impotence' (A. H. Gardiner),[679] 'Faiblesse' or 'Déchéance' (Chr. Cannuyer),[680] 'Ohnmächtige' (K. Sethe),[681] or 'Schwachen' (U. Verhoeven, E. Hornung, Chr. Leitz).[682] Close interpretation is given by R. Hannig: 'Kinder der Schwäche'.[683] U. Rößler-Köhler reads *Bdšt* as 'Müden',[684] the same translation is given in the 'Lexikon der ägyptischen Götter'.[685] Chr. Geisen offers 'Kinder der 'Matten''.[686]

French Egyptologists like P. Barguet and J.-P. Corteggiani translate *mś.w Bdšt* as 'Enfants de la D(/d)échéance',[687] E. Naville, M. Broze, and D. Meeks – as 'Enfants de l'Impuissance',[688] and Cl. Carrier – 'Enfants de la faiblesse'.[689] Otherwise, P. Koemoth proposes the meaning 'enfants du malheur'.[690] In Spanish Egyptology, M. Puvill Donata proposes 'Hijos de la Inercia',[691] while M. Saura i Senjaume for the text in tomb of *Sn-nḏm* (TT 1): 'Fills de la Inèrcia (lit. els nascuts dèbils)'.[692] The original reading was given by A.-A. Saleh: 'Descendants of the Fainthearted'.[693] H. Grapow, who published two translations of BD 17 (in 1912 and 1917), originally reads *Bdšt* as 'Schwachheit',[694] but later he changed his mind and translated it as 'Schwachen'.[695] This version was also added to the 'Berlin Wörterbuch'.[696]

R. Faulkner gives a greater number of translations.[697] For p*Bremner-Rhind* (pLondon BM EA 10188), previously published by him,[698] he indicates that the

676 Le Page Renouf 1904: 39, 44.
677 Allen 1960: 88, 90; 1974: 27, 30, 290.
678 Piankoff 1962: 49, 56; Allen 1988: 32 (4h).
679 Gardiner 1955: 15; Kákosy, Bács, Bartos, Fábián, Gaál 2004 I: 191.
680 Cannuyer 2014: 47.
681 Pyr. Komm. III: 51–52.
682 Ratié 1968: 69; Verhoeven 1993 I: 59; Leitz 1994: 99.
683 Hannig 1995: 266.
684 Rößler-Köhler 1979: 213, 225.
685 LGG III: 422.
686 Geisen 2004: 66.
687 Barguet 1967: 57, 61; 1986: 199, 311, 372, 568; Corteggiani 1995: 145.
688 Naville 1874: 60; Broze 1991: 111–112; Meeks 2006: 10, 11, 199ff.
689 Carrier 2009a: 72, 87; 2010: 15; 2010a: 66; 2011: 194, 206; 2014: 338. Cf.: Carrier 2004 I: 823 (CT Sp. 335); II: 1017 (CT Sp. 409).
690 Koemoth 1993: 20.
691 Puvill Donata 1999: 115.
692 Saura i Senjaume 2006: 108, 109 (CW-VIa).
693 Saleh 1969: 117.
694 Grapow 1912: 2, 36. For *Abschnitt* 22 of BD 17 he leaves *Bdšt* without translation (Ibid: 14–15).
695 Urk. V: II: 3, 22.
696 Wb. I: 488.
697 The same is also true to St. Quirke who propose three different variants of translation *mś.w Bdšt* for three different fragments of the BD text (Quirke 2013: 55 ('children of the rebel' – BD 17), 59 ('the creatures of the evil one' – BD 17), 72 ('the children of the Weary Goddess' – BD 18).
698 Faulkner 1933.

literal meaning of *Bdšt* is 'Faintness',[699] but from the contextual point of view 'Revolt' is more appropriate.[700] In other cases R. Faulkner uses 'Impotence' or 'Weakness' in translations.[701]

M.-L. Buhl reads *mś.w Bdšt* as 'Weak ones', i.e. in the plural form,[702] although the hieroglyphic text in her edition gives no reason for such interpretation.[703] In general, plural indicator I I I (Z2/Z3) of *Bdšt* is quiet frequent.[704] J. Borghouts supports interpretation of I I I as indication of plurality, rather than 'false plural form', which agree in number with the qualitative determination of *Bdšt,* governing noun and subject *mś.w*. He suggests the following translation: 'Children of the Inert Ones',[705] noting that the Ptolemaic texts refer to *mś.w Bdšt* as if to a 'class apart'.[706]

H. Grapow believes that *Bdšt* refers to a kind of goddess,[707] further confirming this interpretation in the 'Berlin Wörterbuch'.[708] E. A. W. Budge also points out that *Bdšt* has female gender in his 'Vocabulary' to the *Book of the Dead* (and in plural as well, although omitting it in his own translations).[709] As already noted, K. Sethe supported the idea of understanding *Bdšt* as a goddess.[710] The opinion that *Bdšt* is a female deity is accepted by Chr. Leitz[711] and D. Meeks[712] which are based on the above mentioned evidence from Pyr. § 558a, and understanding of K. Sethe (as well as forms of writing *Bdšt* in CT I: 253f; IV, 290a; VI, 35o (see below)).[713] The same understanding is given by St. Quirke for *Bdšt* in the BD 18. And he proposes to translate *mś.w Bdšt* as 'the children of the Weary Goddess'.[714]

---

699 Faulkner 1937: 177 (24, 22).
700 Faulkner 1937: 170 (24, 22), 171 (25, 18–19); 1938: 52 (32, 47), 53 (32, 54). The researcher provided the following explanation: '...The expression (*mś.w Bdšt* – M. T.) appears to mean literary 'children of faintness' or the like; in translating these words as 'children of revolt', a rendering which suits the present context better, a confusion of *bdš* 'to faint' and *bšt* 'to rebel' has been assumed, the latter verb being not infrequently written or from the Nineteenth Dynasty onward, see: Wb. *I*: 479 – lacks any determinative, but is doubtless to be read as *ʿdt* 'slaughter'' (Faulkner 1937: 177–178, fn. 24, 22).
701 Faulkner 2001: 44; 1998: pl. 7, 102; 1994 I: 55, fn. 13; II: 62, 119.
702 Buhl 1947: 89.
703 Buhl 1947: 85 (ee).
704 Budge 1911: 139, 185; Shorter 1938: 84; Lapp 2006: 19, 201. Texts on the second shrine of Tutankhamun Cairo J.E. 60666, in the tomb of *Sn-nḏm* TT 1 (form is) (Bruyère 1959: 55, pl. XVIII, nº 3; Saleh 1984: 20; Saura i Senjaume 2006: 108, 109 (CW–VIa)), p*Nḫt-Ỉmn* pBerlin 3002, and p*Ḳnnꜣ* pLeiden T 2 (Lapp 2006: 19, 201), etc.
705 Borghouts 1973: 129, fn. 12.
706 Borghouts 1973: 129, fn. 12.
707 'Name einer Göttin (*bdš.t*); ihre Kinder galten als Feinde des Sonnengottes' (Urk. V II: 3, Anm. 4).
708 Wb. I: 488.2.
709 Budge 1911: 139.
710 Pyr. Komm. III: 52.
711 Leitz 1994: 99, Anm. 20.
712 Meeks 2006: 201. He also transliterated the name of the deity in the papyrus Brooklyn 47.218.84 as '*Bdšt*' while in all three noted references to *mś.w Bdš*(*t*?) in this scroll the female gender ending *=t* was never written.
713 Meeks 2006: 201, fn. 252.
714 Quirke 2013: 72.

The main argument in favor of the female essence of *Bdšt* is the presence of the female word ending *.t*, as well as a number of 'female' determinatives, referred to below. Nevertheless, the ending *.t* is absent in a considerable portion of New Kingdom and Third Intermediate Period BD scrolls (namely: p*Nj3* pLondon BM EA 9929, p*Ḳnn3* pLeiden T 2, p*Hw-nfr* pLondon BM EA 9901, p*Nḫt-Ỉmn* pBerlin 3002, p*P3-ḳrr* pLeiden T 4, p*Nḫt* pLondon BM EA 10471 + 10473, p*Ḫ3rj* pLondon BM EA 9949, pDublin 1661,[715] records in the tomb of *Sn-nḏm* TT 1,[716] p[?]-*Ỉmn.t* pLondon BM EA 10448, and p*P3-di-mw.t* pLondon BM EA 10093,[717] etc.). In general, a number of cases, where male gender defines *Bdš*, corresponds to nearly half of all available New Kingdom copies of BD 17. However, the female ratio for *Bdšt* remains superior (40% to 60% ratio).[718] This is also true for a series of other documents, such as pRamesseum XV recto I, 5[719] or pBrooklyn 47.218.84,[720] were we have the form *Bdš*. The sign 𓏏, written out in part of the documents, as well as the plural marker 𓏥, complicates grammatical identification of the word.

The determinatives could help to clarify the semantics of *Bdšt*. Several were used.

1. 𓁐 / B1. For interpreting the image of *Bdš*(.)*t* as a goddess, as already stated above, the determinative 𓁐 to *Bdš*(.)*t*, confirming this understanding and included into the 'Berlin Wörterbuch',[721] is however rare. It is fixed in CT I, 253f ($B_{10}C^{\underline{b.c.d}}$); IV, 290a ($B_1P$, $BqC^{\underline{a}}$); VI, 35o (B_1P),[722] and in the edition of H. Grapow.[723] The text of the Second Intermediate Period spell on Queen *Mnṯw-ḥtp*'s coffin (13th–17th Dynasties), which gives the earliest known version of BD 17,[724] expresses *mś.w Bdšt* as  (*mś.wt* (?) *Bdšt*), according to the Hieroglyphic transcription of Chr. Geisen,[725] based on the Hieratic copy by J. Wilkinson of 1834, or as  according to G. Lapp.[726] As one can see, the available transcriptions are significantly different.[727] G. Lapp, in contrast to Chr. Geisen:

---

[715] Lapp 2006: 19, 201.
[716] Saura i Senjaume 2006: 108, 109 (CW–VIa).
[717] Shorter 1938: 111.
[718] See also: Budge 1895: 3; 1898: 2 (8); Shorter 1938: 84, 111; Lapp 2006: 19, 200–201. For BD 18 cf.: Lapp 2009: 80–81.
[719] Gardiner 1955: pl. XLVII; 15, fn. 2.
[720] Meeks 2006: 10, 11.
[721] The form (Wb. I: 488.2–3).
[722] I.e. six cases altogether and only two in CT Sp. 335.
[723] Urk. V: Abs. 22; I: 52 (line 3 and 7, again in the 'version of the Middle Kingdom').
[724] It contains only the Version II of the myth under consideration, as in the CT Sp. 335.
[725] Geisen 2004: 34 (12).
[726] Lapp 2006: 200.
[727] For explanation of these discrepancies see: Lapp 2006: 357, Anm. 200, 2–3.

- doesn't distinguish the symbol 𓏏 *t* after 𓏲 *w* before determinatives in writing *mś.w*;
- reads the first phoneme of *Bdšt* as 𓃀 / D58 (as in all known versions of the *Coffin Texts*), rather than 𓂿 / D57;
- reads the determinative to *Bdšt* as 𓀉 / A7, rather than 𓁒 / B3.

If the first two clarifications of G. Lapp to the transcription of Chr. Geisen can be accepted, the third, though, is somewhat unconvincing, when compared with the material of the *Coffin Texts*, where the determinative 𓁒 (in the paleography of the *Coffin Texts* it is respectively)[728] is fixed in T_1S^b (twice),[729] while 𓀉 only in M1N4, but here the sign 𓁒 is given as the determinative to *mś.w*.[730] In the 'Theban Recension' of the *Book of the Dead* the symbol 𓁒 is set forth as a determinative of *Bdšt* only in p*Hw-nfr* pLondon BM EA 9901,[731] as well as the determinative of *mś.w* twice in p*Ḳnn3* pLeiden T 2[732] and the text of spell in the tombs of *Sn-nḏm* TT 1[733] and *Ỉmn-n-ipt* TT 265 (twice).[734] The semantically close determinatives to *mś.w* in p*Nḏ-mw.t* pLondon BM EA 10541 and in p*Nb-snj* pLondon BM EA 9900,[735] are also to be pointed out.

2. 𓀉 / A7. The symbol 𓀉 appears more frequently. It is used in Version I in pParis Louvre E. 11085; p*Ỉmn-m-jpt* pVaticano MGE No. 38 600/1-2; p*Hw-nfr* pLondon BM EA 9901; pDublin TCD MS 1661,[736] p*Nḏ-mw.t* pLondon BM EA 10541,[737] and the BD 17 text in the tomb *Ỉmn-m-ḥꜥt* TT 82.[738] And in Version II, I find it in p*Jꜥḥ-mś* pParis Louvre E. 11085 (repeatedly); p*Nb-snj* pLondon BM EA 9900; p*Nww* pLondon BM EA 10477 (form); p*Ỉmn-m-jpt* pVaticano No. 38 600/1–2 (repeatedly)[739] and tomb of *Ỉmn-m-ḥꜥt* TT 82 (repeatedly).[740]

[728] CT IV: 291, fn. 2*.
[729] CT IV: 290a, 290c.
[730] CT IV: 291a.
[731] Lapp 2006: 201.
[732] Lapp 2006: 19, 201 (i.e. in Versions I and II).
[733] Lapp 2006: 55: pl. XVIII, nº 3; Saleh 1984: 20; Saura i Senjaume 2006: 108, 109 (CW–VIa).
[734] Saleh 1984: 21 (column 1, line 11), 22 (column 1, line 8–9).
[735] Shorter 1938: 84; Lapp 2006: 18.
[736] Lapp 2006: 18–19.
[737] Shorter 1938: 84.
[738] Lapp 2006: 18.
[739] Lapp 2006: 200–201.
[740] Lapp 2006: 200; Cf.: Lepsius 1867: 28, Anm. 'r. D'.

3. 𓅆 / G7. The next sign-determinative of *Bdšt*, recorded already in Pyr. § 558a, and on the coffin of *Mntw-ḥtp*, but never founded in the *Coffin Texts*, is the 'Falcon on the standard' 𓅆 / G7, in use in the New Kingdom' *Book of the Dead,* yet only in p*Jʿḥ-mś* pParis Louvre E. 11085 (twice).[741]

4. 𓀭 / A 40. Along with the sign [hieroglyph], the determinative of 'god' 𓀭 was used already in the *Coffin Texts* (i.e. indicator of male gender despite the ending of female gender!). Thus we have four cases of *Bdšt* with the determinative 𓀭 (three in CT Sp. 335 and one in Sp. 409)[742] in contrast to six with the symbol 𓁐 / B1 (with two in the CT Sp. 335).[743]

Similar situation is found in a New Kingdom BD 17, where 𓃀[hieroglyph]𓀉𓀭 is written in p*Nb.snj* pLondon BM EA 9900.[744] In p*Nḫt* pLondon BM EA 10471 there is twice reference to masculine gender of *Bdš*, the sign 𓀉 A7 is omitted and only the determinative 𓀭 is used: 𓃀[hieroglyph]𓀭 [745] Similar writings of 𓃀[hieroglyph]𓀭 are in p*P3-ḳrr* pLeiden T 4 (twice) and p*Ḫ3rj* pLondon BM EA 9949[746] (i.e. in total: six cases using the symbol A 40). To be added is the preserved determinative 𓀭𓏪 to *mś*[*.w Bdš.*]*t*(?) (probably with ending *.t* (?)) on the fragmentary funerary linen with the BD 17 text (only Version I has been preserved) of the Princess (*ś3.t njśwt*) *Ἰmn-mw-sḫ.t* (QV 8, 18th Dynasty).[747]

In New Kingdom BD 17 copies, the determinative 𓀭 to *Bdšt* is known only from 18th Dynasty documents: p*Jwj3* pCairo CG 51189; J.E. 95839[748] and p*Ḫʿ* pTurin A, Suppl. 8438.[749] In the text of this spell on the linens of Thutmose III's mummy (Cairo CG 40001 + Boston, MFA 82.31) *mś.w Bdšt* is written three times once (Version I)[750] without the determinative and twice with the symbol 𓀭,[751] as well

---

[741] Lapp 2006: 18, 200.
[742] CT IV: 290a (M_8C), 291a (T_3Be); 412 (167) (as *mś.w Bdš.wt!*) (Sq_7Sq); V, 233g (T_1C^b).
[743] CT IV: 290a (B_1P, BqC^a).
[744] Shorter 1938: 111; Lapp 2006: 200.
[745] Shorter 1938: 84, 111; Lapp 2006: 19, 201.
[746] Lapp 2006: 19, 201.
[747] Franco 1988: 78, Figure 3.
[748] Lapp 2006: 18; Munro 1994 II: Taf. 48.
[749] Lapp 2006: 18.
[750] Lapp 2006: 18; Munro 1994 II: Taf. 32.
[751] Lapp 2006: 200; Munro 1994 II: Taf. 33.

as in the BD 18.[752] All cases of *Bdšt* with the determinative come only from the 'Heliopolitan' Version II of the BD 17 mythem, originating from the *Coffin Texts*, where this sign-determinative was also used.

It is obvious that in the *Book of the Dead*, in contrast to the *Coffin Texts*, the feminine word ending *.t* is never found along with the determinative / A40 (i.e. *Bdš* form) and is rarely used with the 'serpent' / I14 determinative (for its variants see below). Yet it is combined with determinatives / B1, / B3 and 'cobra' / I64, and / G7 and frequently / A7, indicating *Bdšt*. A closer look on another widespread characteristic determinative to *Bdš/t* – the symbol of 'serpent' and its species is therefore necessary.

R. Faulkner and R. Hannig suggest for *Bdšt*.[753] Earlier in his 'Vocabulary' E. A. W. Budge considers and as determinatives, as well as .[754] The 'Berlin Wörterbuch' also offers as a later form.[755]

Inscriptions of Late Period, such as BD 17, 18, 140, temple rituals, and calendar texts, one finds such determinatives as , as well as and ,[756] with indication of plural form.[757] For instance, for BD 17:

 – p*Jꜥḥ-tꜣy-ś.t-nḫt* pCologne Colon. Aeg. 10207 (26th Dynasty);[758]

 – pVandier, verso, 1, 3 (26th Dynasty);[759]

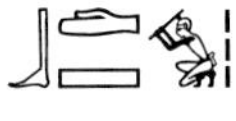 – p*Iw=f-ꜥnḫ* pTurin 1791 (Ptolemaic Period);[760]

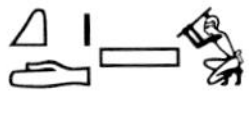 – (*ḳ*[sic] = *dš*) p*Ns-Mnw* pNew Jersey (Ptolemaic Period);[761]

[752] Munro 1994 II: Taf. 35; Lapp 2009: 80.
[753] Faulkner 1999: 86; Hannig 1995: 266; cf. CT IV: 291a, M_1NY, T_2Be(?).
[754] Budge 1911: 139; cf.: LGG III: 422.
[755] Wb. I: 488.2–3.
[756] LGG III: 422.
[757] Cf.: Urk. V: 54 (49, 5), 127 (16).
[758] Verhoeven 1993 II: 13*.
[759] Posener 1985: pl. 10.
[760] Lepsius 1842: Taf. VII (3), IX (48); Urk. V: Abs. 1 (7, 3); Abs. 22 (54, 49).
[761] Clère 1987: pl. IV.

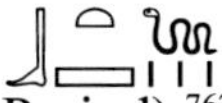 (*Bt*[=sic]*š*) /  – pChicago OIM 10486; pMilbank (Ptolemaic Period).[762]

Thus, this array of variants, both in form of determination, and form of word endings opens a wide grammatical range for determining gender and number (except for dual): *Bdš* /*.t* /*.w* /*.wt* – 'impotent, weak' (male/female/plural forms) that, to put it mildly, makes no contribution to understanding the image. The formula itself *mś*/*.w* + NN, does not facilitate comprehension, since it has been equally used along with male and female names of deities.[763] Whatever, using male singular form is common scholarly practice.

Therefore, considering that it is extremely difficult to pinpoint the exact meaning of *Bdšt* most scholars are unanimous in defining the functions of children of this creature. 'Berlin Wörterbuch' describes *mś.w Bdšt* as 'enemies of the sun god' and 'enemies of the king' within the Late Period.[764] R. Faulkner, K. Sethe and A. H. Gardiner discerns an epithet in them (or 'designation') of enemies of the sun god.[765] H. Grapow, who was the first to study the mythological content of BD 17, understands *mś.w Bdšt* as enemies of the sun god, whose destruction takes place every morning on the eastern horizon of the sky, the place of sunrise, and he also points out relationship between these creatures and some ancient solar Cosmogonic myth.[766] U. Rößler-Köhler, following H. Grapow, interprets them as a group of gods, personifying the enemies of the sun along with Apophis, who had to be defeated at the beginning of each new day.[767] P. Barguet understands *mś.w Bdšt* as kind of evil demons, enemies of the creator, often represented as a serpent.[768] Serpent features of *mś.w Bdšt* were also noted by M. Heerma van Voss,[769] and M. Broze, who understands them as serpentine demons associated with Apophis.[770] This interrelation is also indicated by E. Hornung,[771] J.-C. Goyon,[772] and D. Meeks.[773]

In fact, the serpentine nature of *mś.w Bdšt* is directly confirmed by Egyptian sources. Moreover, the question is not only in the scene of 11th hour of the

762 Allen 1960: pl. LVI, LIX; see also: Budge 1910 III: 196 (529); 209 (67).
763 See: LGG III: 398ff.
764 Wb. I: 488.2–3.
765 Faulkner 1999: 86; Pyr. Komm. III: 52; 93, 15, fn. 2.
766 Grapow 1912: 35–36
767 'Diese Göttergruppe verkörpert neben Apophisdie Sonnenfeinde schlechtin, die täglisch neu bekämpft werden müssen' (Rößler-Köhler 1979: 213, Anm. 5).
768 'Sortes d'anges déchus, ennemis du Créateur; ils sont souvent figurés des serpents' (Barguet 1967: 57, fn. 5).
769 Heerma van Voss 1963: 83.
770 Broze 1991: 111–112.
771 Hornung 1996: 159, fn. 59.
772 'Ce sont les allies d'Apopis dans le cycle solaire de la lutte des origins. Ici, ils doivent designer les serpents maléfiques, incoranation du mal' (Goyon 1972: 9, fn. 14).
773 Meeks 2006: 200.

Book of Gates, but also in a number of contextual indications. For example, in the so-called 'Introductory Hymn of Re' in pꜣnj pLondon BM EA 10470 *mś.w Bdšt* are mentioned among two other serpent-like enemies of Re – *ẖft(j)*[774] and *Śbiw*. Both *mś.w* and *Bdšt* are here determined by the symbols of 'serpents': .[775] However the most clear-cut indication of the serpentine nature of *mś.w Bdšt* is offered in the so-called 'Ophiological treatise' in pBrooklyn 47.218.48/85 (30th Dynasty – early Ptolemaic Period), which describes the various types of poisonous snakes, the effect of the poison and how to deal with it.[776] Although the initial part of the papyrus, presumable describing the type of *mś.w Bdšt*, has not been preserved. There are references to them in relation to other species of reptiles,[777] the study of which gives A. Sauneron grounds to classify *mś.w Bdšt* as vipers.[778]

And finally, O. I. Pavlova and A. B. Zubov have their own understanding of *mś.w Bdšt* – as resemblance to the Hindu demonology. According to these scholars, the 'Children of Weakness' are the 'very close definition to the Vedic 'children of *Diti*', demons *dasyus*. *Diti* is connectedness, limitedness, boundedness'.[779]

Thus, the word *Bdšt*, which I tend to interpret as a proper name, can be translated as 'Weakness / Impotence'. Children of this 'Weakness' had serpent appearance and, being enemies of Re, were identified (at least in Hermopolis and Heliopolis) with the Ancient forces of Chaos, confronting Re (in the quaternary form) on the final stage of Cosmogony. Combat with *mś.w Bdšt* is the first cosmic battle of the young sun god with the forces of Chaos and victory over them in fact completes the myth of creation of the Universe, is its 'happy ending'.

N. Semenov made very interesting observations in this regard in the scope of comparative religious studies,[780] stressing the heterogeneity of cosmogonic myths, which are clearly divided into two stages in the majority of mythologies – the first period, following immediately after the act of creation, with its undifferentiated elements of the Universe (when the sky was not separated from the earth, men and gods lived together, etc.) – a kind of a *Golden Age*; and time, which followed the dramatic separation of these elements, i.e. formation of the Universe on 'the

[774] Literary the 'enemy', but with the determinative of 'serpent'.
[775] Budge 1898: 2 (6); 41, 2–3. Almost the same as in the text of BD 17 in pNjꜣ pLondon BM EA 9929 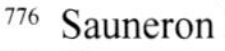 (Lapp 2006: 19).
[776] Sauneron 1989; Leitz 1997; Stegbauer 2010: 274–298.
[777] Sauneron 1989: 14 (§ 20); 15, fn. 6; 74 (§ 48a); 108–109 (§ 80b); Leitz 1997: 146; Stegbauer 2010: 282, 289, 295.
[778] Sauneron 1989: 163.
[779] Павлова, Зубов 1997: 198, прим. 34.
[780] Семенов 2005: 108–121.

way it is now', but violating primitive 'ideal' state of the Cosmos. According to the scientist, the latter should be defined with a special term 'Cosmo-agony'.[781]

Apparently, the fight with *mś.w Bdšt* in the Egyptian notions occurred daily at the sunrise (based on the *Book of Gates*, on the hour before it – the 11th, penultimate hour of the night, when the struggle against the forces of evil ended with victory of Re), since in the morning, according to the Egyptians, the sun is reborn in a young, new form, and this regeneration was perceived as a new act of creation and a new victory over the forces of darkness, where the fight lasted all night while the infernal solar boat was moving in the Underworld from the western Horizon to the eastern.

[781] Семенов 2005: 108–109, 118–120.

Chapter 7

Essence of *mś.w Bdšt* in the Egyptian world view

The question whether there is some relation between the BD 17 mysterious serpent and the text is here discussed. The problem deserves an affirmative answer and, moreover, the name of this snake can be identified. In our opinion, this name was *Bdšt* – 'Weakness'.

This can be confirmed by the determination of the creature's name itself, from early Middle Kingdom data. Thus, on the coffin BH_1Br (*M33*, Brusseles E 5037) in CT Sp. 335 *Bdšt* is written with the 'serpent' determinative / I14,[782] presumably / I64 (?) in T_2Be.[783] New Kingdom and Third Intermediate Period BD 17 determinative of 'serpent' for *Bdšt* in **Version I**[784] is variously written:

– p*Nj3* pLondon BM EA 9929 + 9934A–D + 9935G–H (19th–20th Dynasties),[785] p*3ś.t-m-3ẖ-bi.t* pLondon BM EA 9904 (21st Dynasty);[786]

– p*Ns-Imn* pLondon BM EA 10040 (21st–22nd Dynasties),[787] texts on the 2nd shrine of Tutankhamun (Cairo J.E. 60666),[788] the tombs of *Sn-nḏm* TT 1[789] and *Imn-n-ipt* TT 265;[790]

– p*P3-di-mw.t* pLondon BM EA 10093 (21st–22nd Dynasties);[791]

– p*Nẖt-Imn* pBerlin 3002 (19th Dynasty);[792]

[782] CT IV: 291a. M. Speleers, the first publisher of the coffin, interpreted determinative as by mistake (Speleers 1922: 647), but A. de Buck gives the correct reading of the sign as .
[783] CT IV: 291a.
[784] Urk. V: Abs. 1.
[785] Lapp 2006: 19.
[786] Shorter 1938: 84.
[787] Shorter 1938: 84.
[788] Lapp 2006: 19.
[789] Borghouts 1988: 55, pl. XVIII, nº 3; Saleh 1984: 20; Saura i Senjaume, 2006: 108, 109 (CW–VIa).
[790] Saleh 1984: 21, 22.
[791] Shorter 1938: 84.
[792] Lapp 2006: 19; 149, S. 28, Anm. r) E. (cf. pBremner-Rhind 25, 19: (Faulkner 1933: 54).

 – p*Ḳnn3* pLeiden T 2 (19th Dynasty);[793]

 – p*Hw-nfr* pLondon BM EA 9901 (19th Dynasty); pDublin TCLM 1661 () (19th Dynasty).[794]

 – p*Nb.snj* pLondon BM EA 9900 (18th Dynasty).[795]

In **Version II**[796] the *Bdšt* 'serpent' in BD 17 is thus determined:

 – p[?]-*Ỉmn.t* pLondon BM EA 10448 (21st–22nd Dynasties);[797]

 – text in the tomb *Ỉmn-n-ipt* TT 265 (19th Dynasty);[798]

 – p*P3-di-mw.t* pLondon BM EA 10093 (22nd Dynasty);[799]

 – p*Ḳnn3* pLeiden T 2 (19th Dynasty).[800]

The determinative of 'cobra'  is quiet frequent for writing *Bdš(/t)* in this version:

 – p*Ỉmn-ḥtp* pCairo CG 40002; J.E. 21369 (pBoulaq 21) (18th Dynasty)[801] and text on the 2nd shrine of Tutankhamun (Cairo J.E. 60666);[802]

 – p*Nww* pLondon BM EA 10477 (18th Dynasty);[803]

793 Lapp 2006: 19.
794 Lapp 2006: 19.
795 Shorter 1938: 84; Lapp 2006: 18; cf. Urk. V: 126 (10).
796 Urk. V: Abs. 22.
797 Shorter 1938: 111.
798 Saleh 1984: 22.
799 Shorter 1938: 111.
800 Lapp 2006: 201.
801 Lapp 2006: 200; Munro 1994 II: Taf. 86 (394).
802 Lapp 2006: 201.
803 Lapp 2006: 200.

– p*Hw-nfr* pLondon BM EA 9901 (19th Dynasty).[804]

Apart from BD 17, *Bdšt* is determined by the symbol of 'serpent' or 'serpent, whose body is stricken with knives' ( ) also in BD 140 after p*Iw.f-ꜥnḫ* pTurin 1791:[805] BD 18[806] and 'Introductory Hymn to Re' after p*ꜣnj* pLondon BM EA 10470 in the same p*ꜣnj*,[807] '*Cairo Calendar*',[808] pBremner-Rhind 24, 22; 25, 18–19; 32, 47; 32, 54,[809] pBrooklyn 47.218.84 (IV,4–V,4),[810] 'Ophiological treatise' (pBrooklyn 47.218.48/.85)[811] and some other documents. These 'serpent' determinatives are listed in the 'Berlin Wörterbuch',[812] in the 'Vocabulary' of the *Book of the Dead* by E. A. W. Budge[813] and in 'Lexikon der ägyptischen Götter'.[814] K. Sethe and R. Faulkner paid particular attention to this determinative in writings of *Bdš(/t)*.[815] These facts call for further scrutiny on the 'serpent' essence of *Bdšt*.

We can first conclude that *Bdšt* is an absolutely independent image, whose children can be found in BD 17 and other sources. Therefore, it can be directly depicted in the vignette as a rival of cat-Re. The identification of the serpent with Apophis on vignette BD 17 can not be considered a mistake. As noted above, we have several sources clearly indicating it. The functions of *Bdšt* and Apophis in mythology were undoubtedly similar. The New Kingdom clearly generated the concept that Apophis is the most powerful personification of evil. Therefore, gradual syncretization of Apophis with other mythological serpents, including *Bdšt*, was a natural process, as well as transforming Apophis into the collective image.

In contrast to *mś.w Bdšt*, the independent role of *Bdšt* in sources has not been discerned. The text of BD 17 displays the battle of Re with the 'enemies' and 'children' of the serpent named *Bdšt*, but not with *Bdšt* itself.[816] In my opinion, this is the essence of the vignette BD 17, i.e. it metaphorically depicts the combat of cat-Re with *ḫftj.w* and *mś.w Bdšt*, shown in the form of a serpent.[817] Thus, I can

[804] Lapp 2006: 201.
[805] Budge 1898: 316 (8).
[806] In six documents with BD 18 of the New Kingdom *Bdšt* is determined with the symbol of 'cobra' , while in four scrolls it is written with the sign of goddess (Lapp 2009: 80–81). Probably this was the reason for St. Quirke to translate *mś.w Bdšt* in this spell as 'the children of the Weary Goddess' (Quirke 2013: 72).
[807] Quirke 2013: 74 (13); 2 (8).
[808] Leitz 1994: 72, 94, 102, 321, 341.
[809] Faulkner 1933.
[810] Meeks 2006: 10–11.
[811] Sauneron 1989: 14 (§ 20); 74 (§ 48a);108–109 (§ 80b); Leitz 1997: 146.
[812] Wb. I: 488.2 (4).
[813] Budge 1911: 139, 185.
[814] LGG III: 422.
[815] Pyr. Komm. III: 52; Faulkner 1937: 177, fn. 24, 22.
[816] Zandee 1960: 223–224.
[817] See: Тарасенко 2003: 199–200; 2005a: 104–125; Tarasenko 2006: 345ff. In 2010 the similar idea was also

assume that the function of *Bdšt* is derived from the very name – 'Weakness'. It is necessary to recall here the meaning which the Egyptians attributed to magic and creative power of the name (*rn*).[818]

In Egyptian concepts the name-*rn* was identical to the essence of its carrier, his personality,[819] and unusual common Theophoric names, magically assigned the connection between the man and the divine world.[820] Destruction or change of the name was equal to death of its owner, and even if he was already dead, since the destruction of the name was the result of the so-called 'second' and already irreversible death – *m(w)t(w) m wḥm* – the most dreaded fear of Egyptians.[821] And, as already noted, significant amount of spells and funerary texts were created to counteract irreversible death. Destruction of name meant not only disappearance of the person's individuality, but also disappearance of his/hers memory in society and among their offsprings, and this was an important aspect of funerary cult.[822] There was a special so-called *ritual of Damnatio Memoriae* aimed directly at *destructing* of the name,[823] and it was applied both to the living and to the dead (obviously criminals) through the formula *mt w3 n rn=f r* N / *mtt w3 rn=s r* N – literally 'The deceased, whose name is separated from N', written on special ritual clay figurines (found in the Lisht).[824] In order to protect the deceased from the 'accidental' / 'wrong' destruction of his name in the afterlife (for example, if it coincided with the name of the criminal in the 'curse'), there was a special formula, engraved in one of the Hieratic scrolls with the '*Oracular Amuletic Decree*': *ỉw=n <r> šd=s m ḏrt n3 nṯrw nty ṯ3j rn r rn* – 'We will keep it safe from the gods who take the name of the name'.[825]

Similar mechanism of using magic of the name is characteristic not only for religious and ritual texts. New Kingdom legal documents offer some parallels. In several cases the real names of criminals are deliberately changed to neglectful, 'ungodly', etc.[826] For example, the text of the 'Turin Juridical papyrus' (pJur.Turin) is characteristic[827] outlining the process of harem conspiracy against Ramses III,

independently proposed by M. Kemboly (Kemboly 2010: 336, fn. 1063 ('I do consider *msw bdš* as denoting a single being, that is, the snake, since it is represented so on the vignettes accompanying the spell...')). Cf. also: Corteggiani 1995: 145 ('Un texte court, écrit dans la vignette elle-même, précise parfois que le grand reptile, qui représente ici les 'Enfants de la déchéance', n'est autre qu'Apophis, l'ennemi éternel de Rê, qui doit être à jamais conjuré puisque, n'ayant pas été créé, il échappe à toute destruction définitive et peut, chaque jour, recommencer inlassablement ses attaques contre la marche du soleil').

[818] See: Bonnet 1952: 501–504; Vernus 1982: Kol. 320–326; Taylor 2001: 23–24.

[819] Bonnet 1952: 501–504; Vernus 1982: Kol. 320–326.

[820] Baines 1991a: 176–178.

[821] Bochi 1999: 76–77.

[822] Bochi 1999: 74–75.

[823] Bochi 1999: 73–86.

[824] Plater 2001: 138.

[825] Plater 2001: 146.

[826] Initially this fact was pointed out by G. Posener (Posener 1946: 51–56), and further by D. Lorton (Lorton 1977: 16–19; cf. Taylor 2001: 23).

[827] KRI, V, 350–360; de Buck 1937: 152–163; Peden 1994: 195–210.

and it contains the following names: *Msd-sw-Rꜥ* – 'He is hated by Re', *Pꜣ-in-iwk* – 'Demon', *Pn-ḥwy-bin* – 'Disgusting of Penhevi', *Bin-m-Wꜣst* – 'Disgusting in Thebes', *Pꜣ-Rꜥ-kꜣmn=f* – 'He is blinded by Re' and *Šꜥd-msḏr=f* – 'Cut ear'.[828] It can be inferred from this that distortion of names was aimed at depriving of funerary cult (it can not be 'effective' without the name), but after the execution the convicted 'automatically' went beyond its scope. Still unclear are the criterion for this practice (in pJur.Turin only six out of forty names were changed).

Another example using the same magical mechanism is given in the data of the so-called *Execration ritual* (*Ächtungsritual*).[829] Here, the action was aimed not at immediate physical destruction of 'cursed', but at turning them into *sḳr.w* – i.e. 'killed' (ritually, but not physically!), while such a fate was prepared not for all potential enemies of Egypt and not at once. According to A. E. Demidchik, the 'mechanism' of the 'curse' was activated only in case of 'rebellious' plan and only in relation to those who initiate it'.[830] It was assumed that as a result of the ritual, the 'rebellious' external or internal enemy should loose the ability to resist the punishing will of the king. The figurine of the stranger, used in the *Execration ritual* of the Old Kingdom from the Dakhla Oasis (Balat No. 2326)[831] indicates a special term for identifying the position of 'cursed' (*iꜣm* and *rsy.w*): ***nny*** – denoting a state of 'complete impotence and immobility'.[832] Another term for the ritual state of the 'cursed' was a verb ***rtḥ***, which had a semantically close meaning to *nny* – to 'chain', 'result in petrification', etc..[833] A. E. Demidchik describes the meaning of the verb *nny*: 'medical texts used this word to denote urinary incontinence, heaviness in legs, and even patients who can not eat ... In the funeral texts *nny* – indication of complete powerlessness and immobility, is very harmful for gods and deceased. Such deceased were captured by some terrible 'catchers / fishermen of the *nny.w*-deceased'.[834] The enemies of the solar creator-god were subjected to the same condition *nny*. The lower register of the 2nd hour of the *Book of Gates* (scene No.8) has the image of four enemies in the state of *nny* in front of Atum (***Figure 66,***[835] ***67).***[836]

As a result of the ritual, in case of rebellion the 'cursed' enemy was to suffer the state of helplessness and inability to resist, and therefore become absolutely safe for god, king and state. I believe it to be very close to the serpent-form enemy of Re in the BD 17 – *bdšt* – i.e. 'impotent' in front of the sun-god, which is clearly

[828] Лурье 1960: 299, прим. 4; 300, прим. 1; 302, прим 1–2; 303, прим. 2–3.
[829] See: Ritner 1993: 136ff; Muhlestein 2008; Plater 2001: 124–165.
[830] Демидчик 2005: 145.
[831] Grimal 1985: 112, pl. I; Plater 2001: 158.
[832] Wb. II: 275; Демидчик 2005: 146; Grimal 1985: 116–117.
[833] Wb. II: 460; Демидчик 2005: 147–148.
[834] Демидчик 2005: 146.
[835] Hornung 1999: 60, Figure 27.
[836] Hornung 1999: 67, Figure 31. Cf. Hornung 1979–1980 II: 64–71.

indicated in the passage of the Great Hymn to Re-Horakhty in pBerlin 3050: III,8–IV,1: *mś.w Bdšt nn wsr snm Rʿ m ḫftyw=f* – '*mś.w Bdš* has no more power (*wsr*), Re captured his enemies'.[837] In several texts *nny* literally means the state of death.[838] But what is even more interesting is the first creations of the *demiurge* in Nun – sky, earth, soil and serpents – were created in the same condition of 'impotence-*nnyw*', according to p*Bremner-Rhind* 26, 21–24 and 28, 21–24.[839]

(22) *ʿš3t ḫpr.w m pri m r=i nn ḫpr p.t nn ḫpr t3 nn km3 s3t ḏdf.wt m bt pwj ṯs.n=i ḳm=śn* (23) *m Nw m nnyw*

'(22) Numerous are creations coming out of my mouth: the sky has not been created yet, the earth has not yet appeared, the soil has not been created yet and snakes in this place. I made them in (23) Nun as *nnyw*' (pBremner-Rhind 26, 22–23).[840]

A very close description of the first creations of demiurge as *nny* has been preserved in Demotic pCarlsberg I, II 23–26 (Roman Period).[841] The Hymn to Ptah in pBerlin P. 3048 (IV, 7) describes as *nnyw* the eternal state of the world itself.[842]

FIGURE 66

[837] Sauneron 1953: 85–86.
[838] Zandee 1960: 83–84.
[839] Faulkner 1933: 60, 69–70; Kákosy 2003: 97.
[840] Faulkner 1933: 60.
[841] Kákosy 1998: 97.
[842] Wolf 1929: 23; Kákosy 2003: 99.

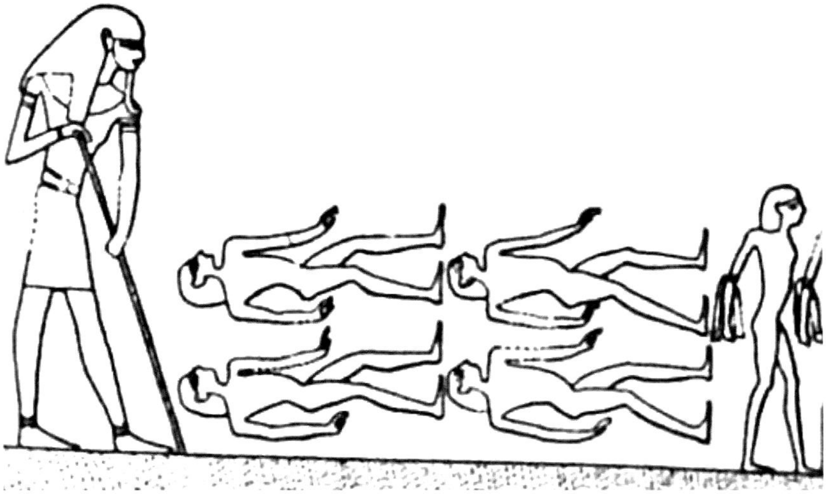

FIGURE 67

Therefore, in my opinion, the name of 'Weakness' (*Bdšt*) directly and intentionally implies the characteristics of this image – its real, magically approved inability to resist the forces of the creator-god, its actual 'weakness / impotence' in front of him. In other words, *Bdšt* is not the direct name of its owner, but rather a name-epithet or nominative characteristic, which goes back to the mythological Cosmogonic history (in fact, the metaphor). The essence of this name consisted in magical weakening, in neutralizing the power of the eternal Chaos, visually perceived in a serpent appearance, making it victory over Re impossible.

Besides Apophis (similar to his positive antipode Re) had his own names-substitutes, which veiled his essence and the knowledge of which was a prerequisite for victory or magical acquisition of power over him. According to pBremner-Rhind, 32, 13–42,[843] there were twenty-nine names of Apophis, but *Bdšt* was not recorded among them.[844] On the other hand, the direct use of the 'true' name could bear a threat. For this reason the determinative 'serpent' to the name of Apophis was often depicted struck with knives . This can be correlated with the phenomenon of 'mutilating' Hieroglyphic signs of animals, birds and serpents in the funerary texts,[845] so that they (the 'revived' forces, embodied in the images) were not able to harm the deceased.

[843] Faulkner 1933: 89–90; 1938: 52.
[844] For more attributes of Apophis, which bring him closer to Re, see: Borghouts 1973: 114–150.
[845] Lacau 1913: 1–64; 1926: 69–81.

Conclusion

Given in this book is a comprehensive study of the scene depicting the cat, cutting off the head of the serpent under the branches of the *išd*-tree found on the BD 17 vignettes. Twenty-six sources were referred to within the source analysis. Seventeen of them are drawings of funerary papyri (fifteen in BD 17 and two are independent scenes; one scroll of the late 18th Dynasty, five of the 19th Dynasty, one of the 20th Dynasty, and ten of 21st Dynasty). Seven are Theban Tomb painted scenes (six of 19th Dynasty, one of 20th Dynasty) and two are known from coffin paintings (21st Dynasty).

The earliest version of the BD 17 vignette was recorded in p*Nḫt* pLondon BM EA 10471 (end of the 18th Dynasty). The majority of the images were created during the 19th Dynasty, when they are also found in tomb paintings (six cases).

During the 21st Dynasty the scene was mainly represented in the papyri of the *Book of the Dead*, including a series of five scrolls with the selected set of BD 17 vignettes, which, in my opinion, represented the last stage in the development of illustrated Hieroglyphic ('Theban') Recension of the *Book of the Dead.*[846]

In p*Nsj-tꜣ-nb.t-išrw* (pGreenfield) pLondon BM 10554 the considered scene is repeated three times in different iconography. The unique composition of the texts and illustrations, as well as an impressive length of the scroll of *Nsj-tꜣ-nb.t-išrw* (40.53 m) can be explained by the fact, that according to its specific title (*bꜣk.t (n.t) pꜣ ipw n Ỉmn-Rꜥ njśwt nṯr.w* – 'Servant of archive of Amun-Re, the king of the gods'), this noble priestess had direct official access to Theban temple archives of Amun, and she could have made use of them when ordering the design of her own funeral papyrus.

Within the Third Intermediate Period the scene with the cat and serpent was used independently from BD 17 illustrations, both in the 'Mythological papyri' and '*Amduat* papyri', and on coffin paintings. But in the Ptolemaic Period this scene appeared only in BD 17 illustrations and its iconography did not essentially go beyond New Kingdom tradition.

According to H. Grapow,[847] this pictorial composition illustrates *Abschnitt 22* of the BD 17 text. Based on the spell, the picture depicts the cat, identified as *miw ꜥꜣ*

[846] pꜥ*nḫ=f-(n-)Ḫnśw* pCologny-Geneva CI, p*Ṯnt-imnt.t-hr-ib* pCologny-Geneva CII, p*Ns*(*j*)-*Ḫnśw* pTurin 1818: p*Ḏd-Ḫnśw* pHermitage No. 18587: p*Diw-sw-n-Mw.t* pLondon BM EA 9948.
[847] Urk. V: 50–54.

– 'the Great cat' = Re, the *išd*-tree and serpent, not named in the text directly. Two hypotheses regarding its personification have developed. M. Mathieu believed it to be *Ỉmj-(w)hn=f*, while most scholars adducing prescripts from the pictures in the tomb of *Nḫ.t-tw-Ỉmn* TT 335 and p*T3w-wḏ3.t-Rᶜ* pCairo S.R. VII. 1149 ('Mythological papyrus'), suggest that the picture shows Apophis. I believe both hypotheses to be disputable since the evidence basis to identify the serpent of the BD 17 vignette as *Ỉmj-(w)hn=f* and as Apophis is taken from indirect sources. The text of the spell shows that the only 'enemy' of Re in this mythem is *mś.w Bdšt* – 'Children of Weakness'. Thus, in my opinion, the main key to understand the vignette and the meaning of the myths is the essence of *mś.w Bdšt*. In Egyptology the study of this subject matter was undertaken only sporadically and was based on limited source materials (H. Altenmüller, Chr. Leitz, D. Meeks). A specific comprehensive study of this image is here developed for the first time.

In the text the *mś.w Bdšt* have been mentioned in two semantic groups of BD 17 (*Abschnitt 1* and *22*), describing the Cosmic Combat, which took place in Hermopolis and / or Heliopolis between Re in the form of the 'Great cat' with the 'enemies' (*ḫftj.w*) and *mś.w Bdšt*. In one case, it is reported on the destruction of *mś.w Bdšt* on the Primeval Hill in Hermopolis, and in another – about the Combat in the Eastern sky, separation of *išd*-tree and further punishment of the rebels in Heliopolis. The first version is not fixed in CT Spell 335, and it is a New Kingdom gloss (although the mythem dates back to the Middle Kingdom). The second, on the contrary, is given in CT Spell 335[848] and in this case we can suggest solar implications – an indication of the area of sunrise. Their Cosmogonic context relates them. To distinguish these two local versions, the following terms were introduced: **Version I** (Urk. V: Abs. 1) = the 'Hermopolitan Version', and **Version II** (Urk. V: Abs. 22) – the 'Heliopolitan Version'.

The first mentions of *Bdšt* are found in PT Spell 343,[849] and *mś.w Bdšt* – in CT spells 60,[850] 335,[851] 409,[852] 477,[853] as well as in the pRamesseum XV verso. In the New Kingdom, Late and Ptolemaic Periods *mś.w Bdšt* are mentioned quite often, but significant similarities with BD 17 cannot be proven. I managed to identify a certain proximity to the BD 17 mythem only in a brief and unclear indication from the so-called 'Cairo Calendar' of the New Kingdom (pCairo J.E. 86637: pSallier IV and pLondon BM EA 10474), where the destruction of *mś.w Bdšt* is reported in six cases.

848 CT IV: 290–291a.
849 Pyr. § 558a-b.
850 CT I: 253f.
851 CT IV: 290a–291a, 290c (T_1C^b), 412h (Sq_7Sq).
852 CT V: 233g.
853 CT VI: 35o.

The available evidences proved to be rather fragmented and contradictory to help us clarify the content of the two BD 17 mythem versions. To interpret the 'Heliopolitan' Version II I have adduced additional sources of contextually-close contents: data of BD 175A, BD 123, CT Sp. 409, pBrooklyn 47.218.84 and the *Book of the Heavenly Cow*, which allowed us to correlate the myth plot of the 'Heliopolitan' Version II about *mś.w Bdšt* BD 17 with Thanatological myth that describes the final stage of Cosmogony associated with the appearance of death and separation of Cosmic spheres of men and gods. The comparative analysis of this source complex demonstrated that this central mythological plot in Egyptian beliefs was preserved in religious consciousness for a long time. It originated in the Middle Kingdom and survived in texts and rituals up to the Graeco-Roman Period. References to the rebellion of *mś.w Bdšt* are quiet numerous in the later periods of Egyptian history, and according to pBrooklyn 47.218.84 (§ 10), the religious festival with a ritual reproducing this rebellion was celebrated in Heliopolis as late as the 30th Dynasty. The *Myth of destruction of mankind*, set out in the *Book of the Heavenly Cow*, was reflected in the '*Book of the Fayum*' of Roman times, while L. Kákosy highlights that the mythem about the rebellion of 'Children of Nut', known from BD 175A, was reproduced in the Hermetic treatise 'Κόρη Κόσμου'. Other replica of this myth is known in Demotic pCarlsberg 462.

According to information from H. Altenmüller and Chr. Leitz, a significant reference to *mś.w Bdšt*, which can be attributed to the 'Hermopolitan' Version I of BD 17, can be found in the text and picture of the 11th hour of the *Book of Gates* (scene No. 69). Characteristic for the visual display of this mythem is the represention of *mś.w Bdšt* in the quaternary form and contrasting them to the four Children of Horus, which is considered as a principle of symmetry by Chr. Leitz. Similar to this motif is the plot of pBrooklyn 47.218.84, indicating that *mś.w Bdšt* are four fingers of the creator-god, who rebelled against him (IV,5–V,4). The pRamesseum XV verso of the Middle Kingdom also denote relation between *mś.w Bdšt* and the fingers of the *demiurge*.

I agree with Chr. Leitz, who sees reminiscences of the Hermopolitan Cosmogonic myth in the images of vignettes BD 30B and BD 125, where the four Children of Horus are depicted next to the throne of Osiris on a lotus flower growing out of the pond or throne symbols. In my opinion, one scene of BD 110 composition (scene '3b' by J. Gesellensetter) and its early prototype (scenes of CT Sp. 465 (V, 357 (XVII), 361 (XVII)) could be ascribed to the same range of graphic replicas of the local myth. They depict the island surrounded by channels, where figures of four deities are usually placed. In the *Book of the Dead*, they are called the 'Great Ennead in the Fields of Offerings', but the *Coffin Texts* marked them as four Children of Horus. The island adjacent territory is designated as *mśḫn* (*nṯr*) – 'Place of birth (of god)' and *ḳnḳn.t* – 'Place of the Combat'. Based on these nominations, which go back to the Cosmogonic legend, in my opinion, this 'territory' was considered to be the mythical place of appearance of the Primeval Hill, birthplace of the young creator-god and battle place of four Children of Horus with the forces of Chaos (probably in the quaternary form of *mś.w Bdšt*) what in its semantics is associated with the BD 17 mythem 'Hermopolitan' Version I.

Therefore, with the aid of the *mś.w Bdšt* image, I reached the following conclusions:

- It was found that *mś.w Bdšt* had serpent appearance. The following Egyptian sources indicate its serpentine nature: the image in the scene of 11th hour of the *Book of Gates*; direct messages of pBrooklyn 47.218.84 and pBrooklyn 47.218.48/.85 (the so-called 'Ophiological Treatise'), where they are described as vipers; the use of the 'serpent' determinative for *mś.w Bdšt* writing in a number of documents.
- As the enemies of Re *mś.w Bdšt* were identified in Hermopolis and Heliopolis with the Ancient of Days forces of chaos, confronting the sun (in the quaternary form) on the final stage of the cosmogony.
- In later sources the image of *mś.w Bdšt*, as the enemies of the sun-god, was naturally merged with the idea of the king's enemies and rebels.
- In the Egyptian beliefs the fight against *mś.w Bdšt* takes place daily at the sunrise.
- Since the text of BD 17 describes the Combat between Re and the Children of *Bdšt,* the same is likely to be reflected on the vignette, i.e. it depicts the battle of Re against *mś.w Bdšt*, metaphorically shown in the form of a serpent.

The word *bdšt*, crucial for clarifying the understanding of the *mś.w Bdšt* image, is derived from the noun *bdš*: 'weakness', 'impotence', 'tiredness', 'lethargy', 'fatigue', etc. The ways of spelling *Bdšt,* here assembled from different sources in the full chronological range of their use, both in the form of determination and in the form of word endings, represent all possible grammatical range to determine the gender and number. On the whole, I can conclude that *Bdšt* acts as a proper name and can be translated as 'Weakness'.

Since the sources do not provide any independent role of *Bdšt* in mythology (except for vague data of PT 343 (Pyr. § 558a-b) for *Bdšt* as a goddess associated with offering ritual), understanding the function of this character in Egyptian religious and mythological beliefs should be derived from the very meaning of the name 'Weakness'. Egyptians considered the *rn*-name to be identical to the essence of its owner. In my opinion, the name 'Weakness' was intentionally given as a metaphorical description of the character: the inability to resist the forces of the creator-god, its 'impotence' before him. Thus, I believe that *Bdšt* is a kind of *epithet*, acting as an abstract allegory to the Cosmogonic myth and neutralizing the forces of the Primordial Chaos, threatening Re.

The typical similar mechanism of applying the magic of name is also noted in legal documents and execration rituals. In the 'Turin Judicial Papyrus', the names of six criminals are deliberately changed to neglectful names. A special term *nny* to describe the position of the 'cursed', denoting the state of 'complete impotence and immobility', was used in such ritual practice. The enemies of the solar creator-god suffered the same condition (2nd hour of the *Books of Gates*, scene No. 8), and in some texts *nny* literally means the state of death. Besides, according to some sources, the first creations of the *demiurge* in Nun (sky, earth, soil and serpents) emerge in the state of *nnyw* (pBremner-Rhind 26, 21–24; 28, 21–24; pCarlsberg I, II 23–26). As a result, the 'cursed' person was turned into a state of impotence, deprived of the ability to resist and became safe for god and the king. This, in my view, is close to the serpent-form enemy of Re in BD 17 as *bdšt*, that is 'weakened' or 'feeble' in front of the deity.[854] Designation of eternal enemies of Re, such as *mś.w Bdšt*, gives this definition a special cosmological value, elevating its origin to the Primeval Chaos, and their rebellion to the times of the mythical *Golden Age* that correlates with the image of *mś.w Bdšt* in the 'Heliopolitan' and 'Hermopolitan' BD 17 mythological plots.

The importance of the discussed myth in Egyptian worldview is determined by its crucial role in Thanatological beliefs (*mś.w Bdšt* are mentioned in about thirty different sources from the Middle Kingdom to the Ptolemaic Period) and the closely related concept of Eternity, displayed in the Egyptian terms of *nḥḥ* and *ḏt*. I agree with scholars, who understand *ḏt* as 'static eternity', as constancy, and *nḥḥ* as 'eternity', expressed by the cyclic flow. Static *ḏt*-eternity characterizes the world created by the *demiurge in illo tempore* in the Waters of the Primeval Ocean – this is the place, where the first creatures, gods and people appeared. As pointed out by Fr. Servajean,[855] this perfect world in the first phase of Cosmogony was 'reorganized' as a result of the rebellion, known to us from the sources given in this chapter (BD 17, BD 175A, the *Book of the Heavenly Cow*). This revolt marked separation of gods and people. The second and final stage of Creation came, destroying the *Golden Age*, the heaven and the celestial bodies were created, as well as the Underworld. From this moment the flow of *nḥḥ*-eternity begins (according to Fr. Servajean) – the cycles of stars, the moon and the sun appeared, forming the basis of measurable flow of time. For mankind it marked the loss of immortality, which is the main essence of the Egyptian Thanatological myth (BD 175^{A} refers to some 'hidden destruction' (*ḥḏi imnt*) performed by 'Children of Nut' in the Universe, created by Atum, resulting in fixing their life

[854] Cf. pBerlin 3050: III,8 – IV,1.
[855] Servajean 2007.

length). Thus, death becomes a kind of bridge overcoming this 'separation' and connecting people with the supernatural world of the First Act of Creation and *ḏt*-eternity. Overcoming the ontological 'separation' of the worlds (that is, in the way of death) itself symbolized victory over *mś.w Bdšt*, who, like *mś.w Nw.t*, were the culprits and participants of the ancient 'rebel' that created this cosmic 'split'.

Placing the Cosmogonic myth in the forms of written description concerning *mś.w Bdšt* mythem and its graphical additions (vignette with cat, serpent and sacred tree of BD 17) into the *Book of the Dead* was intended to overcome death and 'the worlds' split'. It is symbolic, that vignettes displays not the final myth (in this *two* 'horizon trees' of 'current' model of the Universe would be painted, as in some BD vignettes), but its culmination – the cat-Re victory over *mś.w Bdšt* ('horizon tree' on the vignette is not split), in other words – a victory over the Chaos and death forces. The discussed visual representation of the ancient combat had to 'guarantee' the infinite repetition of this mythical victory. Equally, the same 'guaranteed' the essence of the name *Bdšt* – 'Weakness'.

Appendix 1

Catalogue of sources
The scene with the cat, serpent and sacred tree, 18th–21st Dynasties

№	Source	Vignette (Fig.)	Iconography			

Papyri						
18th Dynasty						
1	*pNḫt* pLondon BM EA 10471+10473 end of the 18th Dynasty **BD 17**	**Fig. 1**[855]	+ ←	+ (1)[856]	+ → (2)[857]	–
19th Dynasty						
2	p*Nḫt-ꜥ-Imn* (Ba) pBerlin P. 3002 **BD 17**	**Fig. 2,**[858] **2a**[859]	+ →	+ (4)	+ ← (2)	?
3	pDublin (Da) pTrinity College Library Museum 1661 anonymous **BD 17**	**Fig. 6**[860]	+ →	+ (1)	+ ← (encircling the cat)	+
4	p*Ḳnnꜣ* (La) pLeiden T 2 **BD 17**	**Fig. 3,**[861] **3a**[862]	+ ←	+ (1)	+ → (3)	–
5	p*Hw-nfr* (Ag) pLondon BM EA 9901 **BD 17**	**Fig. 4,**[863] **4a–b**[864]	+ ←	+ (1)	+ → (2)	+
6	p*ꜣnj* (Eb) pLondon BM EA 10470 **BD 17**	**Fig. 5,**[865] **5a**[866]	+ →	+ (1)	+ ← (1)	+
20th Dynasty						
7	p*Pꜣ-ḳrr* pLeiden T 4 (AMS 14)[867] **BD 17**	**Fig. 7**[868]	+ ←	+ (1)	+ → (3)	?

855 © Trustees of the British Museum.
856 Here and hereinafter it is the number of knifes.
857 Here and hereinafter it is the number of bends of the snake corpse.
858 Munro 1997: Photo-Taf. 5.
859 Naville 1886 I: Taf. XXX (Ba); Lüscher 2014: Taf. 12, 13.
860 Naville 1886 I: Taf. XXX (Da).
861 Leemans 1882: pl. XI, 1.
862 Naville 1886 I: Taf. XXX (La).
863 Faulkner 2000: 48; Malek 2000, p. 85. pl. 52.
864 Naville 1886 I: Taf. XXX (Ag).
865 Malek 2000: 85, pl. 51.
866 Faulkner 1998: pl. 10.
867 Unpublished. Totenbuchprojekt Bonn, TM 134347, <totenbuch.awk.nrw.de/objekt/tm134347>.
868 © Photo by Leiden, Rijksmuseum van Oudheden.

	Third Intermediate Period					
8	p*Mw.t-m-wiꜣ* (Bb) pBerlin P. 3157 middle – end of the 21st Dynasty **BD 17**	**Fig. 8**[869]	+ ←	+ (1)	+ → (2)	+
9	p*Nsj-tꜣ-nb.t-išrw* (Ec) pLondon BM EA 10554 (pGreenfield) End of the 21st Dynasty – beginning of the 22nd Dynasty	**Fig. 9**[870] **BD 17**	+ ←	+ (1)	+ → (3)	+
		Fig. 10[871] **BD 124/125**	+ →	+ (1)	+ ← (1)	–
		Fig. 11[872] **Hymns to Re and Osiris**	+ ←	+ (1)	+ → (2)	+
10	p*Tꜣ-wḏꜣ.t-Rꜥ* pCairo S.R. VII. 11496 BD + "Mythological papyrus" middle of the 21st Dynasty **Mythical scene**	**Fig. 12**[873]	+ →	+ (1)	+ → (4)	+
11	p*Ini-pḥ=f-nḫt* pCologny-Geneva C (Bibliotheca Bodmeriana) middle of the 21st Dynasty **BD 17**	**Fig. 13**[874]	+ ←	+ (1)	+ → (3)	–
12	p*ꜥnḫ=f-(n-)Ḫnśw* pCologny-Geneva CI[875] 21st Dynasty **BD 17**	–	+ ←	+ (1)	+ → (3)	+
13	p*Ṯnt-imnt.t-hr-ib* pCologny-Geneva CII[876] (Bibliotheca Bodmeriana) 21st Dynasty **BD 17**	–	+ ←	+ (1)	+ → (3)	+
14	p*Nsj-Ḫnśw* pTurin 1818[877] 21st Dynasty **BD 17**	–	+ ←	+ (1)	+ → (3)	+

[869] Naville, 1886 I: Taf. XXX (Bb) (incorrect orientation of scenes).
[870] pGreenfield, Sh. 11 – © Trustees of the British Museum = Budge 1912: pl. XIV.
[871] pGreenfield, Sh. 37 – © Trustees of the British Museum = Budge 1912: pl. XLIII.
[872] pGreenfield, Sh. 76 – © Trustees of the British Museum = Budge 1912: pl. LXXXVII.
[873] Piankoff 1957 II: pl. 15 (Pap. No. 15).
[874] Bissing 1928: Taf. I; Bickel 2001:128–129, fig. 39.
[875] Unpublished, Totenbuchprojekt Bonn, TM 134678, <totenbuch.awk.nrw.de/objekt/tm134678>.
[876] Unpublished, Totenbuchprojekt Bonn, TM 134677, <totenbuch.awk.nrw.de/objekt/tm134677>.
[877] Unpublished, Totenbuchprojekt Bonn, TM 134600, <totenbuch.awk.nrw.de/objekt/tm134600>.

15	p*Ḏd-Ḫnśw* pЭрмитаж № 18587[878] 21st Dynasty **BD 17**	–	+ ←	+ (1)	+ → (3)	+
16	p*Diw-sw-n-Mw.t* pLondon BM 9948 21st Dynasty **BD 17**	**Fig. 14**[879]	+ ←	+ (1)	+ → (3)	+
17	p*P3-n-pj* pCologny-Geneva CVII (Bibliotheca Bodmeriana) 21st Dynasty **Scene in *Amduat* papyrus**	**Fig. 15,**[880] **15a**[881]	+ →	+ (1)	+ → (3)	–

Tomb decoration						
2	*Pn-bwi* and *K3-s3*[882] TT 10 (PM ²I. 1, p. 20–21) Deir el-Medina 19th Dynasty (Ramses II) **BD 17**	**Fig. 18**[883]	+ ←	+ (1)	+ → (2)	–
3	*Ḏḥwtj-mśw* TT 32 (PM ²I. 1, p. 49–50) El-Khokha 19th Dynasty (Ramses II) **BD 17**	**Fig. 19**[884]	+ ←	+ (1)	+ → (3)	+
4	*Nfr-ḥtp*[885] TT 216 (PM ²I. 1, p. 312–315) Deir el-Medina 19th Dynasty (Ramses II) **BD 17**	**Fig. 20,** **20a**[886]	+ ←	+ (1)	+ → (3)	+
5	*P3-šdw*[887] TT 292 (PM ²I. 1, p. 374–376). Deir el-Medina 19th Dynasty (Ramses II) **BD 17**	**Fig. 21**[888]	+ ←	+ (1)	+ → (2)	–
6	*Nḫt.tw-Imn* TT 335 (PM ²I.1, p. 401–404) Deir el-Medina 19th Dynasty **Spell against Apophis**	**Fig. 22,** **22a**[889]	+ ←	+ (3)	+ → (3)	–

878 Unpublished, Totenbuchprojekt Bonn, TM 134777, <totenbuch.awk.nrw.de/objekt/tm134777>.
879 Shorter 1938: pl. X.
880 Valloggia 1989:131–144, pl. 5.
881 Valloggia 1989: 144, fig. 44.
882 Unpublished. See: Saleh 1984: 18, Anm. 87.
883 © Institut Français d'Archéologie Orientale, Revault.
884 Kákosy, Bács, Bartos, Fábián, Gaál 2004 I: 199.
885 Unpublished. See: Saleh 1984: 18–19.
886 © Institut Français d'Archéologie Orientale, Ihab Mhd Ibrahim.
887 Unpublished. See: Saleh 1984: 18, Anm. 88.
888 © Institut Français d'Archéologie Orientale, Revault.
889 Bruyère 1926: 163, fig. 109; 171, fig. 113.

7	*Ỉni-ḥr-ḫ‘w* TT 359 (PM ^{2}I.1, p. 421–424) Deir el-Medina 19th Dynasty (Ramses III–IV) **Funerary spell, not from the BD corpus**	**Fig. 23**[890]; **23a**[891]	+ →	+ (1)	+ ← (2)	+
8	*Ỉni-ḥr.t-ms* El-Mashayikh 19th Dynasty (Merneptah) **BD 17**	**Fig. 24**[892]	+ →	+ (1)	+ ← (2?)	+

Coffin decoration						
1	*Ḫ3-‘s.t* Cairo J.E. 29665; CG 6076 21st Dynasty	**Fig. 25**[893]	+ →	+ (1)	+ ← (3)	+
2	*Ḫnśw-mś* Turin 2238; CGT 10106b 21st Dynasty	**Fig. 26**[894]	+ →	+ (1)	+ ← (1)	+
3	*P3-di-Ḫnśw* Lyon, Musée des Beaux-Arts H 2320–2321 21st Dynasty	**Fig. 27**[895]	+ ←	+ (1)	+ → (2)	+

890 Cherpion, Corteggiani 2010 II: 65, fig. 98.
891 Bruyère 1933: pl. XXI.
892 Ockinga, al-Masri 1988: 7–8 (Scene 5); pl. 11.
893 Niwiński 1996: 105, fig. 82.
894 Lanzone 1884: Tav. CLII (drawing); Niwiński 2004: Tav. XI. 2 (photo).
895 © Photo by Fr. Jamen.

Appendix 2

Selected texts

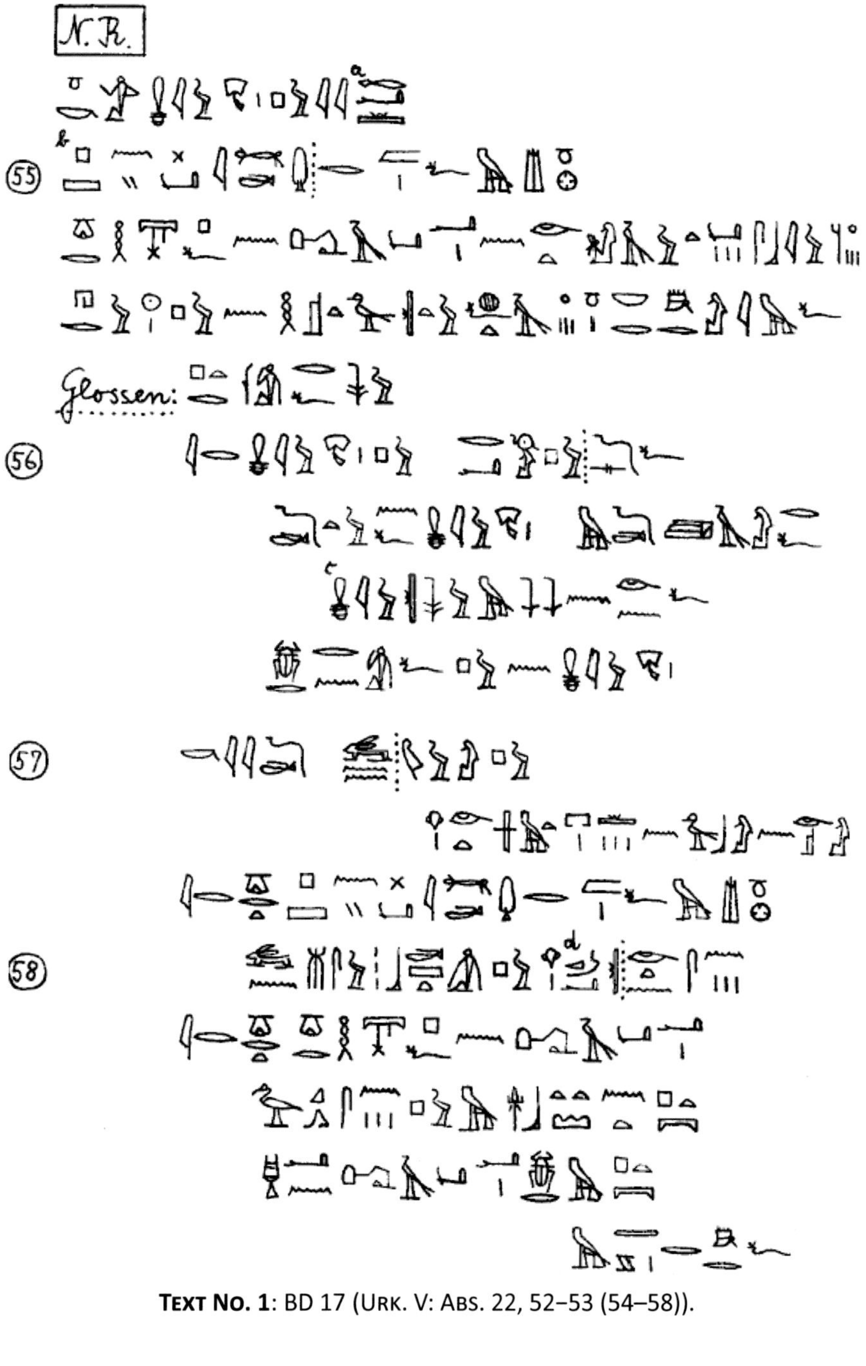

TEXT NO. 1: BD 17 (URK. V: ABS. 22, 52–53 (54–58)).

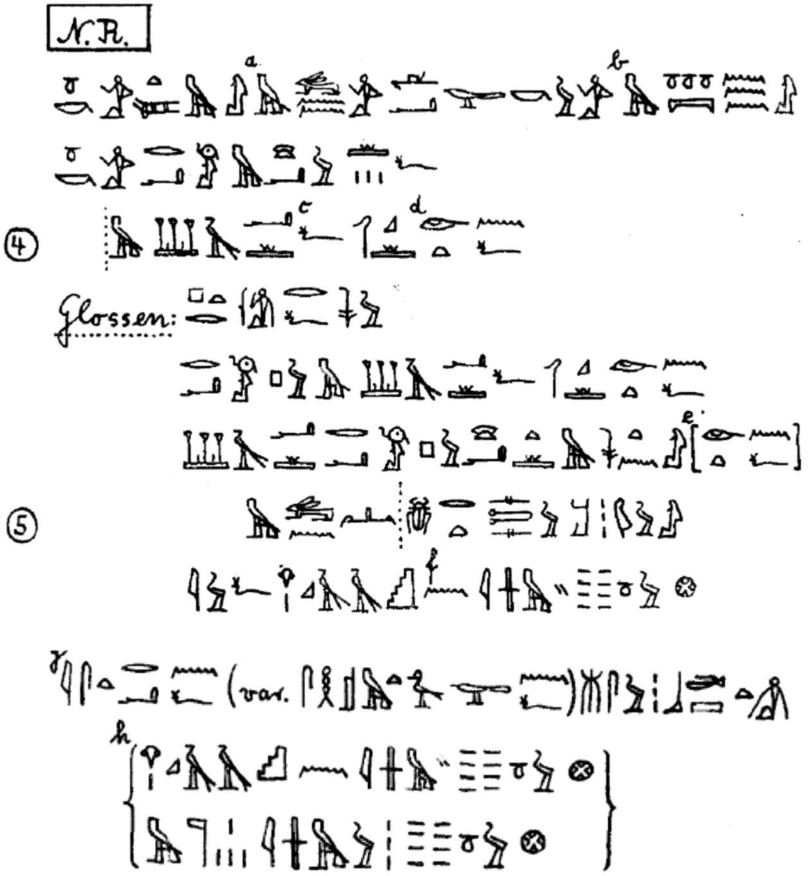

Text No. 2: BD 17 (Urk. V: Abs. 1, 6–7 (3–5)).

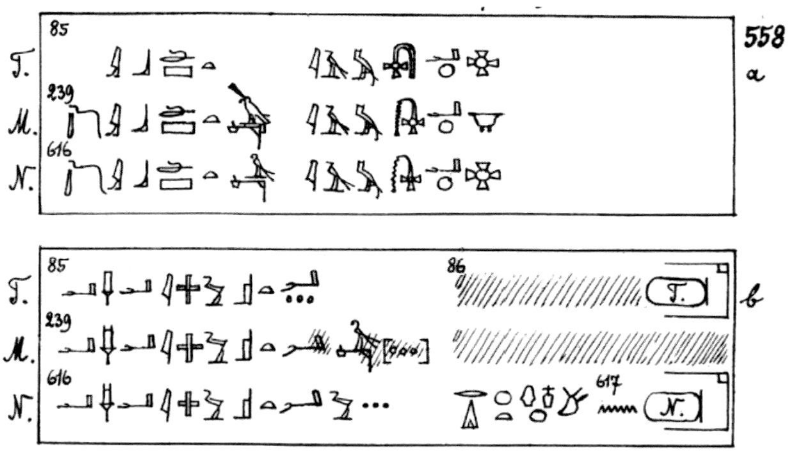

Text No. 3: PT 343, Pyr. § 558 a–b.

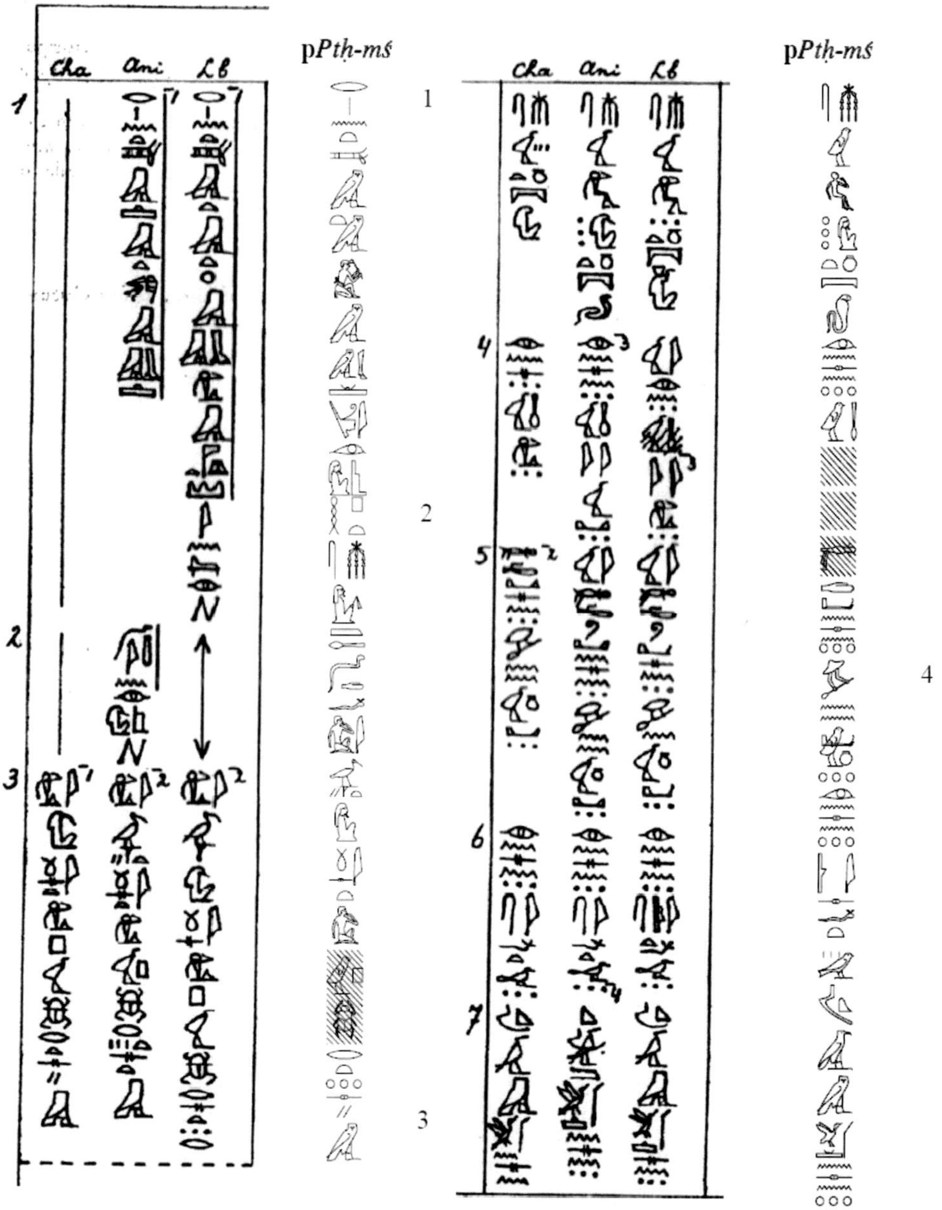

TEXT NO 4, 1. BD 175[A] (AFTER DE BUCK 1950: 86–88, AND LUFT 1977: TAF. III).

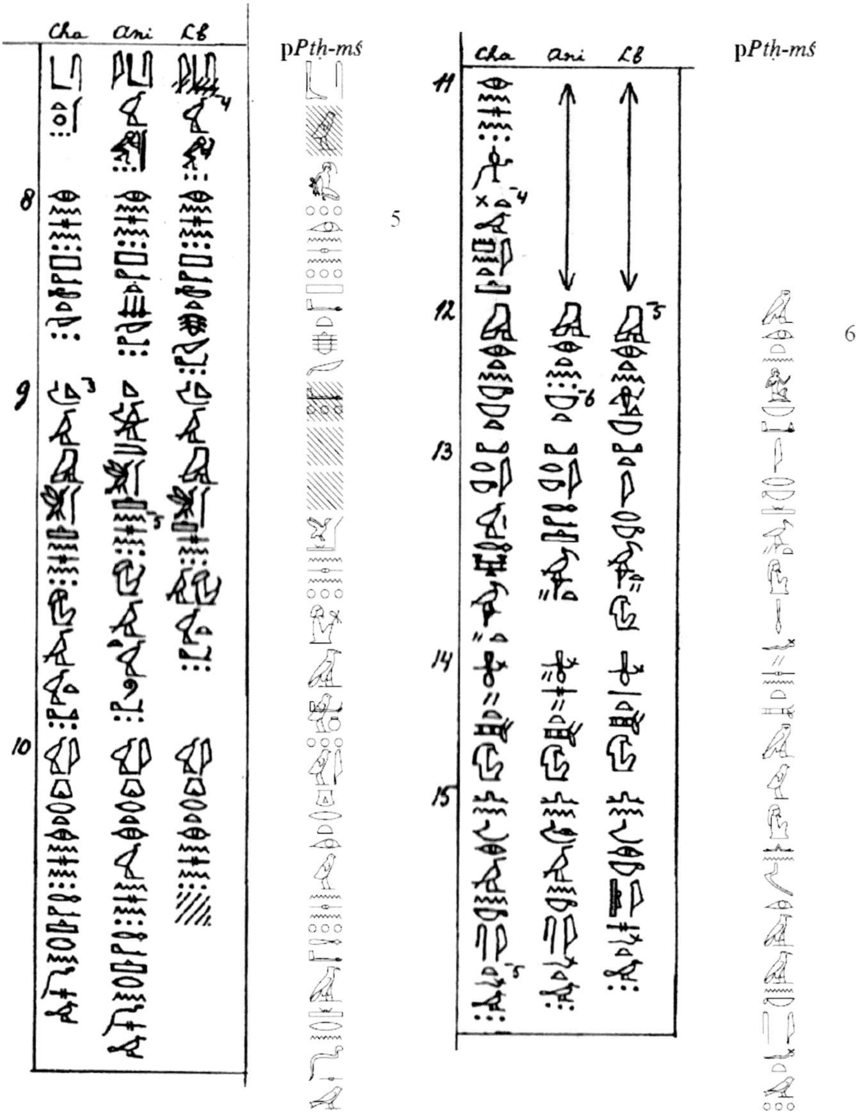

Text No. 4, 2. BD 175^{A} (after de Buck 1950: 86–88, and Luft 1977: Taf. III).

Text No. 5. Fragment of the inscription on the statue of *Nẖṯ=f-Mw.ṯ*, Cairo CG 42206; J.E. 36704, 22nd Dynasty (Osorkon II) (after Jansen-Winkeln 1985 II: 441 (b, 3)).

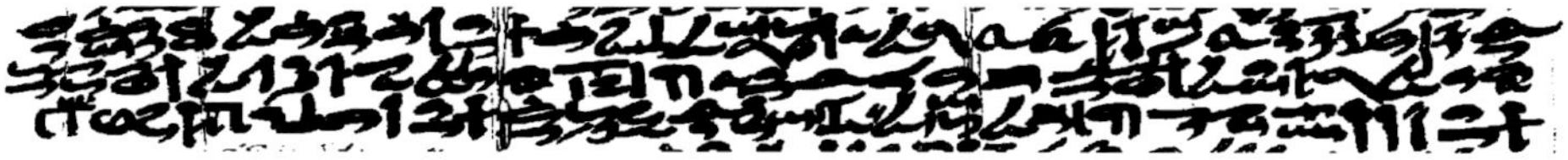

TEXT NO. 6. 'THE TEACHING FOR PTAHHOTEP', 637–644, PPRISSE, 19,6 – 19,8 (AFTER PRISSE D'AVENNES 1926: PL. XIX).

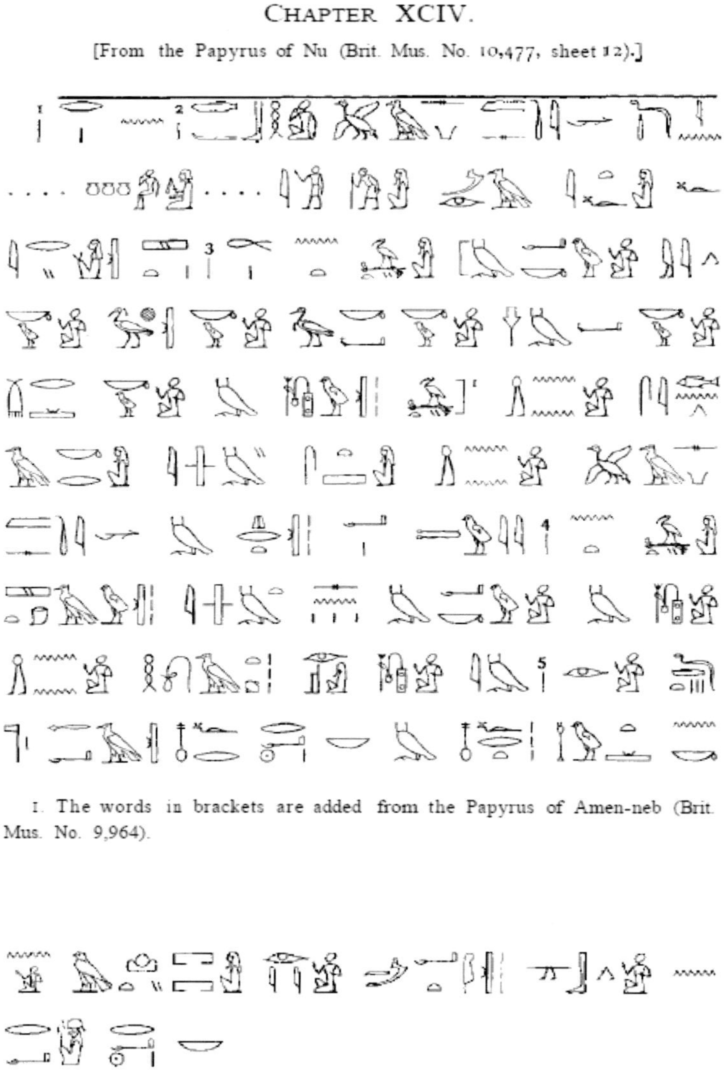

CHAPTER XCIV.

[From the Papyrus of Nu (Brit. Mus. No. 10,477, sheet 12).]

1. The words in brackets are added from the Papyrus of Amen-neb (Brit. Mus. No. 9,964).

TEXT NO. 7. BD 94 (AFTER BUDGE 1898 I: 199–200).

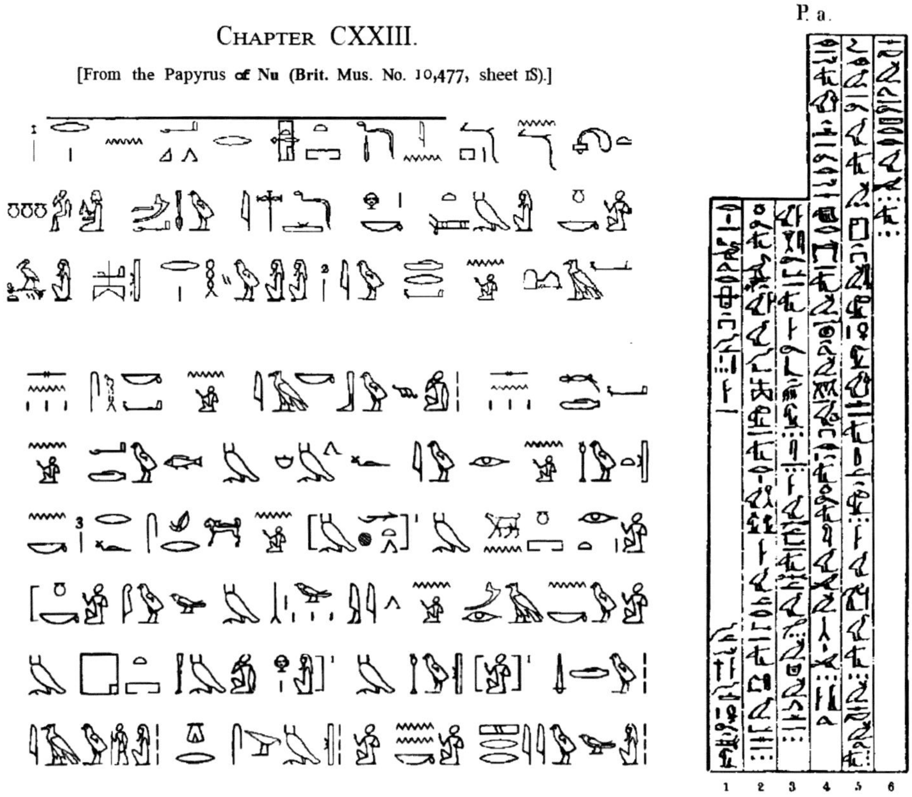

Text No. 8. BD 123 (after Budge 1898: 242–243; Naville 1886 I: Taf. CXXXI).

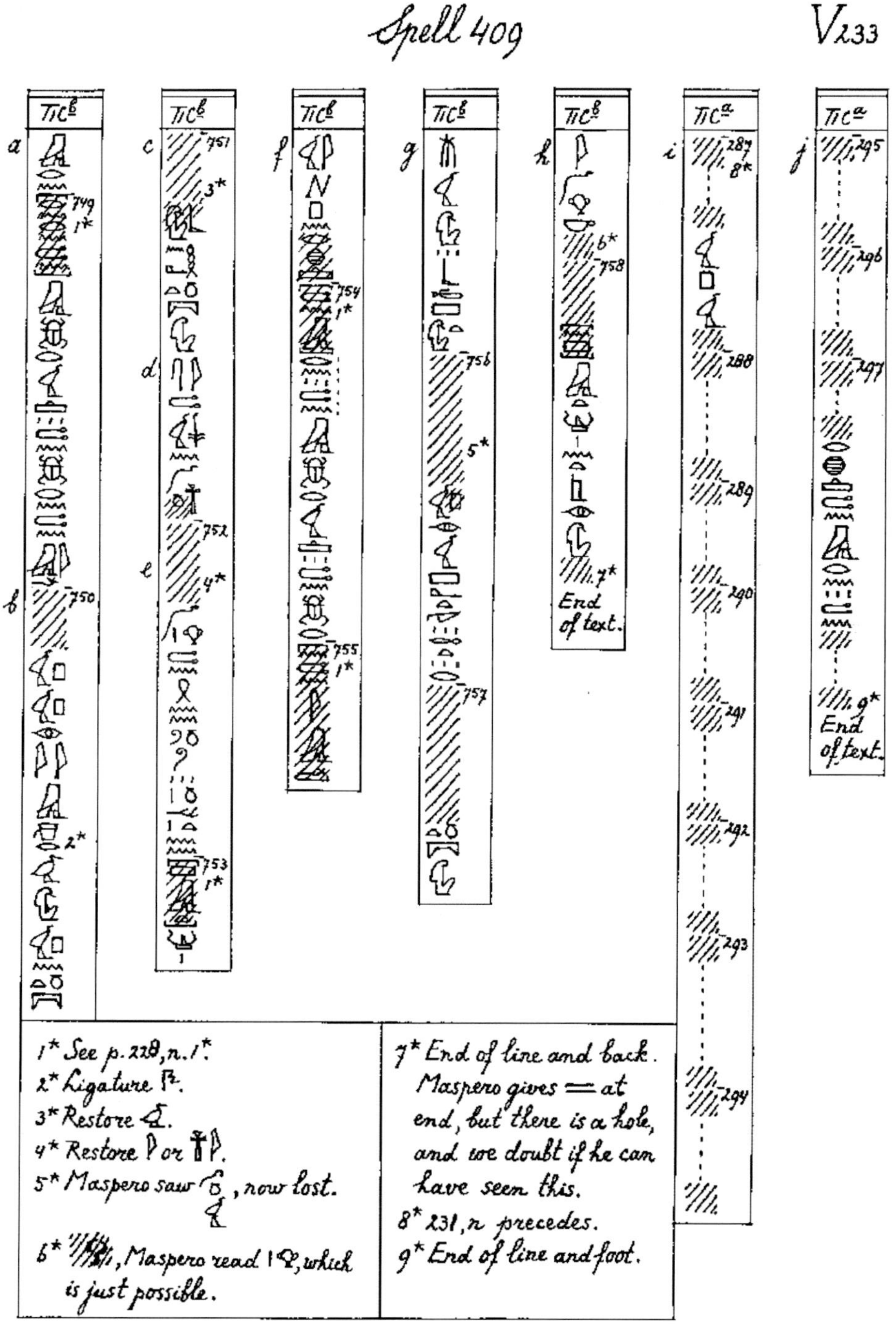

TEXT NO. 9. CT SP. 409 V: 233E-G (T1C^B).

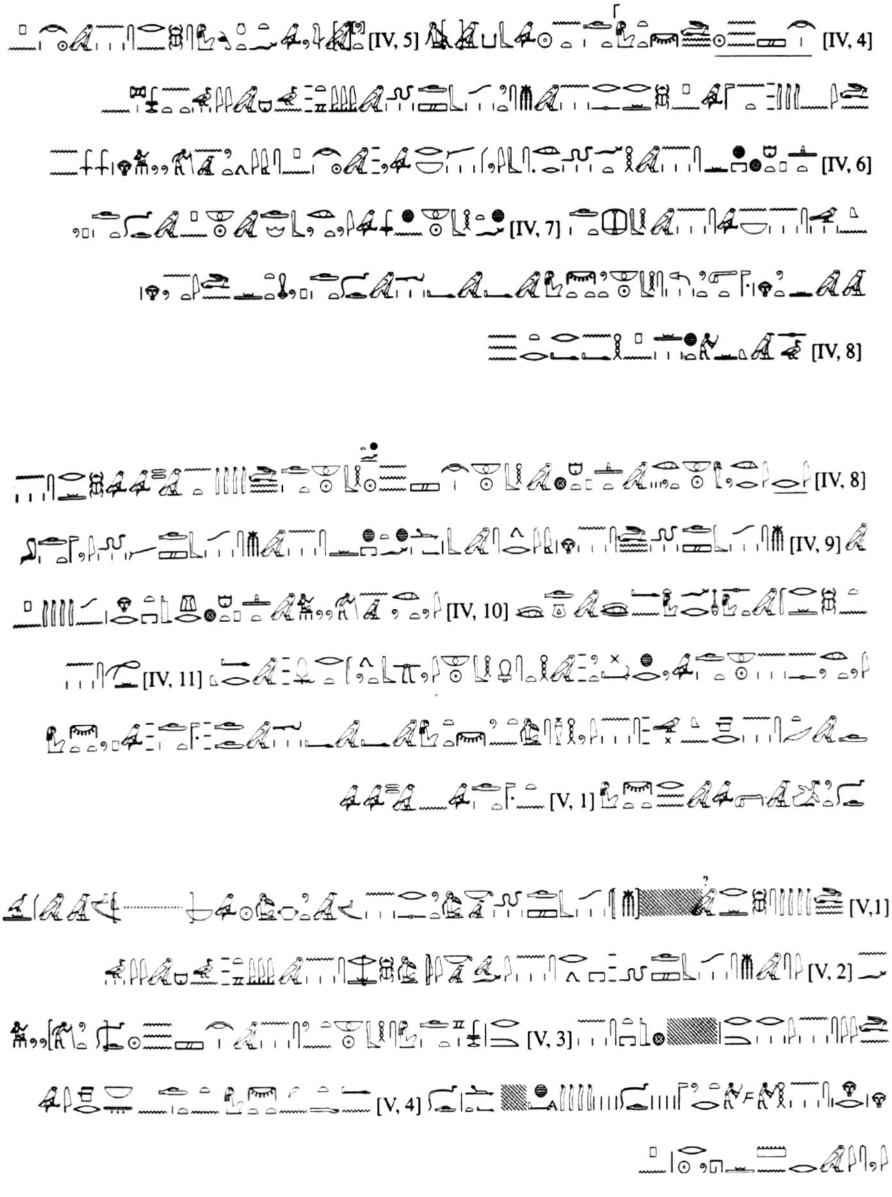

TEXT NO. 10. PBROOKLYN 47.218.84, § 10 (IV, 5 –V, 4) (AFTER MEEKS 2006: 10–12).

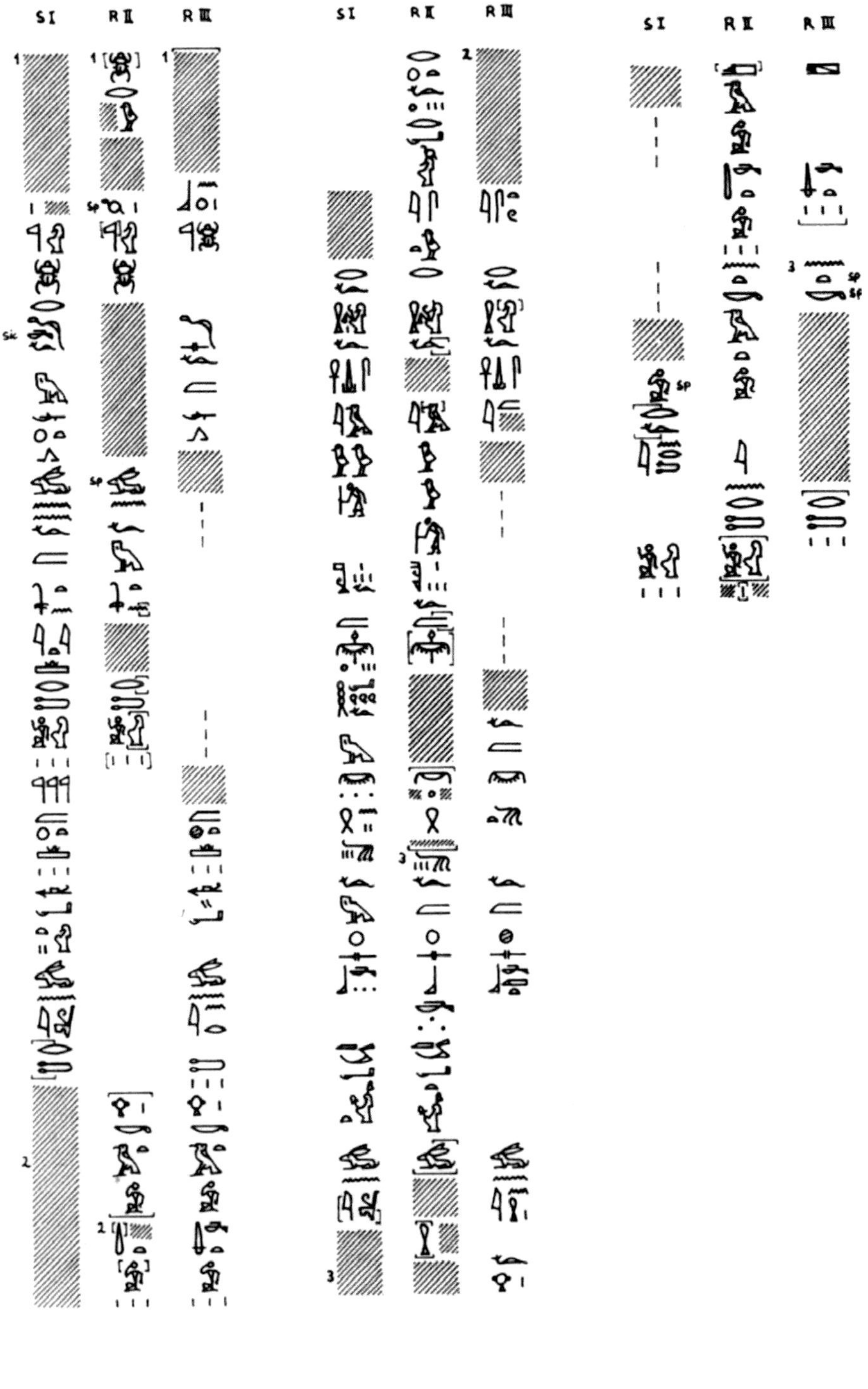

Text No. 11. The *Book of the Heavenly Cow*, 1–9 (after Hornung 1982: 1).

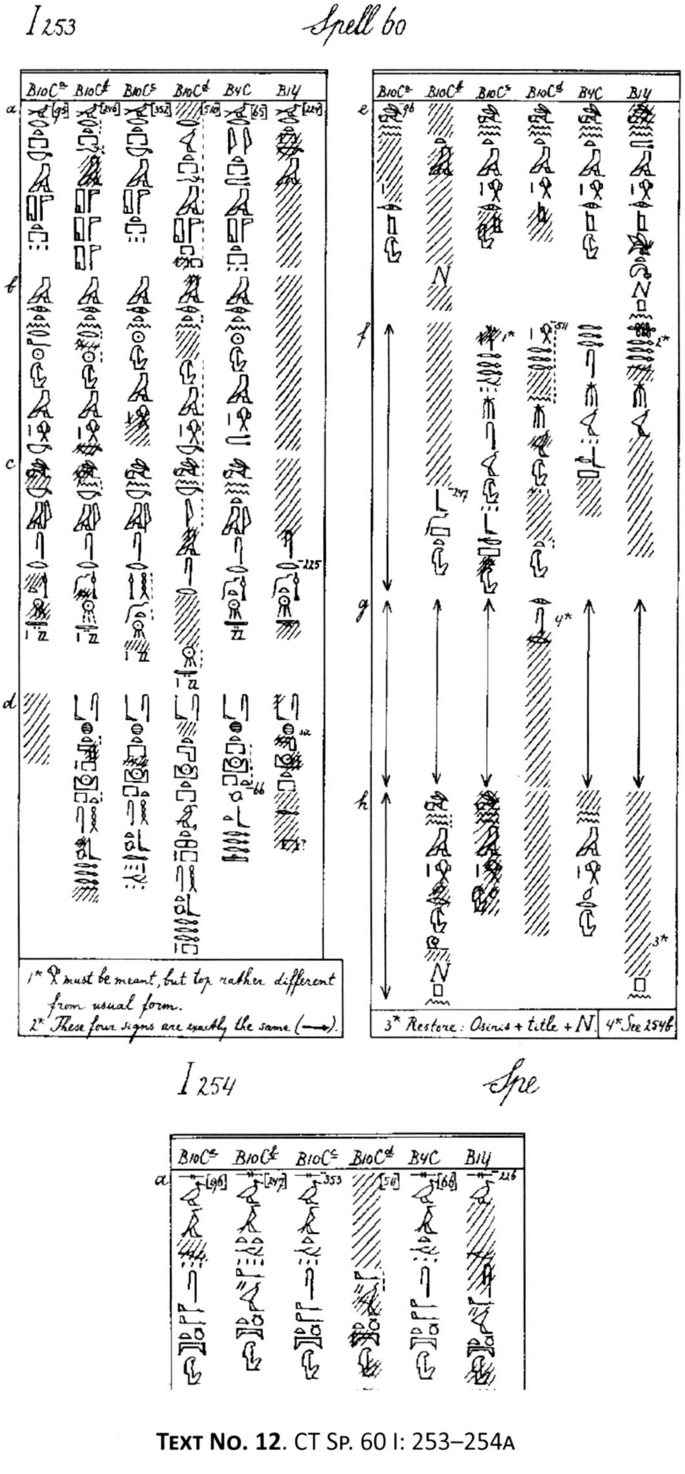

Text No. 12. CT Sp. 60 I: 253–254a

Abbreviations

ВДИ	Вестник древней истории. Москва.
ÄA	Ägyptologische Abhandlungen. Wiesbaden.
ÄAT	Ägypten und Altes Testament. Wiesbaden.
AH	Ægyptiaca Helvetica. Geneve.
APAW	Abhandlungen der Preußischen Akademie der Wißenschaften. Berlin.
ArOr	Archiv Orientální. Praha.
ASAE	Annales du Service des Antiquités de l'Égypte. Le Caire.
AVDAIK	Archäologische Veröffentlichungen / Deutsches archäologisches Institut. Abteilung Kairo. Mainz am Rhein.
BACE	Bulletin of the Australian Centre for Egyptology. Sydney.
BdÉ	Bibliothèque d'Étude / Institut Français d'Archéologie Orientale. Le Caire.
BIFAO	Bulletin de l'Institut Français d'Archéologie Orientale. Le Caire.
BSÉG	Bulletin de Société d'Égyptologie Genève. Geneva.
CdÉ	Chronique d'Égypte. Bulletin périodique de la Fondation d'égyptologique Reine Élisabeth. Bruxelles.
CENiM	Cahiers de Égypte Nilotique et Méditerranéenne. Montpellier.
CT	de Buck A. 1935–1961. *The Egyptian Coffin Texts*, (OIP 34, 49, 64, 67, 73, 81, 87), Chicago.
DE	Discussions in Egyptology. Oxford.
Deir Chelouit II	Zivie Chr. M. 1983. *Le temple de Deir Chelouit. T. II: 56−89. Inscriptions du pronaos*; Dessins de Y. Hamed Hanafi, Le Caire.
Dendera	Chassinat E. Le temple de Dendera / Émile Chassinat. – Le Caire : Institut Français d'Archéologie Orientale, 1934−1952. – T. I−VI. – (PIFAO).
DKAW	Denkschriften der Kaiserlichen Akademie der Wißenschaften in Wien. Wien.
EAO	Egypte, Afrique & Orient. Avignon.
Edfou	T. I–III: Cauville S. Devauchelle D. [2]1987. *Le temple d'Edfou*, Le Caire. T. IV−XIV: Chassinat E. 1928–1934. *Le temple d'Edfou*, Le Caire. T. XV: Cauville S., Devauchelle D. 1985. *Le temple d'Edfou* (MIFAO, 32), Le Caire.

EU	Egyptologische Uitgaven. Leiden.
Esna II–IV, VI	Sauneron S. 1963–1975. *Le temple d'Esna*, II–IV, VI, (PIFAO), Le Caire.
Esna V	Sauneron S. 1962. *Les fêtes religieuses d'Esna aux derniers siècles du paganism*, (PIFAO) Le Caire.
FIFAO	Fouilles de l'Institut Français d'Archéologie Orientale. Le Caire.
GM	Göttinger Miszellen. Beiträge zur ägyptologischen Diskussion. Göttingen.
GOF	Göttinger Orientforschung. Göttingen – Wiesbaden.
HAT	Handschriften des Altägyptischen Totenbuches. Wiesbaden.
IFAO BiblGén	Institut Français d'Archéologie Orientale. Bibliothèque Générale. Le Caire.
JARCE	Journal of the American Research Center in Egypt. Boston – Cairo.
JEA	Journal of Egyptian Archaeology. London.
JESHO	Journal of the Economic and Social History of the Orient. Leiden.
JNES	Journal of the Near Eastern Studies. Chicago.
JEOL	Jaarbericht van het vooraziatisch egyptisch genootschap. "Ex Oriente Lux". Leiden.
JSSEA	Journal of the Society for the Study of Egyptian Antiquities. Toronto.
JSOR	Journal of Society of Oriental Research. Boston.
KRI I–VII	Kitchen K. A. 1968–1969. *Ramesside Inscriptions, Historical and Biographical*, I–VII, Oxford.
LÄ	W. Helck, W. Westendorf (Hrsg.), 1975–1986. *Lexikon der Ägyptologie*; Begr. von W. Helck, E. Otto, I–VI, Wiesbaden.
LAPO	Littératures Anciennes du Proche-Orient. Paris.
LGG	Lexikon der ägyptischen Götter und Götterbezeichnungen / Hrsg. von Christian Leitz ; berabeiten von D. Budde ... [et al.]. – Leuven – Paris – Dudley, MA : Uitgeverij Peeters, Departement Oosterse Studies, 2002–2003. – Bd. I–VIII. – (OLA ; T. 111–116, 129).
MamEdfou	Chassinat E. 1910. *Le Mammisi d'Edfou*, (MIFAO, 16), Le Caire.
MÄS	Münchner Ägyptologische Studien. München – Berlin.
MDAIK	Mitteilungen des Deutschen Archäologischen Instituts, Abteilung Kairo. Wiesbaden – Mainz.
MEES	Memoirs of the Egypt Exploration Society. London.
MIFAO	Mémories de l'Institut Français d'Archéologie Orientale. Le Caire.

NAWG	Naschrichten der Akademie der Wißenschaften zu Göttingen. Göttingen.
OBO	Orbis Biblicus et Orientales. Freiburg – Göttingen.
OIP	The University of Chicago Oriental Institute Publications. Chicago.
OLA	Orientalia Lovaniensia Analecta. Leuven.
OLZ	Orientalistische Literaturzeitung. Berlin – Leipzig.
OMRO	Oudheidkindige Mededelingen van het Rijksmuseum te Leiden. Leiden.
Philae	Benedite G. 1893–1895. *Le Temple de Philae*, 1–2, Paris.
PIFAO	Publications de l'Institut Français d'Archéologie Orientale. Le Caire.
PM ^{2}I.1–2	Porter B., Moss R. L. B. 1970. *Topographical Bibliography of Ancient Egyptian Hieroglyphic Texts, Reliefs and Paintings*, 2nd Edition; Vol. I: The Theban Necropolis, 1–2, Oxford.
PM V	Porter B., Moss R. L. B. 1962. *Topographical Bibliography of Ancient Egyptian Hieroglyphic Texts, Reliefs and Paintings*, Vol. V: Upper Egypt: Sites (Deir Rîfa to Aswân, excluding Thebes and Dendera, Esna, Edfu, Kôm Ombo and Philae), Oxford.
PM ^{2}VI	Porter B., Moss R. L. B. 2002. *Topographical Bibliography of Ancient Egyptian Hieroglyphic Texts, Reliefs and Paintings*, 2nd Edition; Vol. VI: Upper Egypt: Chief Temples, Oxford.
Pyr. Komm.	Sethe K. 1935–1939, 1962. *Übersetzung und Kommentar zu den altägyptischen Pyramidentexten*, I–VI, Glückstadt – Hamburg.
RdÉ	Revue d'Égyptologie. Paris.
SAK	Studien zur altägyptischen Kultur. Hamburg.
SAOC	Studies in Ancient Oriental Civilization. Chicago.
SAGA	Studien zur Archäologie und Geschichte Altägyptens. Heidelberg.
SAT	Studien zum altägyptischen Totenbuch / Studien zu altägyptischen Totentexten (from 2015). Wiesbaden.
SDAIK	Sonderschrift. Deutsches Archäologisches Institut.
SPAW	Sitzungsberichte der Preußischen Akademie der Wißenschaften. Berlin.
Tôd I	Drioton É., Posener G., Vandier J. 1980. *Tôd: Les inscriptions du temple ptolémaïque et romain,* I (FIFAO, 18/1), Le Caire.
Tôd II–III	Thiers Chr., Gout J.-Fr. 2003. *Tôd: Les Inscriptions du temple ptolémaique et romain,* II–III (FIFAO, T. 18/2–3).
Urk. I	Sethe K. 1903. *Urkunden des Alten Reiches* (Urkunden des aegyptischen Altertums, 1), Leipzig.

Urk. III	Schäfer H. 1905. *Urkunden der älteren Äthiopenkönige*, I–II (Urkunden des aegyptischen Altertums, 3), Leipzig.
Urk. IV	Sethe K. 1906–1909. *Urkunden der 18. Dynastie*, 1–16 (Urkunden des aegyptischen Altertums, 4), Leipzig. Helck W. 1955−1961. *Urkunden der 18. Dynastie*, 17–22 (Urkunden des aegyptischen Altertums, 4), Berlin.
Urk. V	Grapow H. 1917. *Religiöse Urkunden nebst deutschen Vebersetzung. Ausgewählte Texte des Totenbuches*, I–III (Urkunden des aegyptischen Altertums, 5), Leipzig.
Urk. VI	Schott S. 1929–1939. *Urkunden mythologischen Inhalts*, I–II (Urkunden des aegyptischen Altertums, 6), Leipzig.
Urk. VIII	Firchow O., Sethe K. 1957. *Thebanische Templeinschriften aus griechish-römischer Zeit* (Urkunden des aegyptischen Altertums ; Abt. 8), Berlin.
VA	Varia Aegyptiaca. Texas.
Wb.	Erman A., Grapow H. [2]1955. *Wörterbuch der ägyptischen Sprache*, I–V, Berlin.
Wb. Belegstellen	Grapow H., Erichsen W. 1940–1958. *Die Belegstellen zu Wörterbuch der Aegyptischen Sprache*, I–V, Berlin.
YES	Yale Egyptological Studies. New Haven.
ZÄS	Zeitschrift für ägyptische Sprache und Altertumskunde. Berlin.

Bibliography

Апинян Т. А. 2005. *Мифология: Теория и событие*, Санкт-Петербург.

Ассман Я. 1999. *Египет: Теология и благочестие ранней цивилизации*; Пер. с нем. Т. А. Баскаковой, Москва.

Большаков А. О. 2003. Изображение и текст: два языка древнеегипетской культуры. In: *ВДИ* 3, 3–20.

Демидчик А. Е. 1999. Несколько замечаний о «родстве» египтян с божеством. In: *Мероэ. Страны Северо-Восточной Африки и Красноморского бассейна в древности и раннем средневековье. Проблемы истории, языка и культуры* 5: Памяти Г. М. Бауэра, Москва, 54–71.

Демидчик А. Е. 2005. *Безымянная пирамида. Государственная доктрина древнеегипетской Гераклеопольской монархии* (Aegyptiaca, 1), Санкт-Петербург.

Коростовцев М. А. 1976. *Религия Древнего Египта*, Москва.

Лурье И. М. 1960. *Очерки древнеегипетского права XVI–X вв. до н. э. Памятники и исследования*, Ленинград.

Матье М. Э. 1956. *Древнеегипетские мифы*, Москва – Ленинград.

Матье М. Э. 1996. *Избранные труды по мифологии и идеологии Древнего Египта*, Москва.

Павлова О. И., Зубов А. Б. 1997. Реальность падшести и парадигма совершенства. In: *Совершенный человек. Теология и философия образа*, Москва, 173–212.

Семенов Н. 2005. Мифоформы священных гор. In: *Київська старовина* 4, 108–120.

Тарасенко Н. А. 2003. Миф о «грехопадении» в Древнем Египте и его коннотации в 17-й главе Книги Мертвых. In: *Вісник Київського Славістичного університету* 14: "Історія", 187–220.

Тарасенко Н. А. 2005. Древнеегипетский *уроборос* – семантика образа. In: *Університет* 4, 14–37.

Тарасенко Н. А. 2005a. *Bdšt* в 17-й главе Книге Мертвых: к вопросу о магии имени в Древнем Египте. In: С. В. Пахомов (Ред.), *Asiatica. Труды по философии и культурам Востока. Вып. I: К 50-летию со дня рождения профессора Е. А. Торчинова*, Санкт-Петербург, 104–125.

Тарасенко Н. А. 2007. Хитрость Исиды. К "игре слов" в папирусе Chester Beatty I, recto, VI. 8 – VI. 14. In: *XI Сходознавчі читання А. Кримського. Тези доповідей міжнародної наукової конференції (м. Київ. 7–8 червня 2007 р.)*, Київ, 53–58.

Тарасенко Н. А. 2009. *Древнеегипетская мифология в изобразительной традиции Книги Мертвых (виньетки глав 16, 17 и 42 в Новом царстве – Третьем переходном периоде)*, Киев.

Тарасенко Н. А. 2009a. *Mḏd*: одна примечательная черта иконографии "демонического" существа в папирусной графике XXI династии. In: *Східний світ* 3, 82–88.

Тарасенко Н. А. 2010. Изобразительная традиция Книги Мертвых (историографический анализ). In: *Сходознавство* 52, 14–40.

Тарасенко Н. А. 2013. Виньетки 17-й главы Книги мертвых в папирусе Нахта (pLondon BM 10471). In: *ВДИ* 2, 3–17.

Тарасенко Н. А. 2015. Казус папируса *Greenfield* (pLondon BM EA 10554). In: М. А. Чегодаев, Н. В. Лаврентьева (Eds.), *Aegyptiaca Rossica* 3, Moscow, 234–258.

Тураев Б. А. 1898. *Бог Тот. Опыт исследования в области древне-египетской культуры* (Записки Историко-филологического факультета Имп. Санкт-Петербургского университета, 46), Лейпциг.

Тураев Б. А. 1914. Изображения Воскресения на египетских памятниках. In: *Сборник статей в честь В. П. Бузескула* (Сборник Харьковского Ист.-Филолог. Общества, XXI), Харьков, 415–422.

Ходжаш С. И. 1960. Жезл и туалетный сосуд с изображением сцены магической защиты. In: *Древний Египет*, Москва, 242–259.

Чегодаев М. А. 2004. *Папирусная графика Древнего Египта*, Москва.

Abdul-Qader Muhammed M. 1966. *The Development of the Funerary Beliefs and Practices displayed in the Private Tombs of the New Kingdom at Thebes*, Cairo.

Allen J. P. 1988. *Genesis in Egypt. The Philosophy of Ancient Egyptian Creation Account* (YES, 2), New Haven.

Allen J. P. 2013. *A New Concordance of the Pyramid Texts*, I–VI, Providence.

Allen J. P. 2014. *Middle Egyptian Grammar. An Introduction to the Language and Culture of Hieroglyphs*; 3rd Edition, Cambridge.

Allen J. P. 2015. *The Ancient Egyptian Pyramid Texts*; 2nd Edition (Writings from the Ancient World, 38), Atlanta.

Allen T. G. 1960. *The Egyptian Book of the Dead Documents in the Oriental Institute Museum at the University of Chicago* (OIP, LXXXII), Chicago.

Allen T. G. 1974. *The Book of the Dead or Going Forth by Day. Ideas of the Ancient Egyptians concerning the Hereafter as expressed in their own Terms* (SAOC, 37), Chicago.

Altenmüller H. 1965. *Die Apotropaia und die Götter Mittelägyptens. Eine typologische und religionsgeschichtliche Untersuchung der sogenannten "Zaubermeßer" des Mittleren Reiches*, I–II; Dissertation, München,

Altenmüller H. 1973. *Synkretismus in den Sargtexten* (GOF, R. IV, Bd. 7), Wiesbaden.

Altenmüller H. 1977: "Gliedervergottung". In: *LÄ* II, 624–627.

Andrzejewski T. 1959. *Le papyrus mythologique de Te-hem-en-Mout (Musée National de Varsovie, no 199 628)* (Académie Polonaise des Sciences. Travaux du centre d'archéologie méditerranéenne, I), Warszawa – Paris.

Angenot V. 2011. A Method for Ancient Egyptian Hermeneutics (with Application to the Small Golden Shrine of Tutankhamun). In: A. Verbovsek, B. Backes, C. Jones (Hrsg.), *Methodik und Didaktik in der Ägyptologie. Herausforderungen eines kulturwissenschaftlichen Paradigmenwechsels in den Altertumswissenschaften* (Ägyptologie und Kulturwissenschaft, IV), München, 255–280.

Angenot V. 2016 (Forthcoming). Hormin. Vignette du Chapitre 17 du Livre des Morts. In: M. Weemans, D. Gamboni and J.-H. Martin (Eds.), *Cent images doubles et paradoxales, Malakoff Hazan*.

Angenot V. in press. Rébus, calembours et images subliminales dans l'iconographie égyptienne. In: Cl.-A. Brisset, Fl. Dumora et M. Simon-Oikawa (Eds.), *Écrire en images: le rébus dans les civilisations de l'écriture*, Paris.

Assmann J. 1975. *Zeit und Ewigkeit im Alten Ägypten. Ein Beitrag zur Geschichte der Ewigkeit* (AHAW), Heidelberg.

Assmann J. 1977. Die Verborgenheit des Mythos in Ägypten. In: *GM* 25, 7–43

Assmann J. 2001. *Maat. Gerechtigkeit und Unsterblichkeit im Alten Ägypten*, München.

Assmann J. 2002. *Altägyptische Totenliturgien I: Totenliturgien in den Sargtexten des Mittleren Reiches*; Mitarbeit von M. Bommas, Heidelberg.

Assmann J. 2002a. *The Mind of Egypt. History and Meaning in the Time of the Pharaohs*; Translated by D. Lorton, New York.

Assmann J. 2003. *Tod und Jenseits im alten Ägypten*, München.

Assmann J. 2005. *Death and Salvation in Ancient Egypt*; Translated by D. Lorton, Ithaca – New York.

Assmann J. 2011. *Steinzeit und Sternzeit. Altägyptische Zeitkonzepte*, München.

Aufrère S. 2004. Taches lunaires, phases de la lune et fécondité des règnes. Lagomorphes, félins divins et hybridations en Égypte ancienne. In : *Res Antiquae* 1, 3–65.

Backes B. 2005. *Wortindex zum späten Totenbuch (pTurin 1791)*; Unter Mitarbeit von I. Munro, S. Stöhr (SAT, 9), Wiesbaden.

Baines J. 1989. Ancient Egyptian concepts and uses of the Past: 3rd and 2nd millennium BC evidence. In: R. Layton (Ed.), *Who need the Past? Indigenous values and archaeology*, London, 131–149.

Baines J. 1990. Restricted Knowledge, Hierarchy and Decorum : Modern Perceptions and Ancient Institutions. In: *JARCE* XXVII, 1–23.

Baines J. 1991. Egyptian Myth and Discourse: Myth, Gods and the Early Written and Iconographic Records. In: *JNES* 50, 81–105.

Baines J. 1991a. Society, Morality, and Religious Practice. In: B. Shafer (Ed.), *Religion in Ancient Egypt. Gods, Myths, and Personal Practice*, London, 123–199.

Baines J. 1996. Myth and Literature. In: A. Loprieno (Ed.), *Ancient Egyptian Literature. History and Forms*, Leiden – New York – Köln, 361–379.

Bakir A. e.-M. 1966. *The Cairo Calendar No. 86637*, Cairo.

Barguet P. 1967. *Le Livre des Morts des anciens Égyptiens. Introduction, traduction, commentaire* (LAPO, 1), Paris.

Barguet P. 1986. *Textes des Sarcophages Égyptiens du Moyen Empire. Introduction et traduction* (LAPO, 12), Paris.

Barthelmess P. 1992. *Der Übergang ins Jenseits in den thebanischen Beamtengräbern der Ramessidenzeit* (SAGA, 2), Heidelberg.

Baum N. 1988. *Arbres et Arbustes de l'Egypte Ancienne. La liste de la tombe thébaine d'Ineni (no 81)* (OLA, 31), Leuven.

Beinlich H. 1991. *Das Buch vom Fayum. Zum religiösen Eigenverständnis einer ägyptischen Landschaft* (ÄA, 51), Wiesbaden.

Berlev O. D. 2003. Two Kings – Two Suns: On the Worldview of Ancient Egyptians. In: St. Quirke (Ed.), *Discovering Egypt from the Neva: The Egyptological Legacy of Oleg D. Berlev*, Berlin, 19–35.

Bickel S. 1994. *La cosmogonie égyptienne. Avant le Bouvel Empire* (OBO, 134), Fribourg – Göttingen.

Bickel S. 1994a. Un Hymne à la Vie. Essai d'analyse du Chapitre 80 des Textes des Sarcophages. In: *Hommages à Jean Leclant* I: Études Pharaoniques (BdÉ, 106/1), Le Caire, 81–97.

Bickel S. 2001. Entre angoisse et espoir: le Livre des Morts. In: *« Sortir au jour ». Art égyptien de la Fondation Martin Bodmer. Catalogue*; Textes réunis et édités par J.-L. Chappaz et S. Vuilleumier (Cahiers de la Société d'Égyptologie, 7), Genève, 117–134.

Billing N. 2003. *Nut – The Goddess of Life in Text and Iconography* (USE 5), Uppsala.

Billing N. 2004. Writing an Image –The Formulation of the Tree Goddess Motif in the Book of the Dead, Ch. 59. In: *SAK* 32, 35–50.

Bissing Fr. W. von. 1928. Totenpapyros eines Gottesvaters des Amon. In: *ZÄS* 63, 37–39.

Bochi P. M. 1999. Death by Drama: The Ritual of Damnatio Memoriae in Ancient Egypt. In: *GM* 171, 73–88.

Bolshakov A. O. 1999. Royal Portraiture and "Horus Name". In: *L'art de l'Ancien Empire égyptien. Actes du colloque organisé au musée du Louvre par le Service culturel les 3 et 4 avril 1998*, Paris, 312–332.

Bommas M. 2004. Zwei magische Sprüche in einem spätägyptische Ritualenbuch (pBM EA 10081): Ein weiterer Fall für die "Verborgenheit des Mythos". In: *ZÄS* 131, 95–113, Taf. IX–XII.

Bonnet H. 1952. *Reallexikon der ägyptischen Religionsgeschichte*, Berlin.

Borghouts J. F. 1973. The Evil Eye of Apophis. In: *JEA* 79, 114–150.

Borghouts J. F. 1978. *Ancient Egyptian Magical Texts* (Religious Texts Translation Series; Nisaba, 9), Leiden.

Borghouts J. F. 1988. An Early Book of Gates. Coffin Texts, Spell 336. In: J. H. Kamstra, H. Milde, K. Wagtendonk, Kampen, J. H. Kok (Eds.), *Funerary Symbols and Religion Essays dedicated to Professor M.S.H.G. Heerma van Voss on the occasion of his retirement from the Chair of the History of Ancient Religions at the University of Amsterdam*, Leiden, 12–22.

Borghouts J. F. 2010. *Egyptian. An Introduction to the Writing and Language of the Middle Kingdom*, I–II (EU, XXIV, 1–2), Leiden.

Brandon S. G. F. 1961. The Personification of Death in some Ancient Religions. In: *Bulletin of the John Rylands Library* 43, No. 2, 317–335

Brier B. 1981. *Ancient Egyptian Magic*, New York.

Broze M. 1991. Le Chat, Le Serpent et l'Arbre-Ished (Chapitre 17 du Livre des Morts). In: L. Delvaux, E. Warmenbol (Eds.), *Les Divins Chats d'Égypte: un Air Subtil, un Dangereux Parfum* (Lettres Orientales, 3), Leuven, 109–115.

Bruyère B. 1925. *Rapport sur les fouilles de Deir el Médineh (1923–1925)* (FIFAO, II / 2), Le Caire.

Bruyère B. 1926. *Rapport sur les fouilles de Deir el Médineh (1924–1925)* (FIFAO, III / 3), Le Caire.

Bruyère B. 1933. Rapport sur les fouilles de Deir el Médineh (1930) (FIFAO, VIII / 3), Le Caire.

Bruyère B. 1959. *La Tombe N° 1 de Sen-nedjem à Deir el Médineh* (MIFAO, 88), Le Caire.

Budde D. 2000. Zur Symbolik der sogenannten Schulterrosette bei Löwendarstellungen. In: *ZÄS* 127, 116–135.

Budge E. A. W. 1895. *The Book of the Dead. The papyrus of Ani in the British Museum. The Egyptian Text with internal Transliteration and Translation, a running Translation, Introduction, etc.*, London.

Budge E. A. W. 1898. *The Book of the Dead: the Chapters of Coming Forth by Day; the Egyptian text according to the Theban Recension in Hieroglyphic, edited from numerous papyri, with a translation, vocabulary*, I, London.

Budge E. A. W. 1898a. *The Book of the Dead: the Chapters of Coming Forth by Day. An English Translation with Introduction, notes, etc.* London.

Budge E. A. W. 1904. *The Gods of the Egyptians or the Studies in Egyptian Mythology*, I–II, London.

Budge E. A. W. 1910. *The Chapters of Coming Forth by Day or the Theban Recension of the Book of the Dead; the Egyptian hieroglyphic text edited from numerous papyri*, I–III (Books on Egypt and Chaldaea, 28–30), London.

Budge E. A. W. 1911. *A Hieroglyphic Vocabulary to the Theban Recension of the Book of the Dead with an index to all the English equivalents of the Egyptian words*, London.

Budge E. A. W. 1912. *The Greenfield Papyrus in the British Museum: the funerary papyrus of princess Nesitanebtashru, daughter of Painetchem II and Nesi-Khensu, and priestess of Amen-Rā at Thebes, about B.C. 970*, London.

Buhl M.-L. 1947. The Goddesses of the Egyptian Tree Cult. In: *JNES* 6, 80–97.

Calmettes M.-A. 2006. La vignette du chapitre 151 du Livre Pour Sortir au Jour. In: *EAO* 43, 23–30.

Caluwé A. de. 1993. Les bandelettes de momie du Musée Vleeshuis d'Anvers. In: *JEA* 76, 199–214.

Cannuyer Chr. 2014. Le génie de Hormin. Le « scarabée-bouquetin » et le « Grand Chat-Âne » (TT 359): deux cas d'hybridation dans la symbolique animalière de l'ancienne Égypte. In: *Mélanges d'Orientalisme offerts à Janine et à Jean Ch. Balty* (Acta Orientalia Belgica, XXVII), Bruxelles, 41–64.

Carrier Cl. 2004. *Textes des Sarcophages du Moyen Empire Égyptien*, I–III, Paris.

Carrier Cl. 2009. *Grands livres funéraires de l'Égypte pharaonique* (Melchat, 1), Paris.

Carrier Cl. 2009a. *Le Livre des Morts de l'Égypte ancienne* (Melchat, 1), Paris.

Carrier Cl. 2010. *Série des Papyrus du Livre des Morts de l'Égypte ancienne. Vol. I: Le Papyrus de Nouou (BM EA 10477)* (Melchat, 3), Paris.

Carrier Cl. 2010a. *Série des Papyrus du Livre des Morts de l'Égypte ancienne. Vol. IV: Le Papyrus de Iouefânkh (Turin, cat. n° 1791)* (Melchat, 6), Paris.

Carrier Cl. 2010b. *Textes des Pyramides de l'Égypte ancienne. T. I: Textes des pyramides d'Ounas et de Téti* (Melchat, 12), Paris.

Carrier Cl. 2010c. *Textes des Pyramides de l'Égypte ancienne. T. III: Textes des pyramide de Pépy II* (Melchat, 14), Paris.

Carrier Cl. 2010d. *Textes des Pyramides de l'Égypte ancienne. T. IV: Textes des pyramides de Mérenrê, d'Aba, de Neit et d'Oudjebten* (Melchat, 15), Paris.

Carrier Cl. 2011. *Série des Papyrus du Livre des Morts de l'Égypte ancienne. Vol. III: Le Papyrus de Nebseny (BM EA 9900)* (Melchat, 5), Paris.

Carrier Cl. 2014. *Les papyrus du Livre des Morts de l'Égypte Ancienne de Neferoubenef (Louvre III 93) et de Soutymès (BnF, égyptien « 38–45 »)*, Paris.

Cherpion N., Corteggiani J.-P. 2010. *La tombe d'Inherkhâouy (TT 359) à Deir el-Medina*, I–II (MIFAO, 128), Le Caire.

Clère J. 1987. *Le Papyrus de Nesmin. Un Livre des Morts Hiéroglyphique de l'Epoque Ptolémaique* (IFAO BiblGen, X), Le Caire.

Corteggiani J.-P. 1995. La « butte de la Décollation à Héliopolis ». In: *BIFAO* 95, 141–151.

Costa S. 2003. El arbol *Ished* en la iconografia real: tres escenas de Rameses IV legitimando su ascenso al trono. In: *Aula Orientalis* 21, 193–204.

Davies B. G. 1999. *Who's Who at Deir el-Medina. A Prosopographic Study of the Royal Workmen's Community* (EU, 13), Leiden.

Davies Th. M. 1908. *The Funerary Papyrus of Iouiya*, London.

Dawson W. R. 1924. A Rare Vignette from the "Book of the Dead". In. *JEA* 10, 40.

de Buck A. 1937. The Judical papyrus of Turin. In: *JEA* 23, 152–163.

de Buck A. 1950. The fear of premature death in Ancient Egypt. In: C. F. Nijkerk, N. V. Callenbach (Eds.), *Pro Regno Pro Sanctuario. Een bundel studies en bijdragen van vrienden en vereerders bij de zestigste verjaardag van Prof. Dr. G. van der Leeuw*, Leiden, 79–88.

de Buck A. 1958. Een Egyptische versie van Achilles' klacht (Od. XI, 489–91). In: *Jaarboek der Koninklijke Nederlandse Akademie van Wetenschappen 1957–1958*, Amsterdam, 74–96.

de Rachewiltz B. 2001. *Il Libro dei Morti degli Antichi Egizi. Papiro di Torino*; Prefazione del Prof. E.Edel, Roma.

Delvaux L. 1991. Les chats et les félins dans les objets magiques du Moyen Empire. In: L. Delvaux, E. Warmenbol (Eds.), *Les Divins Chats d'Égypte: un Air Subtil, un Dangereux Parfum* (Lettres Orientales, 3), Leuven, 93–100.

Demichelis S. 2000. Le phylactère du scribe Boutehamon. P. Turin Cat. 1858. In: *BIFAO* 100, 267–273.

Derchain Ph., Recklinghausen D. von. 2004. *La Création – die Schöpfung. Poème pariétal, ein Wandgedicht. Le façade ptolémaïque du temple d'Esna. Pour une poétique ptolémaïque* (Rites Égyptiens, X), Brepols.

Díaz-Iglesias Llanos L. E. 2005. Commentary on Heracleopolis Magna from the theological perspective (I): the image of the local lakes in the vignette of chapter 17 of the Book of the Dead. In: *Trabajos de Egiptologia* 4, 31–106.

Díaz-Iglesias Llanos L. E. 2014. *El ciclo mítico de Heracleópolis Magna. Continuidad y reelaboración a partir de las fuentes funerarias y cultuales* (Aula Ægyptiaca – Studia, 7), Barcelona.

Dodson A., Ikram S. 2008. *The Tomb in Ancient Egypt. Royal and Private Sepulchers from the Early Dynastic Period to the Romans*, Cairo.

Dondelinger E. 1987. *Das Totenbuch des Schreibers Ani*, Graz.

DuQuesne T. 2002. La Déification des parties du corps. Correspondances magiques et identification avec les dieux l'Égypte ancienne. In: Y. Koenig (Ed.), *La Magie en Égypte: à la rechreche d'une défintion. Actes du colloque organisé par le Musée du Louvre les 29 et 30 septembre 2000*, Paris, 237–271.

Edel E. 1955. *Altägyptische Grammatik*, I (Analecta Orientalia. Commentationes scientificae de rebus Orientis Antiqui, 34), Roma.

el-Sayed R. 1981. À propos de l'iconographie du cercueil no 2238 au Musée du Turin. In: *ASAE* 64, 163–174, 5 pl.

Faulkner R. O. 1933. *The Papyrus Bremner-Rhind (British Museum No. 10188)* (Bibliotheca Aegyptiaca, III), Bruxelles.

Faulkner R. O. 1937. The Bremner-Rhind Papyrus (III). In: *JEA* 23, 10–16, 166–185.

Faulkner R. O. 1938. The Bremner-Rhind Papyrus (IV). In: *JEA* 24, 41–53.

Faulkner R. O. 1962. *A Concise Dictionary of Middle Egyptian*, Oxford.

Faulkner R. O. 1969. *The Ancient Egyptian Pyramid Texts*, I–II, Oxford.

Faulkner R. O. 1994. *The Ancient Egyptian Coffin Texts*, I–III, Warminster.

Faulkner R. O. 1998. *The Egyptian Book of the Dead. The Book of Going Forth by Day*; Introduction and commentaries by O. Jr. Goelet; Preface by C. A. R. Andrews, Cairo.

Faulkner R. O. 1999. *A Concise Dictionary of Middle Egyptian*; 7th Ed., Oxford – London.

Faulkner R. O. 2001. C. Andrews (Ed.), *The Ancient Egyptian Book of the Dead*, Austin.

Franco I. 1988. Fragments de "Livres des Morts" sur toile découverts dans la Vallée des Reines. In: *BIFAO* 88, 71–82.

Frandsen P. J. 2000. On the Origin of the notion of Evil in Ancient Egypt. In: *GM* 179, 9–34.

Frankfort H. 1933. *The Cenotaph of Seti I at Abydos*; With chapters by A. de Buck and B. Gunn (MEES, 39), London.

Friedman F. D. 1996. Notions of Cosmos in the Step Pyramid Complex. In: P. Der Manuelian (Ed.), *Studies in Honor of W. K. Simpson* 1, Boston, 337–351.

Gaber H. 2009. Deux variantes de la scene de la Psychostasie (Chapitres 30 et 125 du Livre des Morts). In: *RdÉ* 60, 1–15.

Gabolde M. 2006. Une interpretation alternative de la «Pesée du Cœur» du Livre des Morts. In: *EAO* 23, 11–22.

Gamer-Wallert I. 1975. Baum, heiliger. In: *LÄ* I, Kol. 655–660.

Gardiner A. H. 1955. *The Ramesseum Papyri: Plates*, Oxford.

Gardiner A. H. 1958. *Egyptian Grammar. Being an Introduction to the Study of Hieroglyphs*; 3rd Ed., London – Oxford.

Gardiner A. H. 1959. *The Royal Canon of Turin*, Oxford.

Gasse A. 2001. *Le Livre des Morts de Pacherientaihet au Museo Gregoriano Egizio* (Museo Gregoriano Egizio; Aegyptiaca Gregoriana, IV), Vaticano.

Gee J. 2010. The Book of the Dead as canon. In: *British Museum Studies in Ancient Egypt and Sudan* 15, 23–33.

Geisen Chr. 2004. *Die Totentexte des verschollenen Sarges der Königin Mentuhotep aus der 13. Dynastie. Ein Textzeuge aus der Übergangszeit von den Sargtexten zum Totenbuch* (SAT, 8), Wiesbaden.

Germer R. 1985. *Flora des pharaonishen Ägypten* (SDAIK, 14), Mainz.

Germer R. 1986. Sykomore. In: *LÄ* VI, 113–114.

Gesellensetter J. S. 1997. *Das Sechet-Iaru. Untersuchungen zur Vignette des Kapitels 110 im Ägyptischen Totenbuch*, Dissertation, Würzburg.

Goebs K. 2002. A Functional Approach to Egyptian Myth and Mythemes. In: *Journal of Ancient Near Eastern Religions* 2, No. 1, 27–59.

Goedicke H. 1998. Ancient Egyptian Vision of Eschatology. In: *JSSEA* 25: Papers Presented in Honour of G. E. Freeman, 38–45.

Goedicke H. 1999. Das ägyptische Credo. In: *SAK* 27, 87–106.

Gourlay Y. J.-L. 1979. Les Seigneurs et les Baou vivants à Chedenou *Hommages à la Mémoire de Serge Sauneron, 1927–1976,* 1: Égypte Pharaonique (BdÉ, 81), Le Caire.

Goyon J.-C. 1972. *Rituels funéraires de l'ancienne Égypte. Introduction, traduction et commentaire* (LAPO, 4), Paris.

Goyon J.-C. 1985. *Les Dieux-Gardiens et la Genèse des Temples (d'apres les textes égyptians de l'éhoque gréco-romaine). Les soixante d'Edfou et les soixante-dix-sept dieux de Pharbaetos. I et II* (BdÉ, 93), Le Caire.

Grapow H. 1912. *Das 17. Kapitel des ägyptischen Totenbuches und seine religionsgeschichtliche Bedeutung*: Dissertation, Berlin.

Grapow H. 1931. Die Welt vor der Schöpfung (Ein Beitrag zur Religionsgeschichte). In: *ZÄS* 67, 34–38.

Griffith F. Ll. 1890. *The Antiquities of Tell el Yahûdîyeh, miscellaneous work in Lower Egypt during the years 1887–1888*, London.

Griffiths J. G. 1960. *The Conflict of Horus and Seth from Egyptian and Classical Sources*, Liverpool.

Grimal N.-C. 1981. *Quatre stèles napatéennes au Musée du Caire, JE 48863–48866* (Études sur la propagande royale égyptienne, 2 = MIFAO, T. 106), Le Caire.

Grimal N.-C. 1985. Les "noyés" de Balat. In: *Mélanges offerts à J. Vercoutter*, Paris, 111–121.

Guilhou N. 2006. La protection du cadavre dans le Livre des Morts : gestes rituels et de devenir de l'être. In: *EAO* 23, 31–38.

Guilhou N. 2014. La Vignette du Chapitre 182 du Livre des Morts. In: М. О. Тарасенко (Ред.), *Доісламський Близький Схід: історія, релігія, культура*, Київ, 63–76.

Guilhou N. 2014a. Les différents supports du Livre des Morts et le devenir du défunt. In: *EAO* 73, 23–32.

Guilhou N. 2015. L'âne, portier et passeur de l'au-delà, ou les metamorphoses. In: M. Massiera, B. Mathieu et Fr. Rouffet (Eds.), *Apprivoiser le sauvage / Taming the wild* (CENiM, 11), Montpellier, 183–196.

Guksch H. 1995. *Die Gräber des Nacht-Min und des Men-cheper-Ra-seneb, Theben Nr. 87 und 79*; Mit Beiträgen von I. Munro und J.H. Taylor (AVDAIK, 34), Mainz am Rhein.

Hannig R. 1995. *Die Sprache der Pharaonen. Großes Handwörterbuch Ägyptische-Deutsch* (Hannig–Lexica 1), Mainz am Rhein.

Hannig R. 2006. *Ägyptisches Wörterbuch II. Mittleres Reich und Zweite Zwischenzeit* (Hannig–Lexica, 5), I–II, Mainz am Rhein.

Heerma van Voss M. 1963. *De Oudste Versie van Dodenboek 17a. Coffin Texts Spreuk 335a*, Leiden.

Heerma van Voss M. 2006. Zur Vignette des Opfergefildes, Totenbuch 110. In: B. Backes, I. Munro, S. Stöhr (Hrsg.), *Totenbuch-Forschungen: Gesammelte Beiträge des 2. Internationalen Totenbuch-Symposiums Bonn, 25. bis 29. September 2005* (SAT, 11), Wiesbaden, 115–120.

Helck W. 1956. *Untursuchungen zu Manetho und den ägyptischen Königlisten* (Untersuchungen zur Geschichte und Altertumskunde Aegyptens, 18), Berlin.

Helck W. 1958. Ramessidische Inschriften aus Karnak. I. Eine Inschrift Ramses' IV. In: *ZÄS* 82, 98–140.

Hellum J. 2014. Toward the understanding of the use of Myth in the Pyramid Texts. In: *SAK* 42, 123–142.

Hermsen E. 1981. *Lebensbaumsymbolik im Alten Ägypten. Arbeitsmaterialen zur Religionsgeschichte. Eine Untersuchung*, Köln.

Hodel-Hoenes S. 2000. *Life and Death in Ancient Egypt. Scenes from Private Tombs in New Kingdom Thebes*; Translated from German by D. Lorton, Ithaca – London.

Hornung E. 1963. *Das Amduat. Die Schrift des verborgenen Raumes* (AÄ, 7), Wiesbaden.

Hornung E. 1965. Zum ägyptischen Ewigkeitsbegriff. In: *Forschungen und Fortschritte* 39, 334–336.

Hornung E. 1968. *Altägyptische Höllenvorstellungen* (ASAW, 59/3), Berlin.

Hornung E. 1977. *Das Buch der Anbetung des Re im Westen (Sonnenlitanei). Nach den Versionen des Neun Reich* (AH, 2, 3), Genève.

Hornung E. 1979. *Das Totenbuch der Ägypter. Eingeleitet, übersetzt und erläutert*, Zürich – München.

Hornung E. 1979–1980. *Das Buch von den Pforten des Jenseits. Nach den Versionen des Neun Reich*, I–II, (AH, 7–8), Genève.

Hornung E. 1981. Die Tragweite der Bilder. Altägyptische Bildaussagen. In: *Eranos Jahrbuch* 48 (1979), 183–237.

Hornung E. 1982. *Der ägyptische Mythos von der Himmelskuh. Eine Ätiologie des Unvollkommenen*; Mitarbeit von A. Brodbeck, H. Schlögl und E. Staehelin und mit einem Beitrag von G. Fecht (OBO, 46), Freiburg – Göttingen.

Hornung E. 1992. Szenen des Sonnenlaufes. In: *Sesto Congresso Internazionale di Egyttologia*, 1, Turin, 317–323.

Hornung E. 1996. *Conceptions of God in Ancient Egypt. The One and the Many*; Translated from German by J. Baines, Ithaca – New York.

Hornung E. 1999. *The Ancient Egyptian Books of the Afterlife*; Translated from German by D. Lorton, Ithaca – London.

Hornung E. 2005. *The Ancient Egyptian Books of the Underworld*; Translated from German by I. Stevens, London.

Hornung E., Abt T. 2007. *The Egyptian Amduat. The Book of the Hidden Chamber*; Translated from German by D. Warburton, Zurich.

Hummel S. 1983. *Vignette zum ägyptischen Totenbuch, Kap. 110*. In: *Orientalia Suecana* XXXI–XXXII, 43–45.

Jamen Fr. 2015. *Le cercueil de Padikhonsou au musée des Beaux-Arts de Lyon (XXIe dynastie)* (SAT, 19). Wiesbaden.

Janák J. 2003. From Dusk Till Dawn. In: *ArOr* 71, 1–12.

Jankuhn D. 1972. *Das Buch "Schutz des Hauses" (sꜣ-pr)*; Dissertation, Bonn.

Jansen-Winkeln K. 1985. *Ägyptische Biographien der 22. und 23. Dynastie* (ÄAT, 8), I–III, Wiesbaden.

Janssen J. M. A. 1950. On the Ideal Lifetime of the Egyptians. In: *OMRO* 31, 33–43.

Jelinkova-Reymond E. 1956. *Les Inscriptions de la Statue Guérisseeuse de Djed-Her-le-Sauveur* (BdÉ, 23), Le Caire.

Junge Fr. 2003. *Die Lehre Ptahhoteps und die Tugenden der ägyptischen Welt* (OBO, 193), Freiburg – Göttingen.

Jürgens P. 1999. Anmerkunden zu Sargtextspruch 335 und seiner Tradierung. In: *GM* 172, 29–46.

Kákosy L. 1964. Ideas about the Fallen State of the World in the Egyptian Religion. In: *Acta Antiqua* 17, Fasc. 2, 205–216.

Kákosy L. 1980. "Ishedbaum". In: *LÄ* III, 182–183

Kákosy L. 1986. "Uroboros". In: *LÄ*, VI, 886–893.

Kákosy L. 1988. Hermes and Egypt. In: Lloyd A. B. (Ed.), *Studies in Pharaonic Religion and Society in Honour of J. Gwyn Griffiths*, (EES Occasional Publications, 8), London, 258–261.

Kákosy L. 1995. Ouroboros on Magical Healing Statues. In: T. DuQuesne (Ed.), *Hermes Aegyptiacus. Egyptological Studies for B. H. Stricker on his 85th Birthday* (DE, Special No. 2), Oxford, 123–129.

Kákosy L. 1998. A New Source of Egyptian Mythology and Iconography. In: C. J. Eyre (Ed.), *Proceedings of the Seventh International Congress of Egyptologists, Cambridge, 3–9 September 1995* (OLA, 82), Leuven, 619–624.

Kákosy L. 2003. Cosmogony in the Pap. Bremner Rhind. In: *Das Alte Aegypten und seine Nachbarn. Festschrift zum 65. Geburtstag von Helmut Satzinger* (Beiträgen zur Ägyptologie, Koptologie, Nubiologie und Afrikanistik, Kremser wissenschaftliche Reihe), Krems, 97–100.

Kákosy L., Bács T., Bartos Z., Fábián Z., Gaál E. 2004. *The Mortuary Monument of Djehutimes (TT 32)* (Studia Aegyptiaca, Series maior, 1), I–II, Budapest.

Kaper O. E. 2002. Queen Nefertari and the fog. On an Amphibious element in the vignette to BD 94. In: *BACE* 13, 109–126.

Karlshausen Chr. 1991. Le Chat dans la Mythologie: les Démons-Chats. In: L. Delvaux, E. Warmenbol (Eds.), *Les Divins Chats d'Égypte: un Air Subtil, un Dangereux Parfum* (Lettres Orientales, 3), Leuven, 101–107.

Keel O., Schroer S. 1998. Darstellungen des Sonnenlaufs und Totenbuchvignetten auf Skarabäen. In: *ZÄS* 125, 13–29.

Kees H. 1927. Ein Klagelied über das Jenseits. In: *ZÄS* 62, 73–79.

Kees H. 1930. Göttinger Totenbuchstudien. Ein Mythos vom Königtum des Osiris in Herakleopolis aus dem Totenbuch Kap. 175. In: *ZÄS* 65, 65–83.

Kees H. 1956. *Totenglauben und Jenseitsvorstellungen der alten Ägypten. Grundlagen und Entwicklung bis zum Ende des Mittleren Reiches*, Berlin.

Kees H. 1964. *Die Hohenpriester des Amun von Karnak von Herihor bis zum ende der Äthiopenzeit* (Probleme der Ägyptologie, 4), Leiden.

Kees H. 1977. *Der Götterglaube im alten Ägypten*, Berlin.

Keller C. 2001. A Family Affair: The Decoration of Theban Tomb 359. In: W. V. Davies (Ed.), *Colour and Painting in Ancient Egypt*, London, 73–79.

Kemboly M. 2005. Iaau and the question of the Origin of Evil according to Ancient Egyptian Sources. In: *Current research in Egyptology 2003. Proceedings of the fourth Annual Symposium at the Institute of Archaeology, University College London 18–19 January 2003* (Current research in Egyptology, 4), Oxford, 89–103.

Kemboly M. P. S. J. 2010. *The Question of Evil in Ancient Egypt* (GHP Egyptology, 12), London.

Kitchen K. A. 1986. *The Third Intermediate Period in Egypt (1100–650 B.C.)*, 3rd Ed., Warminster.

Kockelmann K. 2006. Drei götter unterm Totenbett zu einem ungewöhnlichen bildmotiv in einer späten Totenbuch-Handschrift. In: *RdÉ* 57, 77–94.

Koemoth P. 1993. Du chat à l'uraeus « qui délimite » l'arbe de l'horizon oriental pour Rê et pour Osiris. In: *VA* 9, 19–31.

Lacau P. 1913. Suppression et modifications de signes dans les textes funéraires. In: *ZÄS* 51, 1–64.

Lacau P. 1926. Suppression des noms divins dans les texts de la chamber funéraires. In: *ASAE* 26, 69–81.

Landa N., Lapis L. 1974. *Egyptian antiquities in the Hermitage*, Leningrad.

Langton N. 1938. Further Notes on some Egyptian Figures of Cats / Neville Langton. In: *JEA* 24, 54–58.

Lanzone R. V. 1884. *Dizionario di Mitologia Egizia*, V/2, Torino.

Lapp G. 1997. *The Papyrus of Nu* with a contribution by T. Schneider (Catalogue of the Book of the Dead in the British Museum, I), London.

Lapp G. 2004. *The Papyrus of Nebseni* (Catalogue of the Book of the Dead in the British Museum, III), London.

Lapp G. 2006. *Totenbuch Spruch 17* (Totenbuchtexte; Synoptische Textausgabe nach Quellen des Neun Reiches, 1), Basel.

Lapp G. 2008. *Totenbuch Sprüche 125* (Totenbuchtexte; Synoptische Textausgabe nach Quellen des Neun Reiches, 3), Basel.

Lapp G. 2009. *Totenbuch Sprüche 18, 20* (Totenbuchtexte; Synoptische Textausgabe nach Quellen des Neun Reiches, 5), Basel.

Lapp G. 2015. *Die Vignetten zu Spruch 15 auf Totenbuch-Papyri des Neuen Reiches* (Beiträge zum Alten Ägypten, 6), Basel

Lavier M.-Chr. 2007. La Barque-nechmet dans le Chapitre 409 des Textes des Sarcophages. In: J.-Cl. Goyon, Chr. Cardin (Eds.), *Proceedings of the Ninth International Congress of Egyptologists. Grenoble, 6–12 september 2004* (OLA, 150), II, Leuven – Paris – Dudley, MA, 1083–1089.

Le Page Renouf P. 1904. *The Book of the Dead. Translation and Commentary* (The Life-Work of Sir Peter Le Page Renouf, IV), Paris.

Leemans C. 1882. *Aegyptische hieroglyphische lijspapyrus (T. 2) van het Nederlandische Museum van Oudheden te Leyden* (Monuments égyptiens du Musée d'Antiquités des Pays-Bas à Leide, III, 5 (Livr. 28), Leiden.

Leitz Chr. 1987. Spruch 7 des magischen Papyrus Leiden I 348 (recto, III, 5–8). In: *GM* 100, 47–55.

Leitz Chr. 1994. *Tagewählerei. Das Buch ḥꜣt nḥḥ pḥ.wy ḏt und verwandte Texte. Textband und Tafelband* (ÄA, 55), Wiesbaden.

Leitz Chr. 1997. *Die Schlangennamen in den ägyptischen und griechischen Giftböchern* (Akademie der Wissenschaften und der Literatur, Abhandlungen der Geistes- und Sozialwissenschaftlichen Klasse, Jahrgang 1997, 6), Mainz – Stuttgart.

Lenzo Marchese G. 2004. La vignette initiale dans les papyrus funéraires de la Troisième Période Intermédiaire. In: *BSÉG* 26, 43–62.

Lepsius R. 1842. *Das Todtenbuch der Ägypter nach dem hieroglyphischen Papyrus in Turin*. Leipzig.

Lepsius R. 1867. *Aelteste Texte des Todtenbuchs nach Sarkophagen des Altaegyptischen Reichs im Berliner Museum*, Berlin.

Lesko L. H. 1991. Ancient Egyptian Cosmogonies and Cosmology. In: B. Shafer (Ed.), *Religion in Ancient Egypt. Gods, Myth, and Personal Practice*, London, 88–122.

Logan T. J. 2000. The *Jmyt-pr* Document: Form, Function, and Significance. In: *JARCE* 37, 49–73.

Lorton D. 1977. The Treatment of Criminals in Ancient Egypt through the New Kingdom. In: *JESHO* 20, 2–64.

Lucarelli R. 2006. *The Book of the Dead of Gatseshen. Ancient Egyptian Funerary Religion in the 10th Century B. C.* (EU, 21), Leiden.

Lucarelli R. 2007. The Vignette of Ch. 40 of the Book of the Dead. In: J.-Cl. Goyon, Chr. Cardin (Eds.), *Proceedings of the Ninth International Congress of Egyptologists (Grenoble, 6–12 septembre 2004)* (OLA, 150), Leuven, 1181–1186.

Lucarelli R. 2012. The so-called vignette of Spell 182 of the Book of the Dead. In: R. Lucarelli, M. Müller-Roth, A. Wüthrich (Hrsg.), *Herausgehen am Tage. Gesammelte Schriften zum altägyptischen Totenbuch* (SAT, 17), Wiesbaden, 79–91, Farbtafeln II–III.

Luft U. 1977. Das Totenbuch des Ptahmose. Papyrus Kraków MNK IX–752 / 1–4. In: *ZÄS* 104, 46–75.

Luft U. 1977a. Seit der Zeit des Gottes. In: *Studia Aegyptiaca* II, 47–78.

Lüscher B. 1998. *Untersuchungen zu Totenbuch Spruch 151* (SAT, 2) Wiesbaden.

Lüscher B. 2000. *Das Totenbuch pBerlin P. 10477 aus Achmim (mit Photographien des verwandten pHildesheim 5248)*; Mit Beirägen von U. Rößler-Köhler und M.-T. Derchain-Urtel (HAT, 6), Wiesbaden.

Lüscher B. 2014. *Auf den Spuren von Edouard Naville. Beiträge und Materialien zur Wissenschaftsgeschichte des Totenbuches* (Totenbuchtexte Supplementa 1), Basel.

Lüscher B. 1986. *Totenbuch Spruch 1. Nach dem quellen des Neuen Reiches* (Kleine Ägyptologische Texte), Wiesbaden.

Malek J. 2000. *The Cat in Ancient Egypt*, London.

Maspero G. 1889. *Les momies royales de Deir El-Bahari*, Paris.

Masquelier-Loorius J. 2006. Le Fouet à Double Lanière. In: *RdÉ* 57, 95–107.

Massart A. 1959. A propos des «Listes» dans les textes égyptiens funéreraires et magiques. In: *Studia Biblica et Orientalia* 3, 227–246.

Maystre Ch. 1941. Le Livre de la Vache du Ciel dans les tombeaux de la Vallée des Rois. In: *BIFAO* 40, 53–115.

Meeks D. 1993. Deux papyrus funéraires de Marseille (Inv. 292 et 5323). A propos de quelques personnages thébains. In: E. E. Kormysheva (Ed.), *Ancient Egypt and Kush: In Memoiram Mikhail A. Korostovtsev*, Moscow, 290–299, pl. 14–15.

Meeks D. 2006. *Mythes et légendes du Delta d'après le papyrus Brooklyn 47.218.84* (MIFAO, 125), Le Caire.

Mekhitarian A. 1991. Le chat dans les tombes thébaines privées. In: L. Delvaux, E. Warmenbol (Eds.), *Les Divins Chats d'Égypte: un Air Subtil, un Dangereux Parfum* (Lettres Orientales, 3), Leuven,

Mercer S. A. B. 1927. Some Religious Ideas in the Seventeenth Chapter of the Book of the Dead. In: *JSOR* 11, 217–221.

Mercer S. A. B. 1952. *The Pyramid Texts in Translation and Commentary*, I–IV, New York – London – Toronto.

Meurer G. 2002. *Die Feinde des Königs in den Pyramidentexten* (OBO, 189), Freiburg – Göttingen.

Meyrat P. 2010. *Miw ꜥꜣ*: grand chat ou serval. In: *GM* 224, 87–92.

Milde H. 1991. *The Vignettes in the Book of the Dead of Neferrenpet* (EU, 7). Leiden.

Milde H. 1994. "Going out into the Day". Ancient Egyptian Beliefs and Practices concerning Death. In: J. M. Bremer, Th. P. J. van den Hout, R. Peters (Eds.), *Hidden Futures. Death and Immortality in Ancient Egypt, Anatolia, the Classical, Biblical and Arabic-Islamic World*, Amsterdam, 15–34.

Milde H., 2011. Reading Vignettes. An Approach to Illustrations in the Book of the Dead. In: *JEOL* 43, 43–56.

Morenz L. D. 2004. Apophis: on the Origin, Name, and Nature of an Ancient Egyptian Anti-God. In: *JNES* 63, 201–205.

Moret A. 1902. *Le rituel du culte divin journalier en Égypte d'après les papyrus de Berlin et les textes du temple de Séti Ier, a Abydos* (AMG, Bibliothèque d'Études, 14), Paris.

Mosher M. Jr. 1990. *The Ancient Egyptian Book of the Dead in the Late Period: A Study of Revisions Evident in Evolving Vignettes, and Possible Chronological or Geographical Implications for Differing Versions of Vignettes*; Dissertation, Berkley.

Mosher M. Jr. 2001. *The Papyrus of Hor (BM EA 10479). With Papyrus MacGregor: The Late Period Tradition at Akhmim* (Catalogue of the Books of the Dead in the British Museum, 2), London.

Muhlestein K. 2008. Execration Ritual. In: J. Dieleman, W. Wendrich (Eds.), *UCLA. Encyclopedia of Egyptology*, Los Angeles. (http://escholarship.org/uc/item/3f6268zf)

Munro I. 1994. *Die Totenbuch-Handschriften der 18. Dynastie im Ägyptischen Museum Cairo*, I–II (ÄA, *54*), Wiesbaden.

Munro I. 1996. *Der Totenbuch-Papyrus des Hochenpriesters Pa-nedjem II. (pLondon BM 10793 / pCambell)* (HAT, 3), Wiesbaden.

Munro I. 1997. *Das Totenbuch des Nacht-Amun aus der Ramessidenzeit (pBerlin P. 3002)* (HAT, 4), Wiesbaden.

Munro I. 2009. *Der Totenbuch-Papyrus des Hor aus frühen Ptolemäerzeit (pCologny Bodmer-Stiftung CV + pCincinnati Art Museum 1947.369 + pDenver Art Museum 1954.61)* (HAT, 9), Wiesbaden.

Naguib S.-A. 1990. *Le Clergé Féminin d'Amon Thébain à la 21e Dynastie* (OLA, 38), Leuven.

Naguib S.-A. 1998. The Weighing of the Heart: Iconic Image and Symbol. In: *In Search of Symbols. An Explorative Study University of Oslo, Department of Cultural Studies Occasional Papers* 1, Oslo, 68–88.

Naville E. 1874. Deux lignes du Livre des morts. In: *ZÄS* 12, 57–61.

Naville E. 1886. *Das Aegyptische Todtenbuch der XVIII. bis XX. Dynastie*, I–II, Berlin.

Niwiński A. 2000. Iconography of the 21st Dynasty: its main Features, Levels of Attestation, the Media and their Diffusion. In: Ch. Uehlinger (Ed.), *Images as Media. Sources for the Cultural History of the Near East and the Eastern Mediterranean (1st millennium BCE)*. Proceedings of an International

Symposium held in Fribourg on November 25–29, 1997 (OBO, 175), Freiburg – Göttingen, 21–43.

Niwiński A. 1981. Noch einmal über zwei Ewigkeitsbegriffe. Ein Vorschlag der graphischen Lösung in Anlehnung an die Ikonographie der 21. Dynastie. In: *GM* 48, 41–53.

Niwiński A. 1984. The Bab El-Gusus Tomb and the Royal Cache in Deir El-Baḥri. In: *JEA* 70, 73–81.

Niwiński A. 1988. *21st Dynasty Coffins from Thebes. Chronological and Typological Studies* (Theben, V). Mainz am Rhein.

Niwiński A. 1988a. *Religiöse illustrierte Papyri der 21. Dynastie. Ein Vorschlag der Typologie und Datierung.* In: S. Schoske (Hrsg.), *Akten des vierten internationalen ägyptologen Kongress, München 1985*, 3: Linguistik, Philologie – Religion (SAK–Beihefte, 3), Hamburg, 315–325.

Niwiński A. 1989. *Studies on the Illustrated Theban Funerary Papyri of the 11th and 10th Centuries B. C.* (OBO, 86), Frieburg – Göttingen.

Niwiński A. 1989a. Untersuchungen zur Ägyptischen religiösen Ikonographie der 21. Dynastie (3). Mummy in the Coffin as the Central Element of Iconographic Reflection of the Theology of the 21st Dynasty in Theben. In: *GM* 109, 53–66.

Niwiński A. 1992. Ritual protection of the dead or symbolic reflection of his special status in society? The problem of the black-coated cartonnages and coffins of the Third Intermediate Period. In: Luft U. (Ed.), *The Intellectual Heritage of Egypt. Studies Presented to Lászlo Kákosy by Friends and Colleagues on the Occasion of his 60th Birthday* (Studia Aegyptiaca, XIV), Budapest.

Niwiński A. 1996. *La Seconde Trauvaille de Deir El-Bahari (Sarcophages)*, I (Catalogue Général des Antiquités Égyptiennes du Musée du Caire, N°s 6029–6068), Le Caire.

Niwiński A. 2004. *Sarcofagi della XXI Dinastia (CGT 10101–10122)*; con appendici di G. N. Nikola, T. Radelet e G. Laquale (Catalogo del Museo Egizio di Torino, Ser. 2: Collezioni, IX), Torino.

Niwiński A. 2006. The Book of the Dead on the Coffins of the 21st Dynasty. In: B. Backes, I. Munro, S. Stöhr (Hrsg.), *Totenbuch-Forschungen: Gesammelte Beiträge des 2. Internationalen Totenbuch-Symposiums Bonn, 25. bis 29. September 2005* (SAT, 11), Wiesbaden, 245–264.

Niwiński A. 2008. The funerary stelae and papyri in the burial equipment. An observation on the funerary material of the 21st / early 22nd Dynasty in Thebes as the by-product of the Conference on the Libyan Period in Egypt. In: *GM* 216, 11–12.

Niwiński A. 2009. The so-called chapters BD 141–142 on the coffins of the 21st Dynasty from the Thebes with some Remarks concerning the Funerary papyri of the Period. In: B. Backes, M. Müller-Roth, S. Stöhr (Hrsg.), *Ausgestattet mit den Schriften des Thot. Festschrift für Irmtraut Munro zu ihrem 65. Geburtstag* (SAT, 14), Wiesbaden, 133–162.

Ockinga B. 1988. Totenbuch, Kapitel 175. In: Ch. Butterweck (Hrsg.), Grab-, Sarg-, Votiv- und Bauinschriften (TUAT, II, Liefrung 4), Gütersloh, 518–522.

Ockinga B. G., al-Masri Y. 1988. *Two Ramesside Tombs at El Mashayikh. Part I: The Tomb of Anhurmose – the Outer Room*, Sydney.

Osing J. 1992. *Das Grab des Nefersecheru in Zawyet Sultan*; Mit Beiträgen von B. Dominicus, G. Heindl und D. Salzmann (AVDAIK, 88), Mainz am Rhein.

Otto E. 1954. Altägyptische Zeitvorstellungen und Zeitbegriffe. In: *Die Welt als Geschichte*, XIV, 138–148.

Otto E. 1956. Die Ätiologie des «großen Katers» in Heliopolis. In: *ZÄS* 81, 65–66.

Otto E. 1962. Zwei Paralleltexte zu TB 175. In: *CdÉ* 37, No. 74, 249–256.

Parker R. A., Leclant J., Goyon J.-Cl. 1979. *The Edifice of Taharqa by the Sacred Lake of Karnak*; With translations from the French by Claude Crozier-Brelot, (Brown Egyptological Studies, 8), Providence – London.

Peden A. J. 1994. *Egyptian Historical Inscriptions of the Twentieth Dynasty* (Documenta Mundi: Aegyptiaca, 3), Jonsered.

Piankoff A. 1954. The Tomb of Ramesses VI. Texts (Bollingen Series, XL: Ancient Egyptian Religious Texts and Representations 1), New York.

Piankoff A. 1957. *Mythological Papyri*; Ed. and Preface by N. Rambova, I–II (Bollingen Series XL: Ancient Egyptian Religious Texts and Representations, 3), New York.

Piankoff A. 1962. N. Rambova (Ed.), *The Shrines of Tut-Ankh-Amon*, New York – Evanston.

Piankoff A. 1964. *The Litany of Re* (Bollingen Series, XL: Ancient Egyptian Religious Texts and Representations 4), New York.

Piankoff A. 1972. *The Wondering of the Soul*; Completed and Prepared for Publication by H. Jacquet-Gordon (Bollingen Series, XL: Egyptian Religious Texts and Representations 6), Princeton.

Piccione P. A. 1990. Mehen. Mysteries and Resurrection from the Coiled Serpent. In: *JARCE* 27, 43–52.

Pinch G. 2002. *Egyptian Mythology. A Guide to the Gods, Goddesses, and Traditions of Ancient Egypt*, Oxford.

Plater C. 2001. *Aspects of the Interaction between the Living and the Dead in Ancient Egypt*: Dissertation, Liverpool.

Posener G. 1946. Les criminals débaptisés et les morts sans noms. In: *RdÉ* 5, 51–56.

Posener G. 1985. *Le Papyrus Vandier* (PIFAO, VII), Le Caire.

Prisse d'Avennes E. 1926. *Le Papyrus a l'époque pharaonique et fac-similé du plus ancien manuscrit du monde entier en caractères hiératiques archaiques ou Papyrus Prisse d'Avennes, trouvé à Thèbes. Album*, Avesnes.

Puvill Donata M. 1999. *Textos de la Tumba de la reina Nefertari: revisiyn y traducciyn comentada* (Cuadernos de egiptologнa Mizar, 4), Bercelona.

Quaegebeur J. 1994. La table d'offrandes grande et pure d'Amon. In: *RdÉ*, 45, 155–173.

Quirke S. 1993. *Owners of Funerary Papyri in the British Museum* (British Museum Occasional Paper, 92). London.

Quirke S. 1999. Two Books of the Dead of a Ptolemaic Psamtek. In: *OMRO* 79, 40–42, pl. 20–23.

Quirke S. 2001. *The Cult of Ra: Sun-worship in Ancient Egypt*, London.

Quirke S. 2013. *Going out in Daylight, prt m hrw, the Ancient Egyptian Book of the Dead. Translation, sources, meanings*, London.

Ranke H. 1924. Die Vergottung der Glieder des Menschlichen Körpes bei den Ägyptern. In: *OLZ* 10, 558–564.

Ratié S. 1968. *Le papyrus de Neferouebenef* (BdÉ, 43), Le Caire.

Ricke H. 1935. Eine Inventartafel aus Heliopolis im Turiner Museum. In: *ZÄS* 71, 111–133.

Riggs Chr. 2013. *The Beautiful Burial in Roman Egypt. Art, Identity, and Funerary Religion*, Oxford.

Ritner R. K. 1993. *The Mechanism of Ancient Egyptian Magical Practice* (SAOC, 54), Chicago.

Rößler-Köhler U. 1979. *Kapitel 17 des ägyptischen Totenbuches. Untersuchungen zur Textgeschichte und Funktionen eines Textes der altägyptischen Totenliteratur* (GOF, R. IV, Bd. 10), Wiesbaden.

Rößler-Köhler U. 1980. "Löwe". In: *LÄ*, III, Kol. 1080–1090.

Routledge C. D. 2001. *Ancient Egyptian Ritual Practice: ỉr-ḫt and nt-ʿ*; Dissertation, Toronto.

Sadek Abd al-Aziz F. 1985. *Contribution à l'étude de l'Amduat. Les variantes tardives du Livre de l'Amduat dans les papyrus du Musée du Caire* (OBO, 58), Freiburg – Göttingen.

Saied L. M. 2008. Some remarks on the Egyptian nostalgia or the "Cult of the Past". In: *Tenths International Congress of Egyptologists, University of the Aegan, Rhodes, 22–29, May 2008. Abstracts of Papers*, Aegan, 221–222.

Saleh A. 1969. The so-called «Primeval Hill» and other Related Elevations in Ancient Egyptian Mythology. In: *MDAIK* 25, 110–120.

Saleh M. 1984. *Das Totenbuch in den thebanischen Beamtengrabern des neuen Reiches: Texte und Vignetten* (AVDAIK, 46), Mainz am Rhein.

Sander-Hansen C. E. 1937. *Die religiösen Texte auf den Sarg der Anchnesneferibrê*, Kopenhagen.

Sander-Hansen C. E. 1946. Die phonetischen Wortspiele des altesten Ägyptischen. In: *Acta Orientalia* 20, 1–22.

Sander-Hansen C. E. 1956. *Die Texte der Metternichstelle* (Analecta Aegyptiaca, VII), København.

Sauneron S. 1953. L'Hymne au Soleil Levant. Des Papyrus de Berlin 3050, 3056 et 3048. In: *BIFAO* 53, 65–90.

Sauneron S. 1989. *Un Traité Égyptien d'Ophiologie. Papyrus du Brooklyn Museum № 47.218.48 et .85* (PIFAO, 11), Le Caire.

Saura i Senjaume M. 2006. *La Tomba de Sennedjem a Deir-el-Medina TT 1*; Dissertation, Barselona.

Schäfer H. 1928. *Ägyptische und Heutige Kunst und Weltgebaude der alten Ägypter*, Berlin – Leipzig.

Schäfer H. 1935. Altägyptischer Bilder der auf- und untergehended Sonne In: *ZÄS* 71, 15–38.

Schiaparelli E. 1927. *Relazione sui lavori della Missione Archeologica Italiana in Egitto (anni 1903–20). R. Ministero della Pubblica Istruzione, Direzione Generale delle Antichità e Belle Arti, II: La Tomba intatta dell'architetto Cha nella necropolis di Tebe*, Torino.

Schott S. 1952. Die älteren Göttermythen. In: *Handbuch der Orientalistik* I, Abs. II, Leiden, 67–83.

Schott S. 1956. Totenbuchspruch 175 in einem Ritual zur Vernichtung von Feiden. In: *MDAIK* 14: Festschrift zum 70. Geburtstag von Professor Dr. Hermann Kees, 181–189.

Schott S. 1958. *Die Schrift der verborgenen Kammer in Königsgrabern der 18. Dynastie. Gliederung, Titel und Vermerke* (NAWG. Ph.-Hist. Kl., I, 4), Göttingen.

Seeber Chr. 1976. *Untersuchungen zur Darstellung des Totengerichts im Alten Ägypten* (MÄS, 35), München – Berlin.

Servajean Fr. 2001. Le lotus émergeant et les quatre fils d'Horus. Analyse d'une métaphore phisiologique. In: *Encyclopédie religieuse de l'Univers vegetal de l'Égypte ancienne* II (Orientalia monspeliensia, 11), Montpellier, 261–297.

Servajean Fr. 2007. *Djet et Neheh: une histoire du temps égyptien* (Orientalia monspeliensia, 18), Montpellier.

Sethe K. 1928. Altägyptische Vorstellungen vom Lauf der Sonne. In: *SPAW* XXI–XXII, 259–284.

Sethe K. 1929. *Amun und die Acht Uchtgötter von Hermopolis. Untersuchung über Ursprung und Wesen des ägyptischen Götterkönigs* (APAW, Ph. Hist. Kl., 4), Berlin.

Shorter A. W. 1937. The Papyrus of Khnememheb in University College, London. In: *JEA* 23, 34–38.

Shorter A. W. 1938. *Catalogue of Egyptian Religious Papyri in British Museum. Copies of the Book PR(T)-M-HRW from the XVIIIth to the XXIInd Dynasty, I: Representation of Papyri with Text*, London.

Smith H. 1994. Ma'et and Isfet. In: *BACE* 5, 67–88.

Smith M. J. 1984. "Sonnenauge". In: *LÄ*, V, Kol. 1082–1087.

Smith M. J. 2000. P. Carlsberg 462. A Fragmentary Account of a Rebellion against the Sun God. In: R. J. Frandsen, K. Ryholt (Ed.), *The Carlsberg Papyri 3: A Miscellany of Demotic Texts and Studies* (Carsten Niebuhr Institute Publications 22), Copenhagen, 95–112.

Speleers L. 1922. La Version du Chapitre XVII du Moyen Empire. In: *Recueil d'études égyptologiques dédiées à la Mémoire de J.-F. Champollion*, Paris, 621–649.

Stadler M. A. 2009. *Weiser und Wesir. Studien zu Vorkommen, Rolle und Wesen des Gottes Thot im ägyptischen Totenbuch* (Orientalische Religionen in der Antike, I), Tübingen.

Stegbauer K. 2010. Das Brooklyner Schlangenbuch. In: B. Janowski, D. Schwemer (Hrsg.), *Texte zur Heilkunde* (TUAT, Neue Folge, 5), Gütersloh –München.

Stricker B. H. 1992. The Enemies of Re (I): The Doctrine of Ascesis. In: *DE* 23, 45–76.

Sweeney D. 2009. Cats and their People at Deir el-Medina. In: D. Magee, J. Bourriau, and St. Quirke (Eds.), *Sitting beside Lepsius. Studies in Honour of Jaromir Malek at the Griffith Institute* (OLA, 185), Leuven – Paris – Walpole, MA, 531–560.

Szczudlowska A. 1963. The Fragment of the Chapter CLXXV of the Book of the Dead preserved in Sękowski's Papyrus. In: *Rocznik Orientalistyczny* XXVI, Z. 2, 123–142.

Tarasenko M. 2006. Mythological allusions connected with Cosmogony in Chapter 17 of the Book of the Dead. In: B. Backes, I. Munro, S. Stöhr (Hrsg.), *Totenbuch-Forschungen: Gesammelte Beiträge des 2. Internationalen Totenbuch-Symposiums, Bonn, 25. Bis 29. September 2005* (SAT, 11), Wiesbaden, 339–355.

Tarasenko M. 2007. "Ruti-Scene" in Ancient Egyptian Religious Art (19–21 Dynasties). In: E. Kormysheva (Ed.), *Cultural Heritage of Egypt and Christian Orient*, 4, Moscow, 77–122.

Tarasenko M. 2012. The vignettes of the Book of the Dead chapter 17 during the Third Intermediate Period. In: *SAK* 41, 379–394.

Tarasenko M. 2014. The illustrations of the Book of the Dead chapter 17 during the 18th Dynasty In: M. O. Тарасенко (ред.), *Доісламський Близький Схід: історія, релігія, культура*, Київ, 241–254.

Tawfik T. S. 2008. *Die Vignette zu Totenbuch-Kapitel 1 und vergleichbare Darstellungen in Gräbern*: Dissertation, Bonn.

Taylor J. H. 2001. *Death and the Afterlife in Ancient Egypt*, London.

Taylor J. (Ed.), 2010. *Journey through the Afterlife. Ancient Egyptian Book of the Dead*, London.

Thausing H. 1934. Die Ausdrücke für «ewig» im Ägyptischen. In: *Mélanges Maspero* I (MIFAO, 66), Le Caire.

The Bubastite Portal. 1954. The Bubastite Portal by the Epigraphic Survey. Reliefs and Inscriptions at Karnak, III (OIP, 74), Chicago.

Tobin V. A. 1993. Divine Conflict in the Pyramid Texts. In: *JARCE* 30, 93–110.

Valloggia M. 1989. Le papyrus Bodmer 107 ou les reflets tardifs d'une conception de l'eternité. In: *RdÉ* 40, 131–144.

van Es. M. H. 1982. Das Totenbuch des Ptahmose. Ein Beitrag zur weiteren Diskussion. In: *ZÄS* 109, 97–121.

Vandier J. 1964. Iousâas et (Hathor)-Nébet-Hétépet. In: *RdÉ* 16, 55–146.

Vandier J. 1965. Iousâas et (Hathor)-Nébet-Hétépet. Deuxième article. In: *RdÉ* 17, 89–176.

Vassilieva O. 2010. Cairo statue of resurracted Osiris (CG 38424) and related documents. In: E. Kormysheva (Ed.), *Cultural Heritage of Egypt and Christian Orient*, 5, Moscow, 68–96.

Verhoeven U. 1993. (Hrsg. und Bearb.). *Das Saitische Totenbuch der Iahtesnacht. P. Colon. Aeg. 10207*, I–III (Papyrologische Texte und Abhandlungen, 41 / 1–3), Bonn.

Vernus P. 1982. "Name". In: *LÄ* IV, 320–326.

Westendorf W. 1975. Die Lehre von den zwei Ewigkeiten und ihre Nutzanwendung durch den Toten, dargestellt anhand des 17. Kapitels des Totenbuches. In: W. Westendorf (Hrsg.), *Göttinger Totenbuchstudien. Beiträge zum 17. Kapitel* (GOF, R. IV, Bd. 3), Wiesbaden, 183–206.

Westendorf W. 1980. Leben und Tod. In: *LÄ*, III, 951–954.

Wiebach-Koepke S. 2003. Phänomenologie der Bewegunsabläufe im Jenseitskonzept der Unterweltbücher Amduat und Pfortenbuch und der liturgischen "Sonnenlitanei" (ÄAT, 55), Wiesbaden.

Wilkinson Ch. K., Hill M. 1983. *Egyptian Wall Paintings. The Metropolitan Museum of Art's Collection of Facsimiles*, New York.

Willems H. 1996. *The Coffin of Heqata. A Case Study of Egyptian Funerary Culture of the Early Middle Kingdom* (OLA, 70), Leuven.

Wilson P. 1997. *A Ptolemaic Lexicon. A Lexicographical Study of the Texts in the Temple of Edfou* (OLA, 78), Leuven.

Wolf W. 1929. Der Berliner Ptah-Hymnus (P 3048, II–XII). In: *ZÄS* 64, 17–44.

Yoyotte J. 1981. Héra d'Héliopolis et le sacrifice humain. In: *Annuaire École Pratique des Hautes Études, Ve Section – Sciences Religieuses* (1980–1981), 89, 31–101.

Žabkar L. V. 1965. Some observations on T. G. Allen's edition of the Book of the Dead. In: *JNES* 24, 75–87.

Zaluskowski C. 1996. *Texte außerhalb der Totenbuch-Tradierung in Pap. Greenfield*; Inauguraldissertation, Bonn.

Zandee J. 1960. *Death as an Enemy according to Ancient Egyptian Conception*, Leiden.

Zandee J. 1969. The Book of Gates. In: *Liber Amicurum. Studies in Honour of Prof. Dr. C. J. Bleeker* (Studies in the History of Religions, 17), Leiden, 282–324.

Zandee J. 1992. The Birth-Giving Creator God in Ancient Egypt. In: A. B. Lloyd (Ed.), *Studies in Pharaonic Religion and Society in Honour of J. G. Griffiths* (The Egypt Exploration Society, Occasional Publications, 8), London, 169–185.

Zayed Abd El H. A. 1977. *The Staircase of the God in Abydos*. In: *ASAE* 62, 155–174.

Zeidler J. 1999. *Pfortenbuchstudien. Teil II: Kritische Edition des Pfortenbuches nach den Versionen des Neuen Reiches* (GOF, IV; Reihe Ägypten, 36), Wiesbaden.